The Modern Kiteflier

The Modern Kiteflier

Voices of Those Pulling the Strings

PATTI GIBBONS

Foreword by Bob Ingraham

McFarland & Company, Inc., Publishers
Jefferson, North Carolina

ISBN (print) 978-1-4766-7049-2
ISBN (ebook) 978-1-4766-3367-1

LIBRARY OF CONGRESS CATALOGUING-IN-PUBLICATION DATA

BRITISH LIBRARY CATALOGUING DATA ARE AVAILABLE

Front cover image courtesy Lissa Streeter
and the Dream of Flight Museum and Library,
4007 Old Santa Fe Trail
Santa Fe, NM 87505

Printed in the United States of America

*McFarland & Company, Inc., Publishers
Box 611, Jefferson, North Carolina 28640
www.mcfarlandpub.com*

To Kay Buesing
Imagine if you had given Jim pajamas for Christmas

Table of Contents

1: Friendly Fliers 9

Between pages 42 and 43 are
8 color plates containing 22 photographs

2: Tailors at the Beach 43

3: Canvas in the Sky: Artists and Innovators 74

Between pages 118 and 119 are
8 color plates containing 22 photographs

4: Club Business: The Business of Doing Business   119

5: The Kite Trade   160

Acknowledgments

This project builds on the work Kay Buesing undertook at the World Kite Museum many years ago and, though retired from the classroom, and now also from the Kite Museum, she never lost her teacher magic tricks and taught me all I know about kites, kiteflying, and kitefliers. There are not enough thank-yous to cover all of Kay's contributions to kiting!

Another big shout out to David Gomberg for championing the idea of recording stories and personal histories from VIPs in the AKA and working with the World Kite Museum to launch the oral history program. Thanks also to the AKA members who seconded and supported the idea to collect the memories of influential kitefliers and get some of the club history down on tape. Of course, grateful hugs go out to all the fliers, who usually gave up flying time at festivals to record their oral history interviews.

Much gratitude to the hard working staff at the World Kite Museum, especially to all the folks who searched for photos and sent me tapes over the years, and to Patty Rolfe for opening the museum on her day off to ensure that we could interview fliers. Thanks, too, to honorary Kite Museum associates Pam Buesing and Kim Abel for helping get paperwork to and fro.

Thanks to *Kiting* editors Mike Gillard, Susan Shampo, Phil Broder, and Daniel Prentice for their patience with our perpetual scramble for photos and their 'at-a-girl! encouragement.

A big thank you to Dylan Julian at McFarland for taking interest in this project and helping to share the magic fun of kiting with a wider group of readers, and to Kevin Kimura for his tenacious proofreading and gentle ushering of out-of-place commas.

A special thanks to Bob Ingraham for having a way with words and natural knack for storytelling. Your parents were lovely people, and I, too, am grateful for your mother's hospitality and your father's aviation interests. Unknowingly, your family influenced my interests but, knowingly, I aspire to write like you someday.

Enthusiastic thank-yous to Marla Miller, who knows everyone and generously connected me to fliers, Billy Jones and John Barresi for helping me reach people Marla lost track of over the years, and Suzanne Sadow for her deep phone book, which honestly belongs in the AKA's archive.

Appreciative thanks to Lissa Streeter and Marae Price for keeping kite stories tethered to the memories of their fathers, and Jan Gregor for keeping her mother's kite stories afloat.

Thanks to many, especially Chuck Holmes, Mike Dallmer, Jean Sisson, Rakesh Bahadur, Betty Street, Joe Arrendondo, Tommy Lockhart, Mindy Hogg, Leslie Goldfarb, Sandra Huan, the White Bird Kites Facebook page, Rick Kinnaird, Mi Ann Bennett, Laurel Driskill, Neil Jensen, Donald Jacobs, Jason McCaleb, Terry Officer, Carol Sparks, Bob Rogallo, Cathie Rogallo Fox, Ginny Darcey, Nancy L. Sugden, Elwyn Lynn, William White, Ann Weathers Ebelmesser, Warren Weathers, Nancy Weathers Nicholson, Mikio Toki, Patti Tobakos, John Brazzale, Andrea Tabor Scheib, and Scott Seiwald, for answering my blind correspondence and generously replying back to me with information, photos, and permissions. This book is really possible, only with your help.

Mom, well ... just because you are the best.

At home, I thank the Schicks for tuning out the sounds of screaling cassette tapes rewinding endlessly from my office, and Chin for sleeping through every editorial decision.

Chin, the author's chief editor (author's collection).

Foreword by Bob Ingraham

My father, Robert M. Ingraham—also Bob Ingraham—loved things that flew. Manmade things. It is not that he did not appreciate flying animals, he just liked flying machines, especially kites, a lot more.

Dad was born in Hornell in western New York State in 1911, only seven years after the world's first powered airplane flight. Most of his neighbors probably did not believe that God intended man to fly. Nevertheless, my dad dreamed of flying. When he was five years old, an event occurred that would fire his dreams for the rest of his life.

As his family enjoyed Sunday dinner on November 19, 1916, people in the street outside started shouting and pointing into the sky at something over the nearby fairgrounds. In his unpublished autobiography, Dad describes it as "a giant closed safety pin." That "safety pin" was a Curtiss Model D Pusher biplane, seen from the front as it approached Hornell. The pilot, Ruth Law, had flown non-stop from Chicago. She had planned to refuel at Hornell, but her gas tank had run dry and she was gliding the last two miles to the fairgrounds. At touchdown, she had flown 590 miles without a stop—a new American cross-country distance record.

Dad describes what he witnessed on that day:

> We all hurried to the fairgrounds and got there just as the airplane touched down.... The pilot, dressed in a black leather flying suit, sat on a framework well ahead of the wings and I watched some men lift her from that seat. She was so cold and stiff she could barely walk.... The takeoff before dark was thrilling since she barely made it over the chimney of the first house on our street and adjoining the fairground ... I was greatly inspired and my thoughts were almost endlessly on flying from that time on.

Dad did not exaggerate when he wrote that from that moment on his thoughts were almost endlessly on flying. However, Ruth Law's landing at Hornell should not get full credit for Dad's interest in flying and aviation. As a preschooler, he writes, he conducted "experiments" from the top of a stairwell. "I dropped assorted items to the landing below and observed the results. It was only when my mother caught me about to drop one of the family cats that the experiments were concluded." Moreover, Dad devotes several paragraphs of his autobiography to the excitement he felt as a young boy watching balloon ascensions at the fairgrounds and vicariously enjoying the balloonists' heart-stopping parachute jumps. He writes enthusiastically about visiting Cleveland and the Cleveland Airshow in 1929, where he watched a

Ford Trimotor land and deplane passengers. On the drive home, he was enthralled to see the huge U.S. Navy dirigible *Los Angeles* as it soared low overhead. Dad and his older brother, Lee, once mounted a Brownie box camera on a huge winged box kite that they had built, and designed a shutter release that used a burning cigarette as a timing device to make an exposure once the kite had gained some altitude. It was successful, and a snapshot that has survived provides an aerial view of their school and neighborhood, and, in the foreground, the out-of-focus bridle of the kite, which seems to be 100 or perhaps 200 feet above the ground.

Clearly, Dad wanted to fly, or at least hang around things that flew. He could hardly have lived in a better place than Hornell, 23 miles by air west of Hammondsport, New York. In the 1920s, Hammondsport was a nexus of American aviation. It is where Glenn Curtis built his famous *Junebug*, and where Mercury Aircraft Corporation got its start. Later, Mercury's airplanes and one of their pilots would play a pivotal role in my father's life, but in the late 1920s, Dad's interest in aviation had taken a back seat to two other priorities—Hazel Herrick, and earning money.

Hazel had first encountered Dad at Painted Post High School, which they both attended. She thought that he was very handsome, and they began dating. Eventually she became his wife, and then my mother, but at first, she played second fiddle to Dad's job as a golf caddy at the Hornell Country Club. He even quit school, temporarily, to devote his time to caddying. Then one day an airplane flew over the golf course and landed in a nearby field. As he recalls in his autobiography, "All the afternoon it kept taking off and landing there at about ten to fifteen minute intervals, until I could stand it no longer. When I finished my last nine holes, I made for that field and began a whole new phase in my life."

The plane was a Mercury Standard, consisting of parts from three different aircraft. Its pilot was Harvey Mummert, Mercury's test pilot and engineer. On weekends, he flew to towns in western New York state and northern Pennsylvania, selling rides in order to meet the company's next payroll. He was a barnstormer, one of a new breed of pilots who made ends meet by convincing farmers to let them use one of their fields for a day or two. The pilots would fly circuits over nearby towns to attract attention, and then sell rides to people who might never have seen an airplane, much less ridden in one.

One of Mummert's ground crew, Harold Van Guilder, offered Dad his first job in aviation, spraying water around the area to keep the dust down. Soon, Dad was selling rides, wearing white coveralls and a helmet to impress the customers. His job included a bonus that was better than money: for every five rides he sold, he would get a free ride. Before long, he had taken his first flight, and was hooked:

> It was one of the most thrilling things I had ever done.... The terrible roar of the engine and blasting slipstream combined with the thrill of looking down at the earth the very first time and being able to almost reach out and touch the clouds was something difficult to adequately describe.

Dad soon made friends with another pilot, Jimmy Eyer, who owned a tire shop in Hornell. Eyer had learned to fly at Hammondsport and eventually purchased the same Mercury Standard that Dad had first flown in. He became a barnstormer and Dad became his assistant, often flying with him. Dad was more and more certain that aviation would play the leading role in his career, but he was wrong. By the end of 1929, he had learned an aviation aphorism: there are old pilots and there are bold pilots, but there are no old, bold pilots.

On the same day Dad got his first airplane ride, he sold a ticket to a Hornell jeweler, Merrill McHenry, for *his* first flight. McHenry was so thrilled that he took flying lessons and opened a flying school in Pennsylvania. At an airshow in Hornell, his plane went into an uncontrollable spin. He jumped, but his parachute failed to open and he fell headfirst onto a highway only a few hundred feet from where Dad was standing with McHenry's wife and two-year-old son.

Then, in September 1929, another tragedy would further shake Dad's faith in aviation as a career. That was when the odds caught up with Jimmy Eyer. Soon after Dad had stopped flying with him, Eyer crashed in bad weather over the Allegheny Mountains. But Eyer's death was preceded by another portentous event: on October 29, the stock market crashed. Within days, the Great Depression was spelling the decline of the barnstorming industry and ending Dad's dreams of a career in aviation.

By the early 1930s, Dad had embarked on what he would come to call his "off-and-on-career" as a writer, typing on a Smith-Corona portable typewriter that he bought on an installment plan and paid for with proceeds from sports stories he wrote for the Corning *Leader.*

Between 1929 and 1949, my parents weathered the Depression and the Second World War. They married in 1935. My sister, Helen, was born in 1938, and I arrived in 1943. Except for the war years when Dad worked in the defense industry for Ingersoll Rand, which made air compressors, he continued to hone his writing skills at the *Leader*, winning two editorial awards. Then he hit a wall. He had almost "touched the clouds" in his youthful adventures in aviation, but now he was a flier without wings, yearning for adventure beyond the placid, conservative valleys of western New York State. In 1949, he moved his family to the wide-open spaces and dry, warm climate of New Mexico. It was a kiteflier's paradise, but Dad, with a family to support, had little free time. Besides, by that time, he had probably put kites mostly behind him. Kites were for kids, weren't they?

He was hired as editor of the weekly Silver City *Enterprise*, but resigned after three years, complaining about inadequate pay. He spent an unhappy year as a radio announcer, a happier year driving a dry cleaning truck, and then became manager and eventually owner of Western Stationers in Silver City, working alongside Mom. Western Stationers succeeded, but Dad could never fully dedicate himself to selling office supplies, which interested him less than raising chickens, playing violin in the community orchestra, speaking at local service clubs, or even preaching in local churches. Yet, he never stopped writing and he never stopped dreaming about aviation.

In the late 1950s, he had gotten on NASA's mailing list and began writing for local newspapers, keeping subscribers up to speed on the Space Race. At about the same time he began thinking about a much older aviation technology—kites.

In 1958, we moved into an old brick house in Silver City. It included a garage that Dad soon set up as his workshop, equipping it with a sewing machine (when he was only five, his grandmother had taught him how to sew) and various hand tools that would be useful in building … kites! Soon he had designed and completed a huge winged box kite, using spruce spars and Ripstop nylon.

On the kite's first flight at a disused airport east of Silver City, it soared smoothly into a clear blue sky in a steady, moderate breeze, quickly reaching an altitude perhaps 80 feet. Then it wobbled. Then the line went slack. Then, shockingly, it roared straight down and slammed into the ground, raising a cloud of dust. It had been caught in the vortex of a New Mexico dust devil, a tornado in miniature, which revealed itself only when the cloud of dust began swirling high into the sky. Not one spar survived; even the kite's heavy aluminum brackets were bent and torn.

For Dad, the destruction of his new kite was not a disaster, but an opportunity to make a new, better kite. He had always been a tinkerer, repairing broken things, improving badly designed things, and even inventing new things. In the early 1960s, for example, he became intrigued with the experimental Echo 1 satellite, a huge aluminized balloon that acted as passive reflector for microwave signals. It could not be missed as it soared, night after night, a thousand miles above Silver City.

Dad did not want to miss one of Echo's flyovers, so he built a kludge consisting of a large round mirror, a grid of black electrical tape, a compass, and a clock. With the mirror laid flat on a card table in our backyard and oriented with the help of the compass, and using the clock and data from NASA, Dad could predict exactly where on the horizon, and at what precise minute, Echo would appear. I am not sure how he did that, but it is a good example of the ingenuity that he brought to kite science.

Over the next few years, Dad built and coaxed many types of kites into the sky, but he spent a lot more time thinking about kites than flying them. He wondered why some kites were hard to launch, not much fun to fly, constantly bobbing and jiggling nervously and sometimes committing suicide. He questioned the dogma that kites needed the high winds of spring to fly. He wondered why some kites needed tails and why others of a similar design did not. His questions were mostly rhetorical because he had no one he could ask. And, truth be told, he was just a bit embarrassed to be seen in pubic flying kites like a kid! Why was that?

Then he read a newspaper article about Edward Aff, vice president of the Federal Reserve Bank of Philadelphia, who also was smitten with kiteflying. He wrote to Aff, who agreed that it was time to start an organization for grown-up kitefliers and gave Dad the addresses of several other adult kitefliers. Dad wrote to them, and soon had written a story for United Press International announcing the formation of the American Kitefliers Association, the AKA, even though it existed largely on paper. The story caught the attention of editors across the country. The editor of the *San Francisco Chronicle* featured it on page one. The American Kitefliers Association had been born. By 1964, Dad had designed a classy logo, which survives to this day, and published issue #1 of the AKA's quarterly magazine, *Kite Tales*.

For the rest of Dad's life, kiting would be *the* central theme of not just Dad's life, but Mom's life, too. Mom, as "executive secretary," became the good hostess to increasing numbers of kitefliers, who often just happened to "drop by" in time for lunch or dinner, and she managed the timely mailing of hundreds and then thousands of copies of each new issue of *Kite Tales*. The AKA's membership list grew to include several well-known Americans, among them Charles Schultz, Paul Harvey, and Jimmy Stewart.

Robert and Hazel Ingraham in the mid–1970s.

The AKA was of necessity a labor of love, never providing more than a modest income for my parents. Dad supplemented their income through sales of his wonderful delta kites, which could fly (*without* bobbing and jiggling!) on the lightest of zephyrs (and survive any New Mexico dust devil!). Each kite with its appliquéd design was a "limited edition" of one. Dad could have sold them as expensive *objets d'art*, but he wanted kitefliers to *fly* them, not hang them on a wall. He charged a pittance for them.

Mom and Dad published *Kite Tales* for 14 years, and made and sold hundreds of Dad's delta kites, and came to enjoy a modest sort of fame as the architects of the AKA, which had within very few years become an international community. They attended several kite conventions as honored guests, one time in Hawaii, all expenses paid. Several years ago in Vancouver, I got into a conversation with a kiteflier, and asked if he might know of my father, Bob Ingraham. He was quick to reply: "Bob Ingraham! Well, of course I know Bob! Who doesn't?" These days, not so many people know of Dad and Mom. *Kite Tales* evolved into *Kite Lines* under the editorship of Valerie Govig, who bought the membership list from my parents. *Kite Lines* itself eventually went the way of most magazines to magazine heaven, but the AKA still thrives.

Dad died in 1995, Mom in 2010. You will not find their graves in Silver City, or anywhere. Dad's ashes and then Mom's were tossed into the wind at one of the first spots they visited in the Gila National Forest, soon after moving to New Mexico. That is what they wanted.

Bob Ingraham watched his parents, Hazel and Robert "Bob" Ingraham, turn kite building and kite flying from a pastime for children into the fledgling American Kitefliers Association (AKA). Because of his parents' efforts, kites in the hands of curious adults became efficient flying machines showcasing the marriage of aeronautical science and art.

Preface

It was an idyllic, sun-kissed, breezy day in 1995 and I stepped into what easily could have passed as a postcard scene of the Marina Green park in San Francisco. To my left, towered the Golden Gate Bridge. Down and to my right, Alcatraz glimmered in the Pacific Ocean. But it was head-on that I quickly spotted the California icon I journeyed down the coast to meet, legendary kiteflier George Ham. All smiles, accented with jade jewelry, and radiating goodwill, George met me, a stranger with her tape recorder, and quickly calmed my introverted nervousness with his personal brand of frank friendliness. Easy to talk to, George and I spent the afternoon chatting about kite making, his true blue addiction to parafoils, and the glory he found while showboating for tourists at his home away from home, the Marina Green.

Such was the start of my involvement with kiting and talking to kitefliers. A few months earlier, on a bit of a lark, I applied for an internship at the World Kite Museum. I was midway through a master's degree program at the University of Washington and learned about the summer opportunity. At the time, I knew very little about modern kiting. I was not an avid flier and had never tried my hand at kite making, but I was very interested in learning how museums served the public and collected history. The World Kite Museum's job announcement caught my attention, listing specifically that the ideal candidate must have fun. Fun! Wow. For a tightly wound, bookish type, obligating me to make time for enjoyment was brilliant. And, by the way, I took the requirement seriously. Landing the job, excitedly, I moved to picturesque Long Beach and started a long friendship with museum founder, and now a mentor, Kay Buesing.

From the museum's earliest days, Kay worked to build strong relationships with kite groups, especially the American Kitefliers Association. In the early 1990s, amidst the organized kiting renaissance, then–AKA president David Gomberg and other active AKA members approached Kay to ask how the museum could capture the history of organized kiteflying, especially the stories of the AKA's founding members, who were advancing in years. Facing the cause with a sense of urgency, Kay began an oral history program and set out to first collect the memories of older fliers. For my internship, Kay asked me to "energize and expand" the new oral history program. She encouraged me to research kite history and kiteflier biographies. Without the internet, I jumped in and used the museum's deep library and archive.

A few weeks later, after my crash course in kiting, she sent me down the coast to interview fliers in California. Later that summer, I interviewed fliers visiting the Washington State International Kite Festival. With cassette tapes stacking up, the summer ended, but I did not feel quite finished with the project. In the fall, I consulted with my academic advisor and shaped my thesis project around the museum's oral history program. Over the next year and a half, I continued interviewing fliers, created accessioning policies, and wrote manuals for the program.

After graduation, I moved to Chicago, working in museums, archives, and rare book libraries, and in my off-hours I continued volunteering to help the museum grow its oral history collecting program. Always ready to interview fliers, I kept current on kite happenings and was on the lookout for kite history. In 2002, Kay talked to me about a new opportunity to promote the museum's oral history archive in *Kiting: The Journal of the American Kitefliers Association*. Her idea was to begin a column featuring a different flier's biography in each issue as a way to honor fliers and to promote the oral history program. We named the column *Voices from the Vault*, and our late editor Mike Gillard approved the project and the museum began sharing stories from the oral history interviews with members of the AKA through *Kiting*.

The essays that follow are updated and edited versions of articles I first wrote for *Kiting*, along with new ones based on oral history interviews from the museum's archive. Assembled as a group, I hope the book pieces together high points of contemporary kite history, while telling the unique stories of the modern kiteflier. Just as many fliers express during their interviews, I, too, found that it is the people of kiting that make things special. A hundred interviews later, I have not grown tired of hearing how someone got hooked into kiting, or learning the details about someone's inspiration for an innovation that added to the sport. There is a lovely magic in these accounts, and I find myself so very appreciative of each flier's willingness to follow their kiting interests for reasons none other than the pursuit of pleasure, curiosity, and fun.

Sadly, not everyone who has made organized kiting special is in this book. Some people passed away before we could interview them, other prominent fliers we have not been able to catch up with yet, and some I could not squeeze into this book—though, looking ahead, I hope this book is just the beginning and that future editions will include even more voices. The World Kite Museum's oral history program is ever growing. Please contact the museum if you would like to share your stories, want to suggest someone to interview, or if you would like to research their archive materials.

Did you know the World Kite Museum is the only museum dedicated exclusively to kites in the United States? Open since 1989, this wonderful museum is a kiteflier's paradise. Now hosting a year-round schedule of exhibits, kite making classes, and events, the museum shows how people, named and nameless, use kites. If you have not already, please be sure to visit and support the World Kite Museum.

CHAPTER 1

Friendly Fliers

"Any adult who freely admits to doing something as essentially frivolous as flying a kite tends to be a pretty well-adjusted, happy, goodtime individual. You get a whole bunch of us together, and it is a party." Richard Dermer

Charlie Henderson

Modest to the core, with a heart made of more than just kite string, veteran kiteflier Charlie Henderson has enjoyed a lifetime of kites and sharing whatever needs sharing, with those who tug at the end of a line. A long-time member of the AKA, Charlie's sweet, southern ways brought a slow-steeped pleasure to the flying field and filled the sky with old-fashioned fun.

He was born to parents who, perhaps, had a hunch Charlie would later play in the sky. In 1927, these proud new parents named their son after America's aviation hero Charles Lindbergh only days after the famed pilot completed his record-setting transatlantic voyage. Serendipity or not, Charles "Charlie" Henderson and his kites later crossed the Atlantic several times together, and their time in the air left its own unique mark in the kiting community.

Charlie's story began during the Great Depression in his hometown of Dallas, Georgia. Thrifty times stretched pocketbooks and nurtured spurts of personal ingenuity, prompting Charlie's resourceful mother to head to the cupboards for ingredients essential to her homespun glue recipe. Charlie recalls her sugar and flour paste being tough enough to hold trimmed dog fennel weeds, which he collected from nearby fields, in place to form rudimentary spars on his not-so-fancy barn door kites. Mrs. Henderson, a crafty mother of fun, worked with Charlie to fit worn bed sheets and colorful pages of comics from the newspaper onto three-stick kite frames. Charlie remembered, "We didn't know much about bridling, so we bridled all the tips, all six of them and then we would add or subtract tail from it." Perfect? Not really, but Charlie would let the sticky glue dry and up they'd go.

Winds kicked up perennially during the springs of Charlie's youth, setting the

9

stage for several seasons of kite making, kiteflying, and kite crashing. Kite fatalities were a reality of this pre–Scotch tape era, and Charlie remembers losing many homemade three-stickers and dime store Eddies to rough hands and neighborhood high flying contests. Charlie's father, a machinist at the Goodyear Tire Company, brought home miles of strong twisted cotton cord used at the factory to make road-worthy tire treads. This nearly endless supply of durable line allowed Charlie and his friends to play their "Who-can-fly-the-highest?" game. With so much line at their disposal, the kids eventually ran scared, cautioning one another "not to fly too high, because the sun will burn it up!"

Charlie's boyhood springs eventually gave way to adulthood and its year-round responsibilities. He served as a medical technician in the Medical Corps in the U.S. Navy during the latter part of World War II and afterwards accepted a civil servant post as an x-ray technician for the State of Georgia. After working thirty-four years as a healthcare professional, Charlie retired, but his strong work ethic soon led him to a position in the security department at a local department store, which he happily filled until his second retirement at age sixty-five. Looking back, Charlie enjoyed the lessons of patience and compassion he learned as a caregiver, along with the benefits of his department store pension supplement, about which he quipped, "It's just about enough to cover my cable TV bill each month."

Charlie's healthcare work frequently took him away from home. To combat loneliness on the road, he always packed kites in his traveling bags and popped his favorites out for leisure flies alongside open fields whenever opportunities arose. His first nylon kite, a White Bird, was a staple traveling companion that virtually lived in the back of his station wagon. "A lot of time I wouldn't run into trouble, but I'd be out flying it, and first thing you know here'd come a farmer ... and I'd say 'Is it alright to fly?' and he'd say, 'I just wanted to know what that was up in the air.'" After his traveling days ended, Charlie continued to find pleasure in the skies. With his regimented nine to five days behind him, the world of

Charlie Henderson guiding Adrian Conn's *Dragonfly* kite (courtesy Chuck and Karen Holmes).

organized kiting opened to Charlie. He first learned of other adults passionate about kiting when he came across a copy of *Kite Lines.* He read it cover to cover several times, and inside his well-worn copy, he remembers an advertisement telling readers to "Join the AKA. Be a member of the American Kitefliers Association." Charlie thought, "My gosh that sounds good!" and mailed his "ten or six dollars or whatever it was to someplace in Baltimore" and began his lifelong membership with the AKA.

In the early 1980s, Charlie and a fellow kiteflier from Atlanta planned a road trip to attend his first convention in Detroit. His more experienced friend taught Charlie the convention ropes and encouraged him to make something for the auction block. Charlie, forever claiming his hands were too large for sewing machines, turned to his basement wood working shop to create a little something to support his club. He came up with a winner, *Charlie's Pocket Winder.* This compact, hand-finished red Appalachian oak kite winder not only sold at auction, but started bringing in orders. Much to his surprise, Charlie's attention to detail, skill with woodworking tools, and first-hand experience with tangled lines came together to create a handsome and practical solution that many kitefliers recognize as an item essential for their gear packs. Taking great pride in his work, if Charlie saw a flaw in a winder, he would "put it on my band saw and cut it in two. It's firewood then." He enjoyed his cottage industry but saw it only as a hobby. "If I sell too many its like work. If it ever gets to where I don't enjoy making a kite winder, I've made my last."

Charlie Henderson and World Kite Museum founder Kay Buesing at the AKA convention in Dayton, Ohio, 2003 (author's collection).

AKA convention welcome sign, Dayton, 2003 (author's collection).

When Charlie's daughter Karen was dating her future husband Chuck Holmes, the family met at Chuck's house for dinner. Charlie spotted a kite book on his shelf and said to Chuck, "'Oh, you like kites too?'" Chuck's sister gave him the book when he graduated from college, and that gift jumpstarted a lifelong friendship between the men and, over time, kiting brought the extended family together. In 1980, Charlie and Chuck traveled to the Smithsonian Kite Festival together. Chuck recalls, "We had such a good time, we made it an annual event." Each year, the family invite list grew, and "it was not unusual to have ten to twenty people attending and five to seven members entering the competition." As Chuck notes, "I believe all of my family has at least one trophy" and team Henderson-Holmes tightened family connections through kiting.

Charlie and Chuck bonded over kiting, and years later, when Chuck formed his Rokkaku kite battling team, he named it "Team Charlie Don't Run" and "today we fly a yellow Rok with a 'no running' figure in black emblazoned across it." The kite and the team name are a tribute to a bold declaration Charlie made after he learned a technique for a long-line launch that sidesteps hustling at takeoff. Delighted to learn the method, he proudly exclaimed, "Let me tell you, Charlie don't run!" and coined a heartfelt motto that garnered chuckles and endearment.

Sadly, Charlie passed away in 2011, but his legacy and memory live on in the Henderson-Holmes family and throughout the AKA. Whether it was friendly chatter or much needed flying tips for someone with a shaky kite on their hands, Charlie freely shared his time and experience with those he encountered. As Charlie believed, "It's a good feeling to share with someone."

Bill, Marylu and Bob Sonntag

In 1973, Indiana educators Bill and Marylu Sonntag and their school-aged son Bob spent their family summer vacation in England where they took up kiteflying and beer can collecting because "both were simple, and the beer cans were free." On Sundays, while Marylu and her mother went to church, Bill and Bob slipped off to Kensington Park, where a group of men flew kites. Charmed to see how relaxed the gentlemen were and amazed that they weren't running around, the Sonntag men approached them for flying lessons. Curious and intrigued, their church-dodging outings sparked an interest in kites that blossomed into a lifelong family hobby that the Sonntags enjoyed together for many decades.

Bringing back a piece of summertime fun to the States, Bob later made a kite-themed project for school that got mentioned in their local Evansville newspaper. Early AKA member Jerry Harris read the story and reached out to the Sonntags. Jerry and Bill became friends and Jerry introduced the Sonntags to the national club. In the early 1980s, the family attended the first of many annual AKA conventions, and doors opened as they discovered an irresistible group of fun-loving folks who they looked forward to catching up with each year. Marylu comments, "We loved conventions because there were so many people that were just great fun and they were original." Charmed by the kooky flying antics such as musical night flying, the Sonntags became convention mainstays and looked forward to them each year.

Making the most of the long summer break in the school year, the Sonntags kept up a tradition of traveling and always found room in their suitcases for kites. Having flown in eighty-seven countries and on all seven continents, yes—even Antarctica, the Sonntags personalized a paper travel map to pinpoint the corners of the globe where they've flown, including ocean flies off ship decks and aerial flies accomplished when Bill paced the aisle of an airplane with his kite. Bill usually kept a kite with him at all times, and while traveling with a tour group, while others enjoyed a coffee on the rest breaks, he would pop a kite up for fun. Recalling a trip to the Canadian tundra, Marylu delights in remembering a polar bear that was spellbound by Bill's kite. The bear "stood in awe watching Bill fly his little red kite." The Sonntag family photo album is packed with cherished moments, many punctuated by kites.

Ready for fun at any wind speed, Bill learned to pack kites with different tail

Bill, Marylu, and Bob Sonntag at the Sonntag home in Evansville, Indiana, after their oral history interview for the World Kite Museum, 2012 (author's collection).

lengths. "I look around to see what the trees are doing, how floppy the leaves are, then I pick one of three kites to fly. They are all alike except for the tail." Generous and eager to share, Bill toted extra kites and gave small handmade sleds to tour guides, drivers, and other people they met, to both show gratitude and to leave people with an inspiring souvenir. Something of a global kite ambassador, Bill brought fun to the hands of people the Sonntags met on the road.

Over the years, kiting at home in Evansville was "sporadic, nothing organized," and mainly dominated by dime store kites in the springtime, but the Sonntags enjoyed flying and used kites to invite conversations with passersby. Bob notes, "Most people are surprised when a kite appears" in Evansville, or elsewhere, but as Marylu observes, "Kites make people happy" and prompt many to fondly recall experiences from childhood. Loving that kites get people active and outdoors, the Sonntags appreciate kiteflying as a sport, and as a pleasant icebreaker. Bob notes, "It's hard not to smile and have a good time" when a kite is in your hand.

Taking after his father, Bill kept a lifelong woodworking hobby and somewhere in the 1970s incorporated it with kiting. Knowing his way around a woodshop, Bill began making kite reels because he "wanted to make them prettier." Tinkering and refining his techniques along the way, Bill eventually developed an assembly production system and made beautiful wooden reels in different stock sizes, including a smaller size for ladies. Starting with instructions he found in David Pelham's kite book, Bill began prototyping his own reels and sold around 1,600 of them. Unique to Bill's design is a bicycle axel flange. Bill got the idea to use the bike part after he disassembled a reel and had a vision. Keeping kites close to home, Bill converted his garage into a workshop and hung jigs and pattern parts from the rafters. To ensure high quality reels, Bill made his winders in small batches. Starting with a sheet of plywood, Bill ripped the board down into eight-inch squares and turned the sections into parts. Even in retirement, Bill kept filling orders and made reels that were a cut above stock equipment.

Outside of kiting the Sonntags have lived an involved life and actively participate in civic causes that advance educational institutions and campaigns that improve the lives of the needy. In 2015, sadly, Bill passed away after a long and fulfilling life. Since his death, Marylu reports that "kites have taken a back seat in our lives" and she and Bob spend their spare time giving back to their community. Marylu volunteers at her local library, helps at a soup kitchen, and assists the elderly, while Bob, even with a busy IT career, finds time to serve on two local boards. Whether with a kite, or without, the Sonntag family connects with people in communities near and far from their home.

George Ham

"A product of the midwest," and an eternal child at heart, George Ham relocated from St. Joseph, Missouri to California in 1939. Growing up during the Great Depression, George enjoyed kiting as a frugal hobby that lifted his spirits and gave him a chance to exercise his imagination. Pulling together collected snippets of grocery twine, recycled sheets of newspaper, and splintered sticks from salvaged orange crates, George made his own kites and delighted as they danced in the skies of his childhood. Although George outgrew kiting as he matured into adulthood, after careers in the shipyards and flooring installation business, he eventually returned to kiting in the autumn of his life.

It was around the U.S. bicentennial that George tired of his earlier hobbies, mainly jewelry making and fishing, and was on the lookout for something new and fun to do in his spare time. One fateful day, George happened to be looking up and saw an original Dom Jalbert parafoil squatting in the sky. Friendly and outgoing, George followed the kite line down to the hands of a soon-to-be friend, a labor compensation lawyer recharging his nerves with his favorite kite. George knew at first sight that he had found his new hobby. "'I gotta have one,'" George declared, and set out in search for a parafoil of his own. Quickly learning that "I couldn't find a Jalbert parafoil right off the shelf," George "ended up dealing with Dom myself and he became one of my friends." Smitten with parafoils, George never really took to other types of kites. "They've got no sticks to break" and unlike energetic stunt kites, parafoils allowed him freedom to "lay down and watch the clouds go by and see the kite dance around up there."

In the early days of kiting, parafoils may have been a commercial rarity, but George had the skills to figure out how to make his own. In his youth, George's grandmother taught him to sew and he kept his family cozy with colorful patchwork quilts. Those bright blankets later inspired George's kite making, helped him develop the hand skills needed to create solid and steady fliers, and trained his eye to balance colors. Working without patterns, George studied other people's kites and, with practice, became a kitemaker. "I'm a mechanic, not an artist," but debatable labels aside, George filled the sky with omnipresent parafoils and fun spilled to the ground with the geodesic-shaped bouncing ball toys he made. After making his first sphere, George shamelessly admitted, "I can't quit. If my wife ever found out just how many, I'd have to leave home." Yet, Marion never presented an ultimatum, rather, she often joined George when he flew.

Over the years, George rarely parted with his kites. "I don't sell my kites … a few got away for money, and I regret it," but in some cases, George was open to helping kitemakers. In the 1980s, George designed a 3,640 square-foot kite for the Edmonds Community College kite team in Lynnwood, Washington. With an eye on the Guinness Book, the team flew the kite for seven days, twelve hours, and seventeen minutes. Wind-tested, George's kites could withstand the elements and ensured reliable fun, and George enjoyed sharing the pleasure.

For decades, George enjoyed kiteflying in equal parts to kite making and came to stake out turf in San Francisco's Marina Green. Showboating for park goers, George reveled in the fun kites brought him and the opportunities they gave him to meet friendly folks. Calling the park home, George became devoted to the area and got active in civic initiatives to keep the park tidy and free of riffraff. Locals dubbed him the *Mayor of Marina Green* and this pleased George greatly. "I just love it here." Back in the day, George would fly and entertain passersby seven days a week, but later he scaled back his flying schedule to Sundays, leaving the rest of the week open for kite making at home. For George, kiting was "numero uno. I live the whole week for Sundays." Satisfying himself by amusing others, George was quick to clarify that he "plays to tourists, not a kite crowd" and, for him "the fire under the whole thing is trying to do something different." Bringing kiting to new audiences delighted him. Sadly, George passed away in 2007 but, donning his trademark ten-gallon hat, weighty jade belt buckle, and bolo tie, he continued flying until late in his life.

Richard and Marti Dermer

Before celebrating a half-century in the pizza business, high school sweethearts turned college newlyweds Richard and Marti Dermer started out in the red. Broke but hungry for success, the Stillwater natives ventured into the restaurant industry in their early twenties, financing a dream that pizza would become king on the Oklahoma State University campus. Persistent visionaries, the hustling couple eked through the early lean years and three years later managed a small profit in the a cheeseburger and milkshake diner-dominated landscape. Ultimately their doggedness paid off and the Dermers' Hideaway pizza restaurant flourished, feeding generations of college students. Their once small twelve-seat restaurant grew into a chain crowned by a 360-seat anchor restaurant with sixteen licensed spinoff Hideaways in Oklahoma and Arkansas. "Today, the business is a campus institution."

The hardworking Dermers grew their business over the years but didn't spend all their time in the kitchen. Kite lines eventually untied their apron strings and

Richard Dermer kiteflying in Tiananmen Square, China, 1984 (courtesy Marti Dermer).

pulled them into the world of organized kiteflying. Fortunately, the timing was right and their interest in kiting came when "the restaurant took care of itself" and Richard and Marti could pursue kite interests and travels.

Childhood kite dabblers, Richard and Marti collectively had a buck's worth of dime store kite experience, getting more airtime on their recreational weekend sailing trips, until 1984, when kites courted the Dermers. On a brisk day, a friend passed Richard the lines of his Skynasaur dual-line stunt kite. Richard vividly recalls the power he experienced as he surfed across the grass. "We couldn't hold on to it in that kind of wind. It was incredible!" Richard was hooked and bought his own stunt kite by nightfall.

About four months later, Richard and three other people from Stillwater entered a radio station's kiteflying competition and the Skynasaur-packing team finished 1st, 2nd, 3rd, and 5th. Thrilled, they called the Skynasaur Company to rave about their product and broadcast their sweeping victory. Tickled and impressed, the company said, "'Represent us at the AKA convention'" and Richard guilelessly replied, "'What's the AKA?'" The corporate suits spotted a diamond in the rough and sponsored the Stillwater team's trip to the Nashville convention.

In Nashville, the wind was light on competition day and Richard recalls, "We didn't do worth beans." Empty-handed in the trophy department, the Dermers certainly don't look back on that trip with long faces. On the contrary, they revel in those memories because the trip opened new doors. "We were wowed by all the kites, especially the one-of-a-kind kites that made us realize kiting is a hobby sport." Richard recalls he and Marti "just wandering around wide-eyed the whole time." The couple "didn't know anybody," but that didn't stop them from mingling. On the trip, they met Seattle architect Dave Checkley and learned that he was organizing a kite excursion to China. Richard, on the lookout for a memorable anniversary gift, asked Marti if she would be interested in celebrating their silver jubilee flying kites at a festival in China. Marti jumped at the opportunity and said, "'Let's go!'"

The two traveled to Weifang and Richard awed the crowds flying his American stunt kites. "Of course," the Chinese "invented the kite thousands of years ago, but I had a stack of twenty-four Skynasaurs with sixty-foot tails on each kite that made a glorious sight in the sky." A hundred thousand spectators cheered and Marti boasts that after that trip Richard "says he knows what being a rock star feels like."

The smashing trip fuelled their interest in kites and "gave us instant credibility." They became overnight experts and about a year later, in 1986, the Dermers officially joined the AKA and headed to Rhode Island for their second convention. On their return flight, they met the AKA's southwestern regional director. He was an aircraft company executive from Wichita who purchased an AKA family membership. Over dinner one night, the family talked about the AKA ballots that arrived in the mail, and his son quipped that they each should write in the dad's name on their ballots. This family prank led to victory and the aircraft salesman ascended to the regional director's position with a whopping landslide four-vote victory. The public spoke and in the autumn he decided he better make the trek to his first AKA convention to represent his region. Richard was amused at the hot potato nature of leadership in the early AKA. Not too long after that trip, Al Hargus called the Dermers to see if Richard would be interested in becoming the new southwestern regional director. Richard questioned "'Why me?'" and Al said, "A friend in Wichita recommended you.'" And so it goes, Richard accepted and got involved in the kite club's administration.

Having fun on the flying field and behind the scenes, Richard served nine years as a regional director and eventually assumed the club's top post. As AKA president, from 1997 to 1999, Richard took the job seriously and he and Marti traveled more frequently to represent kiting. In his role, Richard drew from experiences he had as a regional director of the United States Chess Federation. During his time in the chess world, Bobby Fischer rose to fame and club membership swelled from 30,000 to 50,000 people. Richard joked that he wanted to get chess players involved in kiting to bump up the AKA's membership numbers. Kidding aside, Richard and Marti made it their crusade to share the joys of kiting with people and have been known to twist an arm or two to grow the AKA membership roster by buying gift memberships for family and friends, and displaying kites in all the Hideaway stores.

Equally active in kiting on the ground, Marti found a hobby repairing kites. Over the years, she's learned to patch and mend kites, and often ran something of an informal kite hospital. When not tending to needy kites, Marti and Richard also enjoyed teaching kite making classes, especially workshops for schoolchildren. Using Margaret Greger's time-tested plastic bag kite pattern, the Dermers bought takeout bags in bulk through their restaurant supply connections, and created the Dermer sled kite kit for 5th graders. Visiting classrooms, Marti "truly enjoyed" the gigs, especially those at small rural schools throughout Oklahoma, Arkansas, and Texas.

Sadly, Richard passed away in 2014, but Marti continues playing in the sky and cherishes the close friendships she and Richard made through kiting and their restaurants.

Paul Fieber

Although the kiting bug didn't nip Paul Fieber until mid-adulthood, seeds took root during the playground days of his youth. Growing up near the shores of Lake Michigan, a little south of Milwaukee in Cudahy, Wisconsin, Paul and his brothers learned from their father how to construct diamond kites out of butcher paper and sticks. Kite in hand, the family headed to the park to fly, and in those days, thrills for the Fieber boys were found up high. "We flew kites really high," but the currents in the upper atmosphere bullied their handmade kites. "We rarely got our kites back at the end of the day." Scratching his head, wondering why high flies tickled them as kids, Paul declares, "I have no compulsion to fly so high today."

Somewhere, around age fifty, kiting came out of nowhere and enticed Paul at an art gallery. He and his wife Sue visited a kite photography exhibit in Madison and wheels began to turn. As an amateur photographer who enjoyed dabbling with cameras, Paul decided to try his hand at kite aerial photography. He bought what he recalls was "a marginally acceptable kite for photography" and learned to fly it.

In time, Paul's weekend kite outings sparked a broader interest in kiting and the kite photography idea faded away. He reached out to other kitefliers and joined the Milwaukee-based Kite Society of Wisconsin. When the group fractured, Paul joined the newly formed Wisconsin Kiters Club and added the AKA membership card to his wallet. Digging in and becoming an active member, over the years, Paul has held offices in the AKA, including the midwest regional director and chair of the Kite Art Committee. Drawn to service and helping to promote kiting, Paul keeps busy at the club's annual meetings, often volunteering with kite art activities and the Public Services Committee.

Back in the early days of his kiting involvement, Paul developed a strong interest in making his own kites, but quickly realized that he first needed to learn to sew. With practice, Paul mastered the fundamentals and sought out more advanced kite making classes. A familiar face at kite making retreats like Fort Worden and U-MAKE's precursor, the Midwest Area Kite Retreat, Paul learned to build well-made steady fliers, and later produced a number of prize-winning kites. Over time, Paul made his share of deltas but he admits, "I didn't have any one specific kite that I liked to make." In general, though he had a preference for moderate-sized, single-line kites. Kite making eventually led to deeper involvement, and Paul became a kite-making teacher. Appreciating that "it's hard to fly a kite and be tense," he enjoys sharing the magic of kiting with others and freely disseminates his kiting knowledge.

A few years ago, Paul expanded his sewing work beyond kites to include hats. "My friend Nancy Daly is the creator and chief organizer of the Hat Ladies." The thirty-to-forty-member sewing club—comprised mostly of women, with Paul in the *Hat Gentlemen* minority—travels to Madison-area schools and community Head Start programs to create fleece hats for children. "If you think the 'kite smile' is a rush, you ought to see the 'hat smile' when the kids see their finished, one-of-a-kind hats." The group collects upward of 7,000 smiles a year, and through connections in the club, Paul landed a spot on Nancy Zieman's *Sewing with Nancy* television show on PBS. During his segment, Paul showed viewers how to use reverse appliqué on kite sail, expanding the program's range of instructional sewing. The piece originally aired in 2014, but stations across the nation determine local schedules, and Paul continues to get "inquiries from folks around the country" interested in kite making or quilting techniques.

In addition to being a fun pastime, kiting became Paul's passport to travel the globe and he has flown in Europe, China, and South Africa, and enjoyed North American festivals in Montreal, Washington, and many other places. Treasuring the kite community's never-ending camaraderie, Paul's kite travels make him happy and fuel his interest in the sport.

Closer to home, Paul's natural joining spirit helps him create fun in his local community. Active from the ground floor, Paul helped plan *Kites on Ice* with several other kiters. The mega festival, created by Craig Wilson of Madison, ran from 1999 through 2005 and got people out to enjoy kiting during snowy winter days. For the faint of heart and frostbitten, *Kites on Ice* included indoor kite making classes, kite exhibits, and indoor flying demonstrations that were just as popular as the blustery outdoor offerings. In the beginning, the festival had a six-figure budget overseen by a large non-profit management company experienced in running crowd-filled public events. Kicking off the first year, United Airlines generously supported the festival with travel vouchers that organizers used to bring in fliers from around the world. As the years went on and sponsorship waned, the group solicited public donations at the gate before eventually having to end the event. Paul's behind the scenes experience with *Kites on Ice* was advantageous when he and another kiteflier launched Madison's *One Sky One World International Kite Fly for Peace*—a worldwide kite fly, celebrated simultaneously in over thirty countries and countless cities.

Glancing ahead and speculating on the future of organized kiting, Paul notes that it "seems like kiting is stuck, kind of like our economy is stuck right now" but, Paul isn't downhearted because "kiting always has been an up and down kind of thing." Pointing out that kiting is a form of recreation with a low environmental impact, Paul speculates that this may attract young people, who seem increasingly interested in activities with smaller carbon footprints. Retired since 2012 from a career in employment and housing, Paul spends more time on kiting than ever, but he also remains involved in human rights and environmental issues. Paul is an active member of 350.org, an international grassroots group that works to promote awareness about climate change and urges people to "keep fossil fuels in the ground." Although not seeing a direct connection between kites and clean air, the overlap in his passions speaks to Paul's lifelong commitment to justice and being gentle with the earth and sky.

Charlie Sotich

"Born in the house I still live in," native Chicagoan Charlie Sotich called the Windy City home for his entire life outside of a tour of duty when he was in the

Navy, yet he found hometown comforts everywhere he and his kites traveled. Intrigued and enamored with things that fly, kiting was a natural interest for him. "I find it amazing that things are capable of flying," and Charlie enjoyed looking up for inspiration and pleasure. Charlie was a born designer, quick to trim plans down to essentials, a lesson from his professional training as an engineer that left its mark on his success in his skyward hobbies.

Like many, Charlie flew dime store paper diamond kites in the springs of his youth. Extending his backyard to an open field at the nearby grammar school, he and neighborhood friends let out line in highflying contests until vernal winds inescapably guided their rag-tailed toys into budding trees. Frustrated by slippery bridles and lack of guidance with kiteflying, yet drawn to playing in the sky, Charlie joined his brother making model airplanes. Kites drifted out of young Charlie's life but returned in 1973 when coworkers, impressed with his competitive model airplane building skills, approached him to try his hand at kite making. Interested in entering a kite contest sponsored by local radio station WIND, Charlie's colleagues unknowingly hooked him into an adventure that would take Charlie around the world and introduce him to modern kiteflying. For the contest, he built small sled kites from a pattern he found in a book and, from there, he started dabbling with kite making on his own.

With a newfound interest in kite making, Charlie recalled seeing ads for the AKA that Bob Ingraham placed in model airplane magazines to promote the young kite club. Charlie reached out to Bob, and, later, other members, to learn ways to build a better kite. With handshakes from a distance, Charlie introduced himself to the kiting community. Soon, Charlie began attending weekend kiting events in the midwest and then began road tripping a little further out, where he met pen pal friends in person. Nearly always first to say hello and comfortable with introductions, Charlie's keen interest in kites was the common ground that kicked off conversations with friendly fliers wherever he traveled and help forge many long-lasting friendships.

New to modern kiting, Charlie looked to the materials he used in model airplane building for items with kite making potential. Preferring lightweight and lean building supplies, Charlie's future hallmark love of small tissue kites seemed like a logical destiny, but the road to his signature miniature kite wasn't straight. Trying his hands and testing his patience, Charlie created precision-built star-shaped facet kites, but was not enchanted. "I could do it, but it took hours and it was a very stressful time." In the early days, Charlie also experimented with large Rokkakus and a ten-foot delta that, upon completion, he abandoned and lost somewhere in the back of his closet.

Falling in love with the efficiency of simple small light kites, flier friends inspired Charlie to embrace whimsy and turn printed cocktail napkins into playful teeny kites. Up for fun, Charlie and kite club friends celebrated a Chicago Skyliner's birthday at a kiddy pizza parlor arcade and, amid an animatronics concert of singing mice in the dining area, someone handed Charlie a clown napkin and said, "'Why don't you make a kite out of this?'" Like Warhol finding his soup can, Charlie became a skilled mash-up artist breathing new life into ordinary items and punctuated his kite making career with his well-known and prodigious collection of cocktail napkin kites. Finding paper napkins more forgiving than Mylar and easier to work with, Charlie ran with the idea to use napkins as canvases for miniature kites. For spars, Charlie initially turned to bottle rocket sticks that littered the ground after Independence Day, but later stopped sweeping the streets and pared bamboo wok brushes because they cut more uniformly.

Impressing many with his playful kites that peacefully float on the gentlest of breezes, Charlie's sky-bound inspirations persuaded even the shy into trying their hands at kite making. Reflecting on his time in kiting, Charlie taught countless schoolchildren and interested adults but found himself "surprised that I enjoy doing this so much. I was an engineer in real life," and never thought about teaching others, outside a short stint as an electronics instructor when he was in the Navy. Unsure about his instructional credentials, Charlie disclosed, "It doesn't take much knowledge to become an expert among people who know absolutely nothing. So, you are an expert, even if you don't feel you are one." Modesty aside, Charlie's kite making abilities and longtime involvement in kiting made him one of the most qualified teachers around, but it was his frank way of engaging and connecting with people through a shared love of kites that won him a lifetime of sincere and cherished friendships with fliers around the globe.

Marla Miller

"You learn a lot by leaving your country," and with many kite trips to the United Kingdom under her belt, Marla Miller appreciates firsthand how kites and international travel help you better understand the sport and admire other cultures. Never traveling much before kites became her passport to adventure, in the early 1990s, Marla joined the Westport Windriders Kite Club and pored over fellow club member Doug Hagaman's travel slides. Doug flew at a kite festival in England and Marla begged to see his slides over and over and over again. Tired of narrating but recognizing her genuine interest, Doug simply asked, "'Why don't you just go there?'" The proverbial light bulb blazed above her head and "that's when we put the first trip together." Inspired and excited, Marla set out with ten fellow Windriders for England and France on her first foreign kite trip and kicked off a lifelong series of journeys that opened doors internationally, brought her friendships from faraway lands, and inspired her to take up leadership roles in organized kiting.

Looking back, Marla remembers, "I was a spectator until '91" who watched casually from the sidelines. "I was a little intrigued by kites but I never got involved." Marla, a professional florist and wedding consultant, was working on Christmas Eve and "sent all the girls home early" and let one last customer slip into the shop. The collective holiday hustle and bustle verged on chaos in the shopping district, and "people were outside just honking and complaining." With the stress of the season nearing a breaking point, an exhausted Marla remembers telling the last-minute shopper "'I would like to go to the beach and just sit there.'" The man was a beach-goer and told Marla he enjoyed flying kites at the coast. Recognizing a glint of enthusiasm in her reaction, he asked, "'Would you like to go with us?'" The holidays passed and two weeks later, Marla and her husband Ron joined their new friend at the beach in Westport, Washington. Captivated by his stack of three Hawaiians sport kites, her unofficial mentor generously invited her on a test drive. As his helping hands passed the lines to her and he let go, Marla "went about twelve feet down the beach on my bum." People laughed, but Marla dusted herself off and was excited by the fun. Pinpointing the moment her life changed, Marla recalled, "That was it. We were hooked."

Riding the wave of exhilaration, the Millers headed to the nearest kite shop and bought their first kite. Soon after, "we bought more kites and more kites, we kept flying, got more involved with the Westport Windriders," and even "started volunteering a bit." Marla remembers their salad days fondly, especially the trips up and down the west coast where they caravanned in motorhomes with fellow Windriders to kiting events. Marla and Ron joined a merry band and reveled in their newfound kite fun.

Though the Millers mostly tote store-bought kites, Ron's interest in kite making led them to explore the Fort Worden Kitemakers Conference during their first year or so in kiting. While there, newcomer Marla bought tickets for the raffle and ruffled feathers when her terrific beginner's luck won her fourteen kites. More than just a fortunate windfall, her triumph got Marla interested in kite raffles. The following year, while Ron was busy with his kite classes, Marla lent a hand behind the scenes and over the next eighteen years, she learned the ins-and-outs of charity raffling. From there, she got involved with the AKA's convention raffle, which was poised for an overhaul. Marla tinkered with the format, groomed the rules, and in doing so shaved over two hours from the raffle's timeframe. Nearly singlehandedly she helped the club's cash cow grow more successful, but Marla downplays her achievements noting, "I'm just a little aggressive in selling tickets."

Throughout her time in kiting, Marla continued meeting more people and increasingly got more deeply involved with club activities. In 2001, AKA president David Gomberg approached Marla and asked her to take up a board position. Newly entering the post–9/11 world, for Marla, the timing was off. It was a tense period, "I decided to back off for a year" but the following term she accepted the invitation and became a regional director. Serving dutifully, after six years she jumped up to become a director at large and helped the AKA further its kiting mission.

Maintaining a brisk international kiting schedule, while continuing to serve kiting nationally through the AKA, Marla also remains active with her local kite club. In 2007, she began her term as president of the Westport Windriders. With a tireless can-do attitude, Marla won the AKA's Robert M. Ingraham Award for her years of service to kiting in 2008. A well-deserved honor, but one that left her "shocked" yet pumped to contribute more. "I would like to be known as a good volunteer" and "I just promote kiting as much as I can."

Reaching to the future, and outside the net of club membership, these days, Marla dedicates her time and efforts to promoting the AKA's charitable *Thank You Charlie* program that brings kites to groups of kids in schools and clubs worldwide in honor of legendary kitemaker Charlie Sotich.

Marla Miller, Dieppe, France, 2012 (courtesy Marla Miller).

Known for his hallmark miniature kites, Charlie was a giant in the kite world. Sadly, Charlie passed away in 2014 but the AKA keeps his spirit going through the *Thank You Charlie* program, and co-chair Marla enjoys sharing the magic of kites while honoring her dear friend. After his passing, Marla helped his family close up his house, and brought home with her some of Charlie's kite memorabilia. Running a bit of an international kiting B&B, she and Ron host kiteflier friends from around the world who pass through Tacoma, and keep a guest book in their spare bedroom. "Our house kind of looks like a kite museum" and the Millers openly welcome kitefliers. "My whole thing about kiting is the people ... it is not about Marla, it is about kites."

Ed Grys

AKA regional director Ed Grys cannot claim a birthright to his club post, but came to it while pursuing an interest in kiting that escalated somewhere in adulthood. While nurturing his idle curiosity, Ed inadvertently made an unofficial second career sharing kites with others and organizing their fun.

Learning from experience and old-fashioned observation, Ed uses his wits to tinker with kites to get even the peskiest ones flying. As a teen, Ed's father made him a kraft paper diamond kite, modeled after the kites he made himself as a boy in Pennsylvania. Along the way, Mr. Grys forgot some kite building tricks, and his son's acrophobic kite hugged the ground. With pocket change, Ed bought a paper Hi-Flier, popped it up and studied it. Watching its flight patterns and seeing what made it move, Ed diagnosed his dad's kite and made adjustments. "I got it to fly," Ed recalls, and that victory kick-started a lifelong interest in not only kiteflying, but also kite making and repair.

"All through high school I was flying kites" and Ed's encouraging parents donated worn-out bed sheets and chopped the sticks that he and friends collected from the woods to further Ed's kite making projects. Fueled by grand plans, Ed and friends repurposed a haystack tarp and made a colossal flier. Come launch time the wind disappeared and the kite sat in a heap. After a head scratch or two, a light bulb went off over the heads of the resourceful teens and they hooked their kite to the rusty end of a '55 Chevy station wagon. Ed recalls, "When that thing caught the wind, the bumper came right off the car" but their masterpiece flew triumphantly up over the tall telephone poles.

After high school, Ed left the Wisconsin flying fields of his youth and headed to Michigan to study chemistry and pulp and paper technology. Later, as newlyweds, he and his wife lived in Vir-

Closely watched by security, Ed Grys flew a tote-sized Eddy kite at the Eiffel Tower while his wife Gloria laid on her back on the grass to get the shot (courtesy Ed Grys).

ginia for a while, before heading back to the upper midwest to set down roots. At about this time, a new breed of Ripstop nylon and carbon-sparred kites caught Ed's attention and renewed his interest in kiting. Inspired by the innovative kites he saw in books, Ed learned his way around his wife's sewing machine, joined the AKA, and started earmarking vacation time to attend the annual conventions.

Years later, as a card carrying member of kite clubs in Wisconsin, Iowa, Illinois, and Minnesota, Ed's kiting calendar is packed with weekend flies, kite making workshops, and perennial festivals. Finding midwestern winds gusty and unsteady, Ed layers up for *Color the Wind,* a favorite wintertime festival held in Clear Lake, Iowa. Known to most as Buddy Holly's crash site, the lakefront festival grounds are celebrated by robust kite-fliers as a perfect spot to catch "clean winds" that blow steadily off the frozen lake.

Active, with up-rolled sleeves, Ed contributes greatly to the organization and operations of the AKA. "I became involved with the AKA administration when Barb Meyer was elected president of the AKA while she was serving as Region 6 director." Since step-

Ed Grys flying his rainbow Sutton Flowform 125 kite with a 75' (23 m) tail on Bald Head Island, North Carolina, 2005 (courtesy Ed Grys).

ping up to the regional director's office in 2010, Ed has been reelected twice but won't seek another appointment. "This will be my last term. I have enjoyed it immensely but I believe it is healthy for others to bring their ideas and personality to the region." Leaving the office running smoothly, Ed's effective leadership skills help the AKA make it possible to connect with fliers and help them have fun with kites. "Overall, I believe in the philosophy of fewer meetings and more flying on both the local and national level. While meetings are necessary, they need to be efficient and short." Bringing sage management wisdom to his post, Ed furthers the club's core vision and mission for its membership.

When not off on regional kite excursions or filing reports for the AKA, Ed might be teaching a kite history class to 4-H groups or hosting kite making classes in his home. Borrowing tables from a local church, Ed's basement seats fourteen and attracts aspiring kitemakers and sometimes non-fliers interested in learning new needlework techniques. Ed welcomes all and never tires of encouraging budding kite interests.

Retiring from his management position at a large paper corporation in 2009, Ed looked forward to having time to explore areas of kiting, like kite aerial photography, that he hadn't yet mastered. Years later, looking back, Ed notes, "I was gonna have time to do all that stuff, but it hasn't exactly worked out. I'm too busy." Outside of kiting, Ed is a member of two charitable foundations, and "I have been appointed by the mayor to serve on two governmental committees involving power distribution and industrial and commercial development." Additionally, Ed enjoys kayaking, bicycling, beekeeping, and volunteering on social improvement projects in his community. Never idle, Ed is happy with his involvement in kiting and enjoys how it enhances and balances his life.

Pat Daly

Ever-curious, sometimes silly, Renaissance woman Pat Daly's life is woven like a tapestry colored by her many life adventures and trimmed by a legion of friendly well-wishers. Over the years, she has sported several professional hats, deep-dove into varied hobbies, and somewhere along the line allowed kiting to tie her interests together and introduce her to sky-friendly people all around the globe.

The Chicago skyline has been the backdrop for Pat Daly's world for nearly her whole life and home base for her long career in interior design. Primarily focused on office interiors, but with some residential design, Pat's creative juices were focused on mixing and matching color palettes and fabric swatches for over thirty years. During this career, Pat rolled up her sleeves and taught interior design courses at her local college. Like many creative types, Pat enjoys variety over consistency and throughout the years diversified her resume and bankbook with stints as a real estate broker, bartender, and telemarketing agent before leaving design in 1991 to become the editor of the Kite Trade Association International. Reflecting back, "It seems that every seven years I get an itch to do something else." The KTAI evolved into the KTA, and in 2001, Pat left her post to follow a budding interest in gardening. She took a master gardener's course, considered starting a landscape consulting business, and flirted with the idea of returning to school to study landscape architecture. "I went from the sky to the earth."

Kiting once dominated Pat's life, yet the pull into the kite world happened by chance as she followed her interests. In 1984, a friend offhandedly mentioned Elmer Wharton and his delightful dragon kites. Curious, Pat sought out Elmer at the Chicago Skyliners' second annual Sky Circus festival. Bitten immediately by the kiting bug, Pat's art background helped propel her kite making and her handiwork soon became her handshake into kiting circles. For years, Pat enjoyed both kiting and the people she met through the sport.

Though the Skyliners have essentially disbanded, and most of the members from her era have passed or moved away, Pat saw the club's glory days. In the early- and mid–1980s, the Chicago Skyliners kite club was growing and the exquisitely extroverted Pat fit right in with the happy gang. Contributing to fun on the field, Pat's alter ego, a purple wig-wearing, wand-toting weather clairvoyant named Madame Booga Booga, often made appearances. With the wave of her wand, she could offer fliers a wind forecast. Looking back, Pat admits that things "got real silly" but the lighthearted fun kept the tightknit group together.

Pat Daly, always ready to fly a kite, after her oral history interview, Chicago, 1997 (author's collection).

As the Skyliners wandered further and further away from home on road trips, Pat thought it would be fun to capture their escapades and created *Dirty Gertie Gossip,* a column in the club newsletter. As a mascot, Pat dreamed up Dirty Gertie, a wart-nosed feather boa-wearing cartoon, who chronicled the goings on of the roving band of kiteflying friends. Crammed full with old-fashioned name-dropping, Pat realized quickly that people like seeing their name in print and she had fun scooping her friends' kiting adventures. Pat no longer narrates the lives of traveling kitefliers, but keeps busy writing her homeowner association's newsletter.

With Pat's artistic aptitude, her kite making focused on arty features more so than fine craftsmanship. Recalling back to a standout beauty, Pat made a handsome Mayan kite that promptly crashed during its test flight. Rather than trash it with yesterday's newspaper, AKA auction crawlers snagged it for the auction block. Pat estimated its worth at the princely sum of $5, but bidders drove the price up to $70 and when the gavel rested, a Californian gallery owner snatched it up for display. Looking back, over thirty years later, Pat still considers it odd that someone would shell out $70 for a broken kite, but is tickled that her design work commanded that price and keen appreciation.

Throughout her active days in kiting, Pat adored flying, but competitions weren't her cup of tea. In the early days of organized kiting, Pat wondered if competitive flying was a thinly veiled popularity contest. She recalled a pattern where "better known fliers got better points." Over time, judging criteria standardized, but Pat's competitive interests were eclipsed by her broader desire to just have fun and meet interesting people. "Somewhere along the line I quit flying, actually, and got to be more of a public relations ground person." She appointed herself to the welcoming committee and many grateful newcomers shook her hand as they let out their lines. Pat remembers that the flying fields were peppered with "a lot of new people that had no one to talk to." For veteran fliers, "when you're out on the flying field you don't want to take the time or be interrupted or chitchat, and many new people were turned off by that." She and others, eager to share the fun, took turns welcoming new people. This spirit of hospitality was genuine and came easy to Pat. Incurably cordial, she couldn't resist meeting new faces and learning just a little bit about them.

In 2001, as Pat left her job as editor with the KTA, her kiting ties loosened. Outside of a few memorial flies to honor lost Skyliners in recent years, "I have not been active in the kite community or stayed in contact with many kitefliers." Other interests and responsibilities fill her time, but "I still tell new people I meet that kiting once was my favorite thing and they can tell me to 'go fly a kite'" without worries of offending her. For Pat, kiting underscored a pleasant chapter in her life. "I often think about all the friends, people, travels, good times, festivals … they are among my fondest memories."

Mike Carroll

Baby boomer Mike Carroll grew up in a new, tree-less suburb of Dallas, soaking up the fair southern weather before his family headed north to set down roots in northeastern Indiana. Of Mike's four childhood memories, "two of them, interestingly enough, have to do with kites." Once, Mike's playful dad tied a kite to the bumper of the family Jeep. Spellbound, Mike remembers, "It just flew there all day." Then, a few years later the family traded the Jeep in for a Renault and the Carrolls decided to make their own wind. A little older, Mike launched a kite through the sunroof as he and his dad toured the countryside. "I remember having to pull the kite down periodically so we wouldn't hit power lines and telephone lines."

Later, in his early adulthood, Mike tuned into his local radio station, WOWO, and decided to check out the kite festival they were sponsoring in Fort Wayne. Mike remembers "a lot of mud and a lot of madness going on," and "twenty guys from the local frat house with garbage bags and huge sticks trying to get the largest kite award." Mike watched their colossus collapse and crash, but the day's spectacles inspired him to try his hand at kite making. Deciding on Alexander Graham Bell's fairly complex tetrahedral design, Mike used a "really nasty smelling glue and Saran wrap," paired with eight-inch dowels, to make a super heavy dunker. "I remember it actually going up and flying for a minute. I wasn't real sure what I was doing and then it flipped over and ran into the ground." Standing next to his newly created heap of parts, Mike, was "pleased with at least having done that much." Not bad for a first attempt.

Although that chapter of kite making didn't make it through the

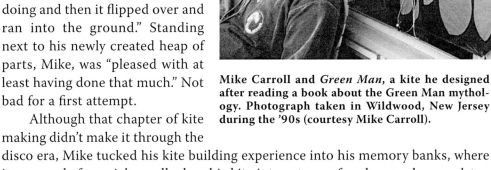

Mike Carroll and *Green Man*, a kite he designed after reading a book about the Green Man mythology. Photograph taken in Wildwood, New Jersey during the '90s (courtesy Mike Carroll).

disco era, Mike tucked his kite building experience into his memory banks, where it was ready for quick recall when his kite interest resurfaced a couple years later. Newly married, and protective of the young couple's pocketbook, Mike found himself in the supermarket checkout and Brummett's *Golden Book of Kites* caught his eye. "Even at the outrageous price of $1.95, I decided to buy it anyway." Investing in his future fun, Mike began building a kite making library and that kept him airborne.

Life later moved Mike to New Jersey and there, Leonard Conover convinced Mike to join Greater Delaware Valley Kite Society, and he "started going to more and more kite festivals, lots of them on the Jersey shore." Needing to increase his kiting gear, Mike learned his way around the sewing machine and figured out "how to do the seams so they usually would hold together." Although Mike is certainly appreciative of fine kite engineering, he found himself "less interested in the archi-

tecture and more interested in what I could put on them." Liking simple kite structures, Mike began using "the surfaces for just free flowing graphics." As Mike's professional career as a software developer took him on out of town on frequent
business trips, he learned to piggyback and manipulate his schedule so he could
squeeze in weekend trips to kite festivals and kite making retreats, like his perennial
favorite at Fort Worden. Being around serious fliers charged Mike up and counter-
acted the effects of sleep deprivation he experience on his frequent red eye flights
back home.

A few years later, Mike tried his hand at a new class of hard pulling, swift twisting sport kites. Something clicked and he found another niche to explore. GDVKS
friends Roger Chewning and Fran Gramkowski "got the idea to hold a competition
dedicated to nothing except stunt kites. They contacted a couple of people to try
and figure out what to do, cause really there hadn't been many, maybe only one
other competition that had been dedicated to stunt kites and we were all making
it up as we went along." Soon Mike found himself sitting in the judge's booth.
Although jazzed at the opportunity, Mike wondered, "What the hell I was going to
do once I got out on the field because we didn't have a clue. Judge a stunt kite competition. What did that mean?"

Prompted to solve a new problem, Mike, Olan Turner, Roger Chewning, Fran
Gramkowski, and George "Corky" Chewning set out to develop the first stunt kite
competition rulebook. Brainstorming for a model, they looked to the competitive
figure skating scoring system. To their dismay, the ice world had little to offer kiting,
so they started from scratch. Some suggested using a ten point system, others were
keen on a twenty-point system, and some lobbied for a 100-point system. Mike
remembers that these discussions came "a couple years after the movie *10* and we
kind of had that in our minds. We decided that we would go with that and tenth
point increments." In the end, mildly influenced by Bo Derek, the group made lasting
strides and outlined a scoring system model that set the stage for today's scoring
framework. In hindsight, "it would have been useful, and less contentious, if we
could have somehow involved other groups in the development of the procedures,
but for at least the first year or two the book was specifically for the East Coast
Stunt Kite Championships and how we worked." Self-critical nitpicking aside, Mike
realizes his contribution to kiting and remarks, "I'm proud of the work the five of
us did in figuring out how to make a stunt competition work and the creation of
procedures to do so, and the idea that those provided one of the starting points for
the current international rules." And many years later, their work continues to guide
the performance of countless competitors around the globe.

As a man of many interests, kiting has shared Mike's leisure time and been
replaced with other hobbies over the decades. "I've had a bunch of interests" including designing and building Japanese paperboard boxes, digital photography, vol-
leyball, creating hanging stain glass art, and guitar. These days, Mike and his wife
live in Port Townsend, Washington and he "volunteers at our local community
radio station as one of their tech guys." While these varied interests do not neces-

sarily overlap or build on each other, "they've each provided an opportunity to visualize something and then create it." And with each, "at some point I seem to reach a plateau of ability or of interest, and subconsciously start looking for something new to learn or play with. Sort of like a shiny new toy." Today, kiting my be the worn old toy in the closet, but Mike's earlier contributions and successes keep the door open for him to revisit kiting at any time.

Pete Dolphin

Born and reared in the Philadelphia area, the youngest of four boys and son of a second-generation funeral director, Pete played the role of fun-loving kid brother

Pete Dolphin (left) with friend Steve Santos, 2017 (courtesy Pete Dolphin).

well and, when looking back, recalls plenty of silly mischief that lightened his schooldays. After high school, Pete headed to Temple University to study engineering and architecture. Four years later, diploma in hand, Pete embarked on his career in the construction industry. For eight years, he apprenticed under two older gentlemen who taught him the tricks of the trade. When they retired, he went to work at a large construction company where, at the age of twenty-nine, he began handling multi-million dollar projects. While tackling these considerable responsibilities, his bank account fattened. In 1982, the Dolphin nest egg was plump enough for him to open his own business. Pete enjoys having his own company because, "There is only one person I can get mad at and that's me."

In 1985, his wife gave him a kite as a Christmas gift. His response was lackluster and untelling of the pull the gift eventually had on his life. "I wasn't very impressed by it until I tried it out, saw the speed, and felt the pull. I was pretty well hooked at that point." Within two years, Pete went from backyard flier to a stunt kite competitor. He competed until 1991 and remembers "some successes and some frustrations."

At around the same time, Pete began traveling to Europe on kiting trips and got exposed to one-of-a-kind handmade kites that wowed and dazzled large crowds of festival goers. Although beautiful, these kites were not for sale. Pete wanted them, so he had to learn to make his own. As luck would have it, Pete lived down the street from a parachute company. Parachute fabric cutoffs make perfect kite cloth, but the company didn't want to sell him their scraps. Turned away from the front door, Pete peeked around to the back where, with flashlight in hand, he hopped into the dumpster to retrieve the mother lode of fabric scraps. Pete squirreled away quite an inventory of cutoffs in his basement. He said the people at the parachute company were not "totally thrilled about someone rooting around the trash, but I was neat about it." To be fair, Pete was also a customer and bought materials from them, but his volume put him in the small potato customer file and many times the sales staff did not want much to do with him.

Not too long after Pete started making kites, he won the People's Choice Award at the Smithsonian Kite Festival. "That fueled the fire," and from there Pete went on to make an endless inventory of signature Dolphin kites. Pete does not consider himself an artist, rather he prefers the tag "clever copier" that Valerie Govig gave him. Pete calls his works *re-Petes* mainly because he gets inspired by something and then riffs off it and transforms the idea into something else.

By the mid–1990s, Pete started "climbing the corporate ladder" and became president of the AKA. When he first started running the AKA he said he treated it like his own company and didn't realize that he had a board of directors to answer to. After hitting a few bumps, "I had to slow down a little bit." Pete enjoyed serving in the AKA, but with two teenagers nearing college, Pete knew he needed to pass the reigns so he could focus on beefing up the family's financial coffers. Reflecting back, his two terms as club president were mostly positive. "I was happy to do it, but it was a huge job."

Over the years, kiting teased out the natural showman in Pete and sparked a love for performing in front of crowds of curious onlookers. A founding member of Team High Fly, he and teammates Fran Gramkowski, Lee Sedgwick, Sue Taft, Ruth Bradley, and Ted Dougherty, took kite showboating to the level of legitimate kite theatre. Pete aptly describes the cast as a "ragtag group who went out and had some fun" while orchestrating theatrical kite skits. Team High Fly cooked up whimsical ways to retell well-known storylines such as *Star Wars* and the *Wizard of Oz* with kites. Set ups were often elaborate and frequently enhanced by full-body costumes, smoke bombs, and show-stopping soundtracks. Over the years, the performance inspired Pete and he enjoyed "putting on a little bit of a show" with kites.

Off the field, Pete shows his kite pride with his extensive kite pin collection. "I'm a pin head." In 1995, at the height of pin mania, Pete ranked his collection as fourth largest in the world—behind David Gomberg, Vic Eshpeter, and Christian Treppner. Pete calmly said he would never chase them because, "I'm never going to catch them. I'm not going to be quite that obsessed." Lugging his seventy-five-pound collection to a kite festival in England, he hefted the load through the airport security, where the screening agents at Heathrow Airport calmly exclaimed "'Oh my, bag check!'" Pete unrolled a sample of his trove on the floor for inspection, and within minutes, a crowd gathered in admiration and curiosity.

Now retired and relocated to Florida, Pete realizes that somewhere down the line he traded his kite passion for a golf obsession, mainly because "there are more opportunities to play golf than kiteflying" in his new town. However, he still finds ample time to fly and occasionally meet up with old friends at select kite festivals. Dabbling also in recent years with kite aerial photography, Pete won a few contests, but those trophies are dwarfed by the Edeiken Award, which crowns his proverbial mantle. Wining the prestigious AKA's lifetime achievement award in 2005, Pete was wowed. "That was quite an honor," and one that continues to tickle Pete and speaks to the deep impact he made in kiting.

John Barresi

Growing up to the beat of a different drummer, master stunt kite flier John Barresi "spent the majority of my time from two and a half to the age of seventeen traveling the country with my father living in a van. Not for a lack of means, just because my father was kind of a unique individual, what I would call a seeker." During his formative years, they trekked to India, Costa Rica, Ecuador, and Mexico, visiting sacred places and meeting progressive thinkers. "That time was mostly about travel and just about learning." Let loose in a playground without boundaries, John experienced the world with an undiluted purity and was trained to recognize, and urged to follow, his life passions.

The first "magical contact" happened in 1990 at San Francisco's Marina Green. John was fifteen and spotted a man flying a "huge giant monster" stunt kite. "It was very interesting, seeing the kite move around and the sound, so I walked out there and said, 'Hey, what's up with that? How does that work?'" The man, an agent of fate, handed John the handles and instructed, "'Right's right, left's left. Here you go.'" Physically outmatched, "the kite just pulled me, I went skiing down the grass." Road wear aside, "I popped up with a feeling that I can still feel today, and that is

John Barresi demonstrating indoor kiteflying with a maneuverable quad line stunt kite (photograph by Kathy Martinelli-Zaun, courtesy John Barresi).

what I'm continually pursuing." Ecstatic, John euphorically recapped the first flight with his dad, and his sage father brought him to Highline Kites in Berkeley where he met Tom McAlister. "I remember he took a lot of time and he explained to me" important kiting fundamentals and sold John his first kite, a "Sky Toys Cheetah." Dedicated, John "flew the better part of every day for the next two and a half years" and embarked on mastering his craft.

Now synonymous with quad-line kites, early on "I did almost everything, very badly," exploring the sport. "That's how you learn." Jumping into kiting during the sport's heyday, John met influential mentors who taught him the technical ropes and started forming a circle of friends he grew to cherish as family. Poring through kite publications like *Stunt Kite Quarterly*, *American Kite Magazine*, *Kite Lines*, and club newsletters, John was a sponge. Unquestionably one of the youngest faces in the sport, John looks back with pride at the egalitarian spirit of kiting, noting the universal support and acceptance he got from other fliers who "never once questioned me standing beside them. That was wonderful."

Thumbing through kite magazines, John learned about competitions. Jumping in, Craig Wong of Paragon Kites sponsored his first trip to the Reno International Kite Festival in 1990. Although they didn't win, John went home high from the experience. In the spring of 1991, he went to San Diego for his first large-scale tournament and was blown away. Though placing around 17th place, the experience kick-started his entry into the sport kiting circuit and marked "the end of my recreational career." Throughout the '90s, John blazed trails, and he and his dad "circled the U.S. three or four times" entering kite contests. Soon, *American Kite Magazine* compared him to his idol and heralded him as "the next Scott Aughenbaugh." Validating his efforts, "that set me on fire, and I just ran, ran, ran." The Air Art team recruited John in 1993 and he has pretty much been part of a team ever since.

Team flying "expanded or clarified things that I did in kiting" and John notes, "I could feel a distinct effect on my ability to output what I wanted to do with kites, that was a pretty notable turning point." A few years later, John moved to Portland. Living on his own for the first time, he got involved with the Invisible Wind masters team. Not long afterward, he moved to Cleveland and lived with his mom and step dad for a year, and Mike Gillard recruited him to Captain Eddies' Flying Circus in Ohio. Helping the team transition from a strictly recreational team to a "fun, kick your butt team," John stuck with them until 1998 when he moved back to Portland.

In these years, the internet was just taking hold and John taught himself coding and web design. "I was just sort of fiddling" but the exploration became relevant when John mixed his computer skills with his love of kites. His first website, Satori Kites, showcased photos and kite competitor biographies. John hoped his site would be a repository of information about individual fliers that would preserve kite history and be a go-to resource for competition announcers. Friend and former teammate Mike Gillard liked what he was doing and reached out to John for help when Mike's duties editing the AKA's magazine kept him from KiteLife, his digital publication venture. The conversation was quick: "'Would you manage KiteLife? Keep the stories coming in?'" As editor, John "just started grabbing pieces of code" and figured out how to rebuild the site and keep it fresh over the years. Ever grateful to Mike, John built in media capabilities, created a member's area, and grew the subscription base. Streamlined and thriving today as an online portal, John packs the site with educational information and partnered with Valerie Govig to digitize and upload every issue of *Kite Lines,* from its start after evolving from *Kite Tales* in 1976 through its swan song release in 1999, as well as archiving *Stunt Kite Quarterly* thanks to the original publisher Susan Batdorff.

In 2007, John and his iQuad team were invited to a festival in Tokyo and his future wife Takako "TK" caught his eye. "She had a lot of style, she looked really good.... I actually snapped a picture of her." Back at home, months later, "she kind of lingered on my mind," and John, wearing his heart on his sleeve, started a long distance relationship. Love blossomed and TK immigrated to the U.S. in October 2009 and stepped right into his life and onto his iQuad team. A kiteflier friend and ordained minister officiated their wedding. "As soon as we finished the ceremony, we stripped out of our wedding clothes and put on our team stuff, went out to the beach and flew kites."

In 2012, the American Kitefliers Association leaders approached John to run the organization. "I took that over at the tail end of some of the AKA's most tumultuous political years." The club is like "a big family, things come up" and John approached the arm wrestle intent on updating seating arrangements, hoping in large part, to give new faces an opportunity to gain firsthand leadership experience from the club's seasoned guard. Reorganizing committees, John searched for newcomers to work with veteran members. By the end of 2013, "I just hit the point where I knew there was nothing else that my skillset could do" and resigned. "Applying a razor" John completely rebuilt his life during the following five months, across 18,000 miles of American road while touring with his wife, giving workshops and private lessons all around the U.S. Focusing on his wife and the things that really inspired him, he divested the weights that held him back.

Over the years, kites have surrounded John and connected every facet of his life. His competitive career, business, marriage, and friendships, are all connected together with a kite line. "I have seen kiting from just about every side, and in spite of politics and business and everything else I have a little pure space inside me which is a fifteen-year-old boy with a Hawaiian kite getting dragged on the grass. So I have always had a pretty conscious protection of the original joy, nothing ever permeates that." For John, kiting is so all encompassing, that "it is actually an absence of concept. It is the real nut that holds me down."

Corey Jensen

With a signature walrus mustache, booming voice, never-ending love of kites, and heart bigger than the sky, Corey Jensen was kiting's impresario and beloved cheerleader. Simply interested in kites and sharing every toy in the sandbox, Corey's all-in involvement in kiting personified modern kiteflying's infectious fun that extends childhood pleasures to every kid at heart.

Born in 1950 in Portland, growing up in Medford, Corey left Oregon "in the late '60s and started traveling all over the world, ending up in Monterey in 1985 after a year up in Santa Cruz and a year up in the Bay Area in a kite manufacturing business." Though later relocating to Las Vegas, Corey for many years anchored himself in Monterey and cultivated it into a kiteflying destination. When he arrived in town, the beachfront was a dump, littered with trash and broken bottles discarded by underage teens and GIs blowing off steam. Looking up past its flaws, Corey flew kites there and little by little started cleaning up the beach. "I didn't put signs up, we just came out here to fly kites," and that spurred people at the State Parks and Recreation Department to develop the site. As plans emerged, the municipal taskforce asked Corey for his feedback. Now with a boardwalk, ADA access, and restrooms, the beach is heavily used and affectionately known to locals as Kite Beach.

Always-impish Corey Jensen surprising the author, Monterey, California, 1995 (photograph by Dinesh Bahadur, author's collection).

"I've been out here flying my kites and looked up and seen some of the most famous kitefliers in the world trudging across the sand to come to this beach to fly with me. It makes my little heart go pitty pat." Seeing the improvements and influencing change "is really gratifying" and helped Corey establish a home base.

Reflecting back, "I got interested in kites because I was a kid, but I got interested in modern kiting and the business in the late '70s with Jane Ambrose in Colorado, making stuff." Jane was manufacturing kites and had a retail store, and at the time, there were very few kite stores. Corey started working for her in 1977, and later in the 1980s, "I made my living solely on kiting because I didn't want to get a real job, grow up, wear a suit, or get into a drudge routine." Opening Windborne Kites in 1985, Corey decided to forego selling toys and novelties at his store, proclaiming, "I believe we are the only truly professional kite store in the country. We wanted to establish that baseline, that this is a sport in and of itself and we don't have to sell hobby gear, boomerangs, or Frisbees." Being a kite merchant suited Corey nicely and allowed him to connect with others. "I'm a very emotional person and kites are something that I'm really passionate about and I want to share that."

Energized by kites and immersed in kite culture, Corey began learning of other adult fliers who shared his passions. "Right off the bat, I started reading *Kite Tales*, a magazine that Bob Ingraham started to augment the American Kitefliers Asso-

Two of kiting's finest, Dinesh Bahadur and Corey Jensen, Monterey, California, 1995 (author's collection).

ciation, and read kite books." Meeting fliers as they visited the store, Corey learned of kite trends by word of mouth. "In 1980 I went to the AKA convention in Seattle, and that changed my life." For the first time, "I realized that there was a whole crowd of people that were just as nuts as the rest of us." Loving the conventions, "I haven't missed an AKA convention since 1980. I missed the first two, but I didn't know about them." Although extroverted and the life of the party, Corey noted, "I don't like crowds, but once a year at the AKA convention, it is like going to St. Peter's for mass, the high altar. I am closer to some of these kiteflying people than I am to some of my own family. I see them more often, too. It is an incredible family that we get to play together with. That is probably the thing I like the best, that sense of family. The inclusion. Those are the rewarding parts that keeps me going day-to-day."

Absorbing goodwill at festivals and committed to helping events succeed, Corey found his niche announcing. "I have no shyness about talking to groups of people, so I just started doing it and kept doing it. Some of the jobs I can't get out of now." In the early days of the Washington State International Kite Festival, Corey stood on a truck bed stage for twelve hours a day, for five days, doing all the sound work, playing the music, and relaying news on walkie-talkies from the field. Although grueling, he did it all to ensure that others could fly. On auction night, to keep club coffers filled, Corey would MC, wearing his trademark loud and colorful Japanese cartoon suit. Always the stand up guy, Corey gave his time and charisma to ensure auction nights were a success.

Corey was a pioneering kite buggy enthusiast. In 1989, Corey saw kite designer Peter Lynn's first prototype, and acquired his by the spring of 1991. "I think I had ordered mine in the fall. It was one of the last prototypes before Peter went into production." Absolutely hooked, Corey blazed trails with traction kiting and fueled an emerging new sport. Simply put, "I love to ride it." Corey enjoyed teaching others how to play and "I publish a magazine called *Buggy News*." As teacher and publisher, "I try to establish an environment where everybody gets to play together and encourage people to learn more about the buggy, so I write articles for kite magazines and spread that around the world." Corey's love of kites and buggying continued for years and he shared the fun with new audiences at Burning Man.

Loving kites and adoring his kite friends, Corey soon found himself traveling as a sponsored guest to festivals around the world. "So, the travel. Boy that is something I didn't expect, but it sure has been grand." Leading tours in Europe, flying in Australia and teaching sport kite clinics in Japan, Corey's playground was boundless. "Everywhere I go, people buy me tequila and beers and let me fly their kites. I'm in heaven. My life is complete. It doesn't take much to make me happy. I like to have fun. I like to see my friends having fun."

Well-known and much loved, Corey was elected AKA president in 1988 through a grassroots campaign. "That was very bizarre, probably my worst year in kiting." Having to do the "things I hate doing, like go to meetings," exhausted Corey, but he toughed it out and helped the club at a time when others could not. Though jesting, "Thank God it was only a year," the experience did not keep him from the boardroom forever. In 2011, Corey headed the Kite Trade Association International for a term and helped promote the business interests of organized kiting.

In 2016, the kiting world lost its fun-loving kid brother and at the AKA convention days after his passing, rather than mourning him, Corey's kite family honored him and gave nod to his pranks by printing Corey's name on the backside of every name badge. For years, Corey enjoyed swapping nametags as an icebreaking conversation starter, and as an impish way to irk orderly organizers who may have been

Honoring Corey Jensen days after he passed, all attendees played Corey's name badge swapping game at the 2016 AKA convention (courtesy Rick Kinnaird).

taking things too seriously and needing a reminder to have fun. "I like the memories. When we go to conventions, I swap nametags. I'll swap 200–300 times during the course of the convention because in twenty years when I open up my box of memorabilia I don't want to pull out my nametag, I know who I am. I will pull out somebody else's nametag and all those wonderful memories will come flooding back."

Don Tabor's Hawaiian masterpiece.

Steve Brockett's *No Two Feathers* kite (courtesy Steve Brockett).

Expert Edo kitemaker Mikio Toki keeps Japanese kite making traditions alive (courtesy Mikio Toki).

Steve Brockett's *Feather Woman*, screen inks on Rip-stop, carbon fiber, 7' (2 m), 2016 (courtesy Steve Brockett).

Steve Brockett's *The Fledgling*, screen ink on polyester fabric, carbon fiber and fiberglass, 59" (150 cm), 2017 (courtesy Steve Brockett).

John Pollock's *Caretaker of the Legend*, acrylic on nylon, 4' x 6' (122 × 183 cm) (courtesy John Pollock).

Van Sant's *White Bird*, Jon Burkhardt (courtesy Jon Burkhardt).

Ralf and Eva Dietrich's bear family: Frederik (32'/10 m), Frederikke (32'/10 m), and Fenja (10'/3 m), during Frederikke's first flight at a kite festival in Fréjus, France (courtesy Ralf and Eva Dietrich).

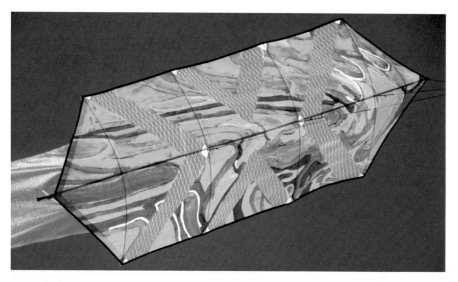

Part of a four-part series called *The 4(5) Elements* that Ralf and Eva Dietrich created for a kite making competition in Dieppe, France, 2012. A Frenchman declared space as the fifth natural element, and for the contest, Ralf decided to use transparent parts that infuse color into kites and honor their place in space (courtesy Ralf and Eva Dietrich).

Ralf and Eva Dietrich's *Hang Bao Singh* star kite flying in San Vito, Sicily. The kite's name translates from Chinese to "Big Red Eight Times Star" and is also a Chinese emperor's nickname (courtesy Ralf and Eva Dietrich).

C4

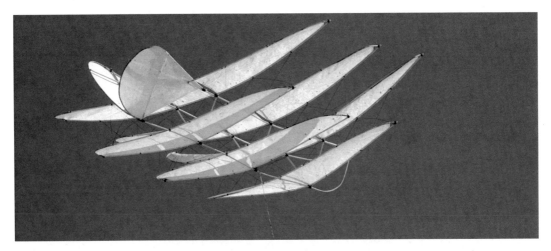

Ralf Dietrich built this beauty out of bamboo and Japanese washi paper (31" × 256"/80 cm × 650 cm). His elegant kite won the German Championship (courtesy Ralf and Eva Dietrich).

Cat Gabrel's snapshot of a trio of kites made by Robert Brasington of Tasmania at the Fanø Kite Meeting in Denmark, 2017 (courtesy Cat Gabrel).

Leaf kite by Bernhard Dingwerth of Germany, snapped by Cat Gabrel on Fanø Island, Denmark, 2015 (courtesy Cat Gabrel).

Kites in the Sky sells this train kite from Windlove Kites as a kit. Out of the box, it arrives all white. Cat Gabrel decorated it with permanent markers and assembled it with Jim Day before flying it in Stillwater, Oklahoma, 2013 (courtesy Cat Gabrel).

Germany's Arthur Skibb's bird kite in flight and photographed by Cat Gabrel at the Fanø Kite Meeting, Denmark, 2015 (courtesy Cat Gabrel).

Two 82-foot-long (25 m) *Spirit Man* kites, designed by Martin Lester of England and made by Dirk Stübinger of Germany, dancing hypnotically at the Fanø Kite Meeting, Denmark, 2015 (courtesy Cat Gabrel).

The Longbottom *Phoenix* kites being flown as part of the main arena display at the 31st RICV in 2017 in Berck-sur-Mer, France. The kites won the Andre Cassagnes Trophy for innovation (courtesy Sara and Karl Longbottom).

Phoenix Number 11 prior to its first flight at the Longbottom home in Dorstone, England, 2017 (courtesy Sara and Karl Longbottom).

Kathy Goodwind enjoying a day at the beach in Wildwood, New Jersey, at the 2011 AKA convention (photograph by Cat Gabrel, courtesy Kathy Goodwind).

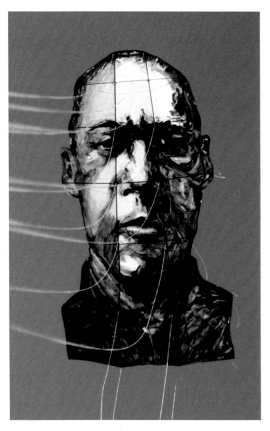

Artistic and haunting, Robert Trépanier's face kites look at you from above (courtesy Robert Trépanier).

Peter Lynn, dragons over kite beach, Dubai (courtesy Peter Lynn Kites).

Always impressive, Peter Lynn Kites animate the sky, Berck-sur-Mer, France (courtesy Peter Lynn Kites).

CHAPTER 2

Tailors at the Beach

"I'm a mechanic, not an artist." George Ham

Cliff Quinn

Living life in three acts, longtime kitemaker Cliff Quinn left two careers before plunging into a kite avocation that won him awards and put smiles on the faces of thousands of children living with serious medical conditions. Long before mastering the intricate art of kite making, Cliff worked for nearly two decades at a large industrial corporation in the northeast that manufactures power plugs and connectors, first as a sales engineer, and then as a product manager. He liked the job, but could do without the corporate hassles. At about the time his son left for college, Cliff became his own boss, and moved his family to Pennsylvania to open a pair of automotive repair centers in Allentown. After graduation, his son joined Cliff at the shops, and in his off time became a NASCAR modified racecar driver and relied on Cliff in his pit crew. Over the years, as Cliff set his sights on retirement, his son learned the ropes and eventually bought the business. Passing the company reins left Cliff with time for himself, and soon kiting took center stage in his daily schedule.

Finding pleasure in kite making from an early age, Cliff's grandfather introduced him to kites when he was about six years old. Together, they constructed kites from household scraps. Reclaimed dowel rods, newspapers, flour paste, and string his grandmother saved from feedbags, all found second lives as kite parts that caught flight above the fields of Cliff's youth. Looking back to these special play dates, Cliff remembers relaxing with his grandfather and being captivated by their morning's work. "We lay in the grass and look up at the kite, see it soaring back and forth, tugging on my finger. It was a great thrill." After his grandfather passed away, "kiting stopped for me," but in the 1990s, when Cliff himself became a grandfather, he re-discovered kiting and this third act pulled him further into kiting than any of his childhood dabbling. Adult kiting began unexpectedly and "came at the right time of my life." While vacationing in Ocean City, Maryland, Cliff and

Cliff Quinn leading a kite making workshop in a fifth grade classroom in Dieppe, France, where the students learn kite making and practice conversational English, 2012 (courtesy Cliff Quinn).

his wife Joyce were dazzled by a sea of magnificent kites that danced above them at the beach. Looking up, "I said to my wife, 'We can do that.' She said, 'You're crazy.'" But, later that day the couple wandered into a kite store and Cliff left with magazines and inspiration. At home, Cliff started learning about kiting, bit by bit. Soon, he discovered the Lehigh Valley Kite Society nearby in Bethlehem and was curious enough to attend a meeting. Quickly hooked, he recruited Joyce, and together they explored their local kite scene and met new friends. "For many years, I wanted to do everything associated with kites, it was like chasing my tail. After awhile I realized you can't do it all and expect to master everything."

With time and exposure, Cliff began focusing on kite making. Leafing through one of his new kite magazines, a pattern caught Cliff's eye. With a can-do spirit, he cut out fabric and asked his wife to sew the kite. Mainly interested in cellular kites, Cliff enjoys the challenge of building these precise and unforgiving fliers. Noting, "I'm not an engineer, but I like mechanical things," Cliff's lifelong interest in woodworking and metalworking likely helped him construct his maiden kite project. That kite was well-received, and fellow club members suggested that the Quinns take it to the Smithsonian Kite Festival. Deciding to compete, "we got in

Cliff Quinn flying a newly constructed diamond kite that he made during his kite making workshop for fifth graders in Dieppe, France, 2012 (courtesy Cliff Quinn).

line, got a number, and we went through the judging tables." After a critical reception by a fussy line judge, Cliff didn't dream they'd place, but asked his wife to stay to the end of the event to see the winning kites. Pleasantly surprised, Cliff was thrilled to take home the Paul Garber bronze medallion. "That was kind of like sinking the hook in." Back home, the couple made a second kite, but by the third, Joyce told Cliff he had to learn to sew himself.

Cliff's accomplishments at the sewing bench are numerous and his firsthand journey learning how to make kites helped him as a teacher. Beginning as a workshop instructor, Cliff taught interested adults how to make kites, but eventually found his niche teaching kids, and later he focused on sharing the magic of kiting with disabled and ill children. "I just love making a difference in their lives" and the opportunity to help came about unexpectedly. One day, while shopping at his local art store, Cliff left his card on the public bulletin board. A few months later, "along came a lady" who asked him if he would like to display his kites at a charity event she was organizing to support the Ronald McDonald House in Philadelphia. He did, and later she invited him to a summer camp to teach kids how to make kites. Opening his heart and rolling up his sleeves, Cliff taught pediatric cancer patients and left the camp deeply satisfied and inspired.

Convinced that kites could also pull smiles from other kids, Cliff searched for similar children's wellness organizations and discovered Paul Newman's Hole in the Wall Gang Camp. Cliff contacted their activities director and traveled to their camp in Connecticut to teach kite making classes to kids with life-threatening illnesses. "What a thrill" it is to teach the children to make kites, and then there is a "second thrill when they go out and fly." Witnessing firsthand how kites bring "smiles from ear to ear and joy into their hearts," Cliff knows he has "made a difference in their difficult lives" and when he travels around the country to "kite festivals I go on the internet and look for children's hospitals in the area." Working with hospital program coordinators, Cliff creates kite making events for kids facing grim medical prognoses. "My batting average is 1000, everybody accepts my offer with open arms." In 2011, the AKA honored Cliff's significant outreach efforts and presented him with the Robert M. Ingraham Award. Never resting on his laurels, Cliff continues to share kites with ill children, seniors in assisted living centers, and museums looking to enrich the lives of their members.

As a go-to kite expert, Cliff's kite making skills helped producers at the History Channel demonstrate a visual perception experiment. Cliff built an enormous condor kite, and the show's producer filmed a segment of their *Birdzilla* show in a Minneapolis park and recruited fellow AKA flier Barbara Meyer to fly it. Isolated upward, without nearby objects as size references, onlookers were asked to estimate the wingspan. Most guesses were far off, and only "one older gent" correctly guessed its 25-foot wingspan. Cliff's handiwork helped the show discuss the vagaries of human optical perspectives and found an offbeat use for kites that only enriched Cliff's portfolio of kite making expertise.

Bobby Stanfield

Born with nimble hands and a mind for design, master kitemaker Bobby Stanfield tapped into kiting as an adult and discovered a little outlet for his huge talent. Son of a nurse and a Baptist minister, brother to five siblings, Bobby grew up in the southeast. As a child, Bobby preferred balls to books, action to rest, and creating things from his imagination over thinking through stale instruction. A little bit of a rebel, but mainly a spunky kid, Bobby wheeled through his childhood days remembering more fun times than hard times.

While working in a professional cabinetry shop, Bobby stumbled onto a life-enriching opportunity. Between large millwork orders, his easygoing boss let everyone ride the clock and use the shop tools to tackle personal projects. During a downtime patch, Bobby listened when "an old man in the shop said, 'Why don't you go fly a kite?'" Bobby thought, "'You know, I could build one.'" Twenty minutes later he had a kite and was flying it behind the shop. By the next day, all the cabinetmakers had kites and shop work was temporarily roofless. Bobby never looked back and charged headlong into a life with kites.

Bitten by the kite making bug, Bobby quickly amassed a stable of paper kites. One afternoon, his wife came home with festively colored fabric and said, "'What do you think of it?'" Being an honest man, Bobby confessed, "'Well it is kind of wild, isn't it? What are you going to do with it?'" A coach by nature, his wife countered, "'I'm tired of looking at brown paper. You're going to build a cloth kite.'" This leftfield idea caught Bobby off guard. Not knowing how to sew, he hadn't thought much past sticks and paper. Bobby's wife did not fuss over his lack of sewing skills and simply instructed him to "'use glue.'" Around this time, Bobby's kite making expanded to French military kites and other kite patterns he found in David Pelham's time-tested kite making book. Looking back, his wife's prodding heralded what he calls "the cotton and poplar wood phase" of his kite making career.

As Bobby's kite making skills grew, so did his kiting network. He met people in the AKA and club membership opened new doors. Bobby remembers meeting Charlie Henderson early on and Charlie invited him to kite events at Stone Mountain, Georgia. Ultra competitive, Bobby vowed to become a winner and record breaker. While sizing up the competition, Bobby unanimously heard that Adrian Conn was the best kitemaker around. Immediately, Bobby knew, "I'm gonna take him on!" In preparation, Bobby worked on a special kite for seven months and hauled it to his first AKA convention in San Diego. During this time, the legend grew. Bobby imagined Conn to be "a seven-foot-tall giant," but was, "surprised when it turned out he was four-foot eleven, barely 100 pounds, and the sweetest guy in the world." Months of honing his competitive bravado went unneeded for his meeting with Adrian Conn, and Bobby quickly learned that "kiting is loaded with wonderful, down to earth, sincere people." Over the years, Bobby has remained impressed by the goodwill in kiting circles and fondly recalls how kite friendships helped soothe the sting of emotional rough periods in his life. World-round, the camaraderie he's experienced is consistent and genuine, making kiting both irresistible and comforting for Stanfield.

Long after Bobby's formative kraft paper days, he reached for high tech materials and let himself experiment. His tinkering evolved into intricate yet streamlined cellular kites. "My first love is lightness, so I build clean kites that fly in the widest range of winds." By streamlining construction, Bobby guesses that his kites "have a look that lends itself to flight and that takes on a look of its own." When fine tuning his designs and selecting color swatches, Bobby listens to his moods and pulls confident blues, hopeful yellows, and fired up reds together to express the feelings that swell during the kite making process. For Bobby, "it is a combination of things give my kites a certain look." His crisp line work is distinctive and, in 2015, the AKA recognized Bobby's contributions with the Lee Toy Award. Celebrating his outstanding skills, shortly afterward, Bobby retired from kite making at the top of his game.

Charm and Ron Lindner

Kites strings don't tie up too many childhood memories for St. Louis natives Charm and Ron Lindner, yet the couple later blossomed into fine kitemakers. Ron recalls, "kites never crossed my mind" until later in adulthood when he and Charm were walking on a beach in San Diego and happened upon a guy doing loop-de-loops with a sport kite. Without hesitation, Ron approached the flier and asked if he could fly his kite. The flier passed the handles and the kite went up, up, up, and then crashed into the ocean. A little deflated, with his tail between his legs, Ron figured he'd just bought his first stunt kite, but the beach flier was easygoing and said, "'No harm done.'" Red faced but interested, their beach stroll introduced Ron and Charm to a new breed of kites and shortly afterward Ron "was hooked on sport kites," and ended up purchasing several dozen kites over the next six months.

Infectiously fun, Charm and Ron Lindner enjoy making kites and being together (courtesy Charm and Ron Lindner).

Attracted to stacks of kites, Ron's budding interest in kiting initially left Charm a little nonplussed. Later she saw that, unlike the unreliable kites of her youth, these modern kites "really did fly." She got interested and joined in on the fun, first flying and then making kites. As Charm warmed to kites, Ron enjoyed pleasing crowds at kite events and teamed up with Glenn Mueller to fly stacks in duet over the next five years until Glenn fell ill and succumbed to cancer. Thinking back to his days of tandem flying, Ron remarks, "Glenn was an excellent flier and I was and excellent follower." The two dazzled crowds and their groundbreaking routines stumped judges and wowed spectators. They got

Dinner in Chicago's Chinatown, Patti Gibbons, Charm and Ron Lindner, 2017 (author's collection).

"standing ovations, but no points, because there wasn't yet a way to score" routines consistently, but victories did not matter. The thrill of pushing the kiting envelope jazzed and motivated them to try new things.

Merely knowing how to fly kites well did not satisfy Ron and Charm, and soon they got a full-blown case of the kiting bug and began making their own creations. Charm, with her lifelong interest in studio arts, especially pencil illustration and Japanese sumi-e painting, took to kite making easily. One winter, people from their local kite club got together to make stunt kites, and Charm recalls that with their first kite, "We made every mistake you could have made on it, but it flew." Encouraged, Ron and Charm kept going and came up with an assembly system for their next kite where Ron "cut out the material and marked it" and Charm later sewed the parts together at home. The finished kite looked like stain glass with individually numbered color panels, and people later nicknamed it the "paint by numbers kite." Their technique may have been naive, but the quality of their work held up over the years.

In addition to stunt kite making, Charm developed a romance with miniature kites. She has won awards for her tiny creations and some have found their way into museum collections. She enjoys the challenge of creating petite fliers and as a kitemaker, Charm especially appreciates creating "something a little unusual." One year, after placing in an international kite making competition, Ron was quick to point out that only two Americans received accolades, "and Charlie Sotich was the other person." Legendary miniature kitemaker Charlie Sotich, mentored Charm and she and Ron cherished their friendship with the late kite making luminary. Recalling back to a time when Charlie visited them in St. Louis, and knowing Charlie was an active model airplane builder, the couple suggested they visit a model airplane event happening nearby that day. The Lindners were floored at the rock star reception Charlie received. "I had no idea he was so famous in the ultralight field. He drew a crowd and the event came to a standstill." Beloved by kitefliers and airplane builders alike, Charm and Ron remember Charlie fondly and Charm took her second place finishes to him as honors, because, "Charlie, you just couldn't beat him."

Throughout the late 1980s, the Lindners progressively became more active with organized kiting and turned up regularly at festivals and kiting events. With exposure, the couple absorbed a great deal about the sport and learned how to manage and organize kiting events. Longtime members of the St. Louis Gateway Kite Club, Ron spent a few years as president and advanced kiting in their metro area. In addition, the Lindners kept an active schedule in national kiting circles, volunteering annually at the AKA convention's Fly Mart and helping behind the scenes with tasks only dedicated volunteers would even notice during the club's busiest get-together. As accomplished kitemakers, Ron and Charm continually share their knowledge and regularly teach kite making classes at U-MAKE. The AKA honored the Lindners in 2008 with their Volunteer of the Year Award and the Robert M. Ingraham Award a year later.

Active fliers and club members, somewhere down the line, the Lindners also inadvertently backed into the kite trade, as owners of Flying High with Charon—the kite store they launched to help them, and fellow fliers, get higher quality kites than they could readily acquire through other retail avenues. Looking back, Ron comments that they approach the store like a hobby. Busy with his electrical contracting business, and Charm occupied throughout the years as a housewife, dog groomer, office manager, and bus driver, the store was never something the Lindners saw as a viable business pursuit. "I got other things to do" but the toehold into the kite trade helped the Lindners get quality kites into the hands of interested fliers and, although the store space is really a spare bedroom, they continue to fill orders upon request.

Married for more than sixty years, life together "just keeps getting better." Ron and Charm enjoy sharing leisure interests, and as hobbies go, organized kiting suits them perfectly. Over the years, the sport has allowed them to travel and form important and lasting friendships with interesting people who have enriched their lives and met them on common ground. The Lindners are drawn to kiting and, even though their kite making is beginning to slow, Ron notes he and Charm are "basically just having fun with it all."

John and Marzlie Freeman

"Like everybody else in the world, when I was a kid my dad made a kite out of newspaper and kindling wood," and, "no, it didn't fly." Though he was unimpressed with failed father-son craft projects, that dud did not dampen master kitemaker John Freeman's aerial curiosities later in life. As a married couple, John and Marzlie Freeman always kept a store-bought kite in the car in case a nice breeze crossed their path. Their casual preparedness took a turn around 1990 when their daughter came home from a beach outing, a bit breathless and bedazzled by her day with a Trlby sport kite, and said, "'You gotta try this!'" The tug was strong and the Freemans purchased a Trlby that opened doors to kite experimentation. From Trlbys to Skynasaurs and then through Catch the Wind's line of sport kites, in a short time, the die was cast and this foundry artisan by day began an informal second career in kiting and Marzlie found another creative outlet to showcase her sewing talents.

As sport kites opened his eyes to what kites could do, John, a do-it-yourselfer, got curious to the possibility of making his own kites after seeing an advertisement for the Fort Worden Kitemakers Conference. Up until this point, John had never sewn, and he looked to Marzlie to teach him to thread the machine before heading to class. Sewing since she was five and seamstress to her family, Marzlie helped John figure out kite making, and thought through projects one by one, as she did with clothes for the family, formal dresses for her daughters, and tailored suits for John. Together, they explored kite making, and little by little,

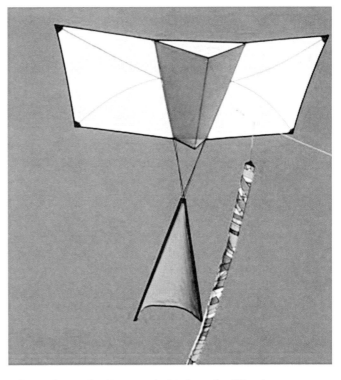

John and Marzlie Freeman's *Bird on the Wire* (courtesy Marzlie Freeman).

In his trademark stocking feet, John Freeman teaches kite making classes at the World Kite Museum, 2005 (courtesy Marzlie Freeman).

John learned to sew kites. Starting with smaller fighter kites and working up to large fliers they dubbed *Not Peter Lynn Kites*, they dabbled, developed skills, and nurtured a budding interest in kite design.

Strongly drawn to quilting techniques, John experimented and found that Bargello and log cabin patterns were perfect for kite making. Mastering a range of styles, John began leaving his patchwork trademark in the sky and others quickly got interested in his craft. In nearly a dare, World Kite Museum director Kay Buesing approached John with an idea to teach a weekend kite making class and prefaced her appeal with a "'Why don't you...'" dare. Gauntlet thrown, John started teaching complex kite making workshops at the Kite Museum. For over a decade, each Presidents' Day weekend, John kicked off his shoes and taught students in his stocking feet. Snubbing the restrictiveness of business attire, John embraced informalities and remarked, "It is just comfortable and it is what I do at home. When I'm teaching a class, I'm at home, so why not?" For the record, John never stepped on a pin, showing naysayers that coziness and caution can coexist.

Jumping off from the success at the World Kite Museum, John went on to teach classes at Fort Worden, the Oregon Kitemakers Retreat, AKA conventions, and internationally during kite travels to Australia. As an instructor, John's philosophy

John and Marzlie Freeman, World Kite Museum workshop, 2008 (courtesy Marzlie Freeman).

was to guide his students. "I don't make artistic decisions," yet, he was often pleasantly surprised with their finished work. As a teacher, John found that graphics challenged beginners, but with practice "there's no end to what you can do quilting." A fan of variety but with respect for tradition, John favored ingenuity over custom. "I look at places like Indonesia who have century-old traditions of kite making, and for the last 500 years they built the exact same kites. If it were that way here, I wouldn't be interested." For John, "it is the continual variation, variety, discovering

Vertigo 2, **John and Marzlie Freeman (courtesy Marzlie Freeman).**

something new and different" that fueled him. "The ingenuity you can pour into it" is endless and John experimented without repetition.

In addition to building kites, John nurtured a concurrent passion for fabricating paper models. Not as well known in North America, this whimsical hobby is beloved in Europe and Asia. Using card stock and a desktop computer printer, John built models of everything from beetles to bombers, perhaps inspired by hand skills he honed in kite making. Crafty, dexterous, and with a natural eye for color, John sculpted fun for the tabletop and the sky.

Native west coasters, John and Marzlie moved around from California to Oregon and retired in British Columbia. Married over fifty years, the college sweethearts explored kiting together and shared a pastime that brought them pleasure and allowed them to build cherished friendships. Looking back, as winds pulled kites up and away, the Freemans recall chasing entertainment and joining clubs to meet fellow fliers. Enjoying the friendships they made as much as the prized kites they stitched, John remarked, "There is something about this hobby that doesn't seem to attract obnoxious people." Over the years, John and Marzlie met many fun-loving people in kiting, and because "you just can't have too many friends," the Freemans joined five kite clubs. In 1994, Marzlie "started editing the Oregon Kiters newsletter" and began editing the Washington Kitefliers Association's club newsletter in 2007. To date, editor Marzlie is ever in contact with fellow fliers "trying to get members to send in articles and photos" for the AOK and WKA newsletters. Her friendliness and interest in people's kite doings keep her active in kiting and help others stay connected. Unfortunately, John passed away in 2010, but his expert instructions keep patchwork kites coloring the sky, and Marzlie sweetly comments, "I always feel he is looking over my shoulder when I am working on my embroidery digitizing designs."

Nancy Lockwood

Native to the Buckeye State, Nancy Lockwood spent most of her life chasing the American dream around the greater Cleveland metro area. After raising six children and a long career in journalism, Nancy caught the kite bug and cheerfully welcomed a little color into her world. Ace kitemaker, team flier, and friend to everyone she meets, Nancy Lockwood's kite odyssey enriches her life, and helps keep her forever young. As many kitefliers can readily confirm, Nancy notes that "Peter Pan is not the only boy not to grow up. There is a child inside every one of us." And, Nancy's inner child is certainly familiar with kite lines and fabric tails.

In the 1980s, recently divorced and involuntarily downsized from the rapidly shrinking world of journalism, Nancy found herself in a bit of a blue period. Down and disoriented, Nancy could have tossed in the towel, but instead kept her chin up and remained open to friendly suggestions. In an effort to ease her woes, her good pal Harry Gregory suggested, "Let's go fly a kite." Nancy was game, so Harry grabbed the Hi-Flier that had decorated his wall and the two went flying. A short time later, they discovered the Ohio Society for the Elevation of Kites and went to one of the club's daylong kite events in Cleveland. They met people and "it's just been up from there on out." Nancy looks back on that time and realizes "I sort of reorganized myself and reinvented myself" through kiting.

Nancy Lockwood modeling *Chinese Bugs Fly on Strings,* a period happi coat she made for the World Kite Museum's auction, 2009 (courtesy Nancy Lockwood).

Coinciding with Nancy's entry onto the Cleveland kite circuit, her younger brother, a sail maker, visited from North Carolina and plunked a huge box of Ripstop nylon scraps on her table and said, "'Here, do something with this.'" Nancy opened the box, fingered through the colorful swag, and her imagination percolated. The fabric booty was perfect for kite making. Nancy's first creation was a Chinese three-stick kite sporting an American quilt design. Nancy was pleasantly pleased with her patchwork creation and began her journey into kite making.

Calling upon her Pennsylvania Dutch heritage, Nancy researched traditional graphic images and incorporated symbols of good fortune and friendship into her early kites. Her inaugural line of windsocks sported Dutch motifs and caught the eye of a friend who asked to buy the friendship sock. Surprised, Nancy admitted, "I never thought of selling them," but her persistent friend replied, "'Well you better start. How much do you want for one?'" Soon after her first sale, Nancy discovered a budding market for windsocks at craft fairs, art stores, and kite shops, as well as word of mouth custom-design orders.

Granddaughter to a professional seamstress, Nancy learned "what was excellent, what was good, and what was acceptable sewing" as a young girl. Through her grandmother's instructions, coupled with years of making Halloween costumes, curtains, school clothes, and quilts, Nancy learn to sew anything, and her experience came in handy as Nancy experimented with kite making. Nancy notes, "I approach windsocks the same way I did kid toys and stuffed animals." Armed with an idea, she sketches a general outline, pieces together parts drawn on template paper, and connects the dots as she works. In the early days complicated figures, such as her Uncle Sam windsock, took months of tinkering to get the scale and pocket openings just right, but with each project Nancy picked up technical tricks that shortened her time at the proverbial drawing board. Nancy's sewing proficiency, along with her innate art sensibilities, have given her a leg up in kite making ventures. She recognizes her natural "eye for art," but aside from afternoon art classes taken at a local museum as a girl and training in journalistic photography in college, the graphic arts did not dominate Nancy's word-driven professional life. Kiting nurtured her natural creative talents and put her skills to work.

While Nancy certainly excels in kite making, she made a name for herself making kite accessories. In the '90s, AKA president David Gomberg put out a call asking members to design a banner for the AKA. Nancy submitted the winning design, and at final count, she made 103 sixteen-foot long banners that helped the AKA's branding campaign. Throughout the '80s and '90s, stunt kite fliers and teams were looking for colorful ways to mark spaces in the flying fields, and Nancy's custom feathers and banners delighted people. Swamped with orders, in 1993 Nancy published an article in *American Kite Magazine* titled "Sewing the Flag" to share her knowhow. Fliers from countless fields tried her advice and Nancy is forever thrilled when people send her pictures of their creations and pull her aside at events to show off their handiwork.

When Nancy isn't behind her sewing machine, it is very likely that she's lending a hand at kite events. Besides hosting "make it, take it" workshops and being a nurse in the kite hospital tents at club-sponsored kite events, Nancy also brings the world of kiting to the general public through her touring workshops at local schools and libraries. As she teaches people to build kites, Nancy shares general kite history that she enjoys researching "because I would hate to find the knowledge of kites fade into nowhere." Knowing that "early kites came from China and other Asian countries, I began to look for how they got to Europe and then the Americas." Nancy has traced the "routes, the dates, and parts of human history between 1300 and 1650 that played a role in how we got kites. Since some of it is stories rather than solid facts, verifying what I've found is still incomplete."

In between banner making and teaching workshops, Nancy revels in joyful times at kite events near and far. Being a bit of a social butterfly, Nancy quickly made friends through kiting and looking back, recognizes that it is kiting's camaraderie that feeds her. "It is just so special. I think that is what I've enjoyed the most about getting into this entire world.... Walk up to somebody at a festival, say, 'Hi' and you've got a hug."

Margaret Greger

A beloved pioneer in the kiting world, Margaret Greger found a knack for writing transparently clear kite making instructions that have helped generations of newcomers, day fliers, and expert kitemakers alike get new kites up and soaring.

Born in the 1920s in Nebraska, Margaret "never saw a kite until I was thirteen" but learned to make two-stick kites from "honey brown wrapping paper from mailing packages" and willow poles under the guidance of a boy who moved to their town. "We didn't know much about what we were doing" but, Margaret recalled, at the edge of the Dust Bowl, "We had wind." Imperfect but fun, Margaret "always liked kites" and her fond childhood memories helped her welcome kites back into her life later in adulthood.

Bright, with a can-do spirit, Margaret was the valedictorian of her high school class and, at seventeen, left home to study journalism at the University of Nebraska. There, she met George Greger, and the couple married in 1947. The newlyweds moved to New York. While in college, Margaret learned her way around a linotype machine, and joined the Typographical Union, and quickly found a job in New York setting printing type for a newspaper. A few years later, when George got a job on the nuclear Hanford Project, the couple relocated to west-

Carefree Margaret Greger flying *Sky Window* in Richland, Washington, 1979 (photograph by Greg Greger, courtesy Jan Gregor).

ern Washington and set down roots, raising seven kids, and championing social causes and civil rights. Margaret was a teacher, writer, and later a volunteer librarian for her local chapter of the Audubon Society.

Kites reentered Margaret's life when her children enrolled in summer camp and she was looking for a new craft activity to teach them. Kites came to mind, jumpstarted by their recent visit to the Seattle's World's Fair, where she bought them a snake kite. "I was so amazed at how it flew" and later, at home, Margaret noticed her bamboo blinds and, in an aha moment, "realized I could make that kite" and switch to curtains. Summertime camp activities kicked off the beginning of her kite making with kids and her own involvement with organized kiteflying.

Margaret Greger flying a *Joseph Lee Delta Bird* kite, Richland, Washington, 1985 (photograph by Greg Greger, courtesy Jan Gregor).

A teacher and den mother, Margaret's lessons evolved into kite making workshops—thousands of them, and later Margaret sought to partner with educators who could teach kite making to children in their classrooms. As her workshop work grew, Margaret began writing down instructions, not only for her students but also to help her build her tools and materials list. "These instructions have been vetted by many, many people who didn't know anything when they started out and were able to succeed." Class after class, Margaret observed where students got hung up and she polished and refined her instructions to make learning seamless. "After a few years of that, I realized I was halfway through a book of instructions."

In 1977, Margaret published *Blown Sky High*, the first of four instructional kite-making books she would write. "Self published all the way," Margaret "worked with a small local press to get it into shape." Looking back, Margaret recalled it was "not hard to sell," largely because she knew her market. Starting with a modest 500-book print run, the title sold out, and the feedback she received was excellent. "What happens, to my surprise, when you publish a book is that other people who have kites in the same genre will write to you and say, 'You might like to know about this one.' People are extremely generous, they know they aren't going to do a book

Margaret Greger flying a *Lynn Lary Delta-Conyne* kite, Richland, Washington, 1985 (photograph by Greg Greger, courtesy Jan Gregor).

but they would like to share" their favorite kites with people. Gathering ideas for other kite making projects, Margaret tested and perfected instructions for new kite styles and added them to her repertoire. "As I began running out" of printed books, "I combined them all into *Kites for Everyone.*" With a non-stop circuit of testing new ideas in workshops, for children, teachers, adults, and seasoned kitemakers, Margaret went on to write *More Kites for Everyone* and *Simple Fabric Kites,* leaving her mark as the preeminent person for kite making instructions. "The pleasure of getting a good, lucid set of instructions down is tremendous," and motivated Margaret to articulate the time-honored secrets of kite making.

Making a name for herself as an expert kitemaker and instructor, Margaret joined the AKA early on and corresponded frequently with influential kitefliers.

One of the club's pillars, Margaret helped take frustration out of kite making and ensured that fliers found fun. "I have come to enjoy watching other people fly and make kites, and helping them with their kites is almost more fun than flying them myself. It is a pleasure being with a bunch of people with kites because they are happy people, they are pleased with themselves, and they are enjoying what they are doing." In 1996, *American Kite Magazine* named her their person of the year, and the World Kite Museum inducted her into kiting's hall of fame in 2002. Sadly, Margaret passed away in 2009, but her books remain the definitive source for kite making instructions.

Gary Engvall

Looking to the sky with fascination, native New Englander Gary Engvall has pulled cherished friendships and a lifetime of fun from the kite lines he's launched over the years. Growing up near Worcester, Massachusetts, the kiting bug bit Gary in childhood and he has maintained a keen interest in kites throughout his life. "I was always fascinated with things that flew and kites were the next best thing to airplanes."

In his formative years, young Gary flew traditional dime store paper and plastic Hi-Flier and Gayla variety kites. "You bought them in March or in April because that's when kite season was" and Gary perennially tinkered with his stockpile, modifying bridles and tails to optimize flight. Somewhat of a loner, Gary enjoyed the freedom of experimenting without boundaries and without meddling mentors. "There was nobody telling me to run ... or to 'hold it this way'... and I didn't get any bad advice. I was able to figure it out by myself." Self-directed exploration fueled Gary's imagination and kick-started a lifelong odyssey that only grew stronger in adulthood. For Gary, kiting remains new. "I'm still waiting for the wonder to wear off."

Always with kite in hand, it was not until he was in his 30s that Gary discovered "anything other than paper and plastic" kites. While driving about 100 miles from his home, Gary unexpectedly happened upon World on a String, a small kite and aerial toy store. Astonished by the variety of kites, Gary circled through the store flooded with inspiration and awe. Joyfully admiring winged box kites and two-line Trilby kites, Gary recalls, "I walked around with my mouth open." Wide-eyed and overjoyed, Gary kept his cool and didn't let the experience tank his pocketbook. "Some people are thrifty, but I'm cheap. I didn't buy a kite, I bought a book." With David Pelham's timeless *Kites* in hand, Gary "started building from day one and never looked back."

Eager to expand his instructional library, Gary soon picked up Wayne Hosking's *Kites: Aussie Style* and Margaret Greger's *Kites for Everyone* and pushed on with his skyward experiments. First welding faceted kites from plastic trash bags, Gary later advanced to fabric box kites. Overall, looking back Gary notes, "I did what everybody does. I took out the wife's sewing machine and put it on the kitchen table" and dabbled. Quickly becoming proficient at sewing, he snapped up his aunt's Pfaff cabinet machine and developed a preference for these resilient workhorses. Though he does not tote these brutes to workshops, he found room for three at home.

Generous and open to sharing his kite knowledge, Gary frequently teaches

Rhode Islander Gary Engvall and his red, white and blue cellular kite *Mirage* (courtesy Gary Engvall).

Seasoned kitemaker Gary Engvall doesn't shy away from complex cellular kites (courtesy Gary Engvall).

kite making workshops. "Being at the front of the room was new to me" but he quickly got the hang of guiding people through the steps of kite making. For Gary, there is a three-stage learning curve. First, you follow patterns to the letter, no matter how nonsensical they sound. Next, you open up to improvisation and change plans to fit your own method of building. Then, the last stage is where you get inspired and just figure it out, without any printed plans. Over the years Gary has taught many and delights when "my protégées graduate" to the "see one, build one" level. Furthering his instructional reach outside the classroom, Gary freely publishes kite making advice and plans on the internet. He has made instructional videos that he shares on YouTube where he narrates DIY instructions with sideline tips that teach newcomers about sewing techniques and product information. Beyond a simple how-to approach, Gary makes sure people understand the fundamentals of kite making in hopes that they will have fun.

Soon after discovering the World on a String store and exploring kite making, Gary began meeting other adult kitefliers and joined kiting clubs whenever he learned about them. Though not a glad-handing politico, Gary served as the American Kitefliers Association's president from 2008–2009 and furthered the club's mission to reach out to fliers and celebrate kites. "I don't understand politics ... but if you want to get something done, I'm your guy. If you want to talk about it for two weeks, I'm probably not your guy." His straight shooting brand of leadership helped Gary's administration get kites launched across the country.

Whether helping kiting from the president's office or from a flying field, Gary's undeniable passion for kiting attracts and welcomes newcomers. "There is something in kiting for everybody. Anybody, whatever your ability, whatever your activity level, there is something in kiting that you can excel at, at every age." This universal even playing field tickles Gary and fuels him to keep on pulling strings.

Stormy Weathers

Longtime fixture on west coast flying fields and early AKA member Warren "Stormy" Weathers was an ever-curious problem solver who started asking questions whenever he flew a kite. "How does this work? Why does it work?" Then thinking, "What would happen if I changed *this* just a bit? Would it fly better?" Down to earth, approachable, and kind, this Oregonian left his mark on kiting, patenting kite plans, challenging a century-old altitude flying records, and creating workhorse kite reels that continue to help today's fliers stay afloat.

With practice, patience, and a heavy dose of stick-to-it-ness, technical writer and Navy veteran Stormy became a superb kitemaker later in life after overcoming his share of amateur kiting flops. In childhood, kites were part of afternoon fun for young Stormy, but he did not think about them again until he retired from the Navy and wanted to go fishing. While stationed in the Solomon Islands on a tour of duty in 1942–43, Stormy heard about kite fishing. Back stateside, without plans or instructions, Stormy picked up a Hi-Flier and gave kite fishing a blind try. Wind conditions were rough as Stormy tied his fishing line to his kite, and fifteen minutes later, "the kite was in the drink." After some experimentation, Stormy found that a half-filled plastic jug kept "the kite from flying away with your bait and kept the fish from drowning the kite." Stormy's nickel solution

Stormy Weathers flying a steady kite at the beach (courtesy Ann Weathers Ebelmesser).

allowed "absolute control over the bait." Green before his time, Stormy encouraged people to go kite fishing, noting that, "it's safe for the environment and you can get stuff as good with a kite as you do in a boat."

Aside from sneaking up on fish, Stormy's kite interests blossomed over time and, in 1975, he and his son competed in a local kiting event. Looking around, Stormy saw a sea of flimsy reels and got an itch to come up with something better. That afternoon, Stormy mingled, meeting people and collecting their contact information. Back at work, his company was tossing out a mound of plastic spools. Stormy asked if he could have a few and his gleeful manager said, "'Take all you like.'" Armed with raw materials, Stormy mocked up test reels and sent them to fliers along with a questionnaire. About a month later, Stormy analyzed the results and determined that people were asking for something that did not exist. Parsing ideas, Stormy determined that the perfect reel had to be comfortable, easy to use, and have a locking spool. After some tinkering, he created a champ and began selling them. Later on, Stormy continued to fiddle with reels and retooled a Honda steering wheel to let out three lengths of line for every full turn. With a mindset that improvements are always possible, he modestly remarked, "the world still needs a good kite reel."

As Stormy explored reel building, he learned more about kites and started experimenting with kite making. After a couple lackluster diamond kites, he discovered the Allison polymorphic—his all-purpose favorite go-getter. Early on, Stormy saw many kites go up and suddenly collapse. Perplexed and hungry to solve the problem, Stormy zoomed in for a closer look. Making a large kite and flying it low, Stormy saw how his kites buckled under wind pressure. Wheels turning, the "Aha!" light bulb went off above his head, Stormy cut a V in the leading edge and cured the problem. Others elsewhere came up with similar solutions, such as notching semicircles, but Stormy's V was simple and effective. Years later while reading a story about South American kiteflying, Stormy noted with pride that they, too, clip Vs in their leading edges.

Always inching toward improvements, Stormy's crowd-pleasing Star Victory evolved from the simple Allison polymorphic body that he modified to launch from the ground. To gain air he put wings on the Allison, and from there a star was born when he notched two Vs in the leading edge, and added a soda straw mast in the center to hold the canopy open around a star-shaped body. Worrying needlessly that it would collapse in the wind, he "took it out and it flew beautifully." Believing in his design, he made samples and shipped them to AKA friends for feedback. AKA club founder Bob Ingraham test-drove an ill-fated early star. Up in the air something went wrong and the kite spun. Bob fed it line, only to have it spiral faster with slack. "For the first time in his life, he wound up with a kite in a power line. I heard about that one!" Setbacks like that may discourage some, but Stormy weathered them well. "I always shared my developments with respected kite builders and fliers so I could get feedback. I take criticism as well as the next person, which means I get mad as hell." Though irked, Stormy teased good from negative comments and used suggestions to slowly reach solid results. Stormy's kiting knowledge matured through the seasons but his designs always remained streamlined and economic. "I like things that are simple. I'm a simple person myself."

Stormy's eye for improvements produced results. His kites were stable and flew well. For a time Stormy held the high altitude kite flight record, and he impishly enjoyed involving kites in semi-mischievous pranks. For kicks, around Halloween Stormy made an oversized kite

Even in death, Stormy Weathers encourages kiteflying (courtesy Ann Weathers Ebelmesser).

out of clear plastic and decorated it with a luminous painted cross and flew it at night over a well-trafficked walking path. Flying in the dark, Stormy's glow-in-the-dark kite was an eerie sight that spooked passersby but delighted him as he watched the lightning quick exits the frightened made and surmised that "more than a few people that night 'got religion.'" During the gloomy Oregon winters, Stormy frequented the Clackamas Town Centre with a palm-sized sled kite that only needed a whisper of air to fly. His minuscule kite bobbed merrily above his shoulder as he surprised mall walkers with his seemingly magical indoor kite. Stormy's well-crafted kites brought enjoyment to him as well as to onlookers.

Warren "Stormy" Weathers, 1921–2003, loved sharing kiteflying and his gravestone reads, "Stormy Says Go Fly A Kite."

Bill Bigge

Reared in suburban Washington, D.C., Bill Bigge set down roots in an area that later blossomed into a kiting hub at a time when Bill's professional and leisure interests coalesced. Bill grew up with an eye on the sky and hands that could tame the wiliest of kites.

The son of educators who met at the Ferris Institute, Bill inherited a nimble mind and keen intellectual abilities. While studying physics at the University of Michigan, Bill began making kites. Inspired by simple nylon thread he saw at a store, the inventive Bill got an idea "to make lighter and smaller kites." He knew he could "make a real neat kite using nylon thread as a line." That was the first of his many fliers. Kites accompanied Bill throughout his adulthood, and became a pleasurable part of his larger life's work.

Initially interested in joining the Air Force and becoming a pilot like his older brother, Bill, unfortunately, was not able to serve in the military. Yet, even with dreams of being a pilot dashed, Bill played in the sky and studied aerodynamics throughout his long career at the National Bureau of Standards as a physicist specializing in measuring temperatures. As an avid model airplane builder and kitemaker, Bill cross-pollinated his pockets of knowledge, letting his work influence his play and his play influence his work. During the weekday, Bill often sketched kite designs during his lunch breaks. Later these ideas moved from the drawing board to testing and scientific scrutiny. Bill's understanding of physics and aerodynamics helped him shape ideas into working solutions, and some kite-related projects unknowingly intersected with his daytime projects.

Bringing model airplane making techniques to a new audience, Bill introduced innovative solutions and construction materials to kite making. As a materials scientist, Bill fearlessly coupled composite materials to improve flying performances, showing that high-tech epoxies and plastic films are cozy bedfellows with traditional wood and wire parts. A believer in exploring a never-ending series of adjustments, Bill's constant adaptations made his kites fly better and better. A working scientist and a walking encyclopedia on how to fly kites, Bill tinkered with wobbly kites and learned to make even duds soar.

Known for his trademark elastic bridle on his Mark Airplane and Janus kites, Bill's kites took on an extraordinary wind range with ease. As a master designer, experienced with success in the model airplane world, Bill built kites that could smoothly traverse blustery days or float effortlessly in whispers of air during still weather. Always improvising, Bill became known for his kiting innovations and inventions. The homespun, somewhat steampunk solutions in Bill's kite bag reflected his keen understanding of mechanics and his eye for simplicity. Looking back, Bill points out how his interests in model airplanes influenced and advanced his kite making, "and vice versa."

Gracious and loved by many fliers and kitefliers, Bill met many people over the years at kite gatherings and became a bona fide icon at the Smithsonian Kite Festival. Bill made friends one at a time, often after observing someone's kite and offering simple suggestions for minor adjustments that helped wobbly kites fly better. In 2009, the AKA honored Bill with its Steve Edeiken Award to celebrate Bill's design contributions and the legion of friendships he quietly cultivated. Bill took the well-deserved accolade in stride, and quickly found his way back to the flying field to help others enjoy the sky.

Walter Mitchell

Before picking up kite strings in adulthood, Walter Mitchell had only fleeting practice flying kites as a youngster. Remembering his formative years, Walter can pinpoint perhaps the beginning of his kinship with larger fliers, as he fondly recalls the majestic four-foot diamond kite his father flew on his day off. "It seemed like each time we came home, we brought a huge ball of knotted-up string. In the evening I sat on the bed undoing that ball of string." Tangles and bumps aside, Walter relished kiteflying and enjoyed spending time with his dad. The Mitchells moved around a lot, and Walter gladly unpacked their kite and flew it with his father at each new neighborhood park.

Interested in the sky, Walter enlisted in the Air Force and traveled the world.

In the early 1980s, about a decade after returning stateside, he began dabbling in kite making. Flipping through *Mechanics Illustrated* magazine, Walter spotted a small ad for *Kites,* David Pelham's now classic kite book. A month later, while reading *National Geographic,* he spotted an advertisement for the Nantucket Kiteman's handmade deltas. Curiosity piqued, things began to connect and Walter realized "I can do this. I can make this because I can sew. My momma taught me to sew on a pedal machine when I was about ten years old." Charmed by the thought of making his own kite, Walter mailed away for the Pelham book, picked up some cotton fabric, and made his first kite. Taking to kite making quickly, Walter developed a fondness for large cotton kites and delighted in scouring secondhand stores for brightly colored bed sheets and fabric with large stripes that he could upcycle into kites.

Retiring from the Air Force, Walter jetted into a second career in the oil industry. As a road warrior, kites became Walter's trusted traveling companions and he took his sewing machine with him on trips. During downtime back in his motel rooms, Walter would roll up his sleeves and make large kites. During one memorable stay when he was working on a twenty-four-foot kite, Walter outstretched the fabric and hit the walls. Pinched for workspace, scratching his head, and looking out the window, Walter noticed the freshly paved parking lot. The pristine field of clean asphalt was irresistible and the ever-resourceful Walter found a local hardware store and bought chalk and a tape measure. Tools in hand, he carefully lined up complex pattern lines and traced outlines for his kite on the pavement. Happily working away, the cheery mood changed suddenly. Walter recalls looking up after hearing an exasperated manager bellowing, "'Mr. Mitchell, what are you doing on my parking lot?'" The answer, "'making a kite'" prompted a line of follow up questions, but the manager eventually cooled. The manager conceded, "'You know that's a pretty good idea'" and let Walter proceed. Walter still has the kite and is sure it outlived that driveway.

About five years into kite making, Walter met kite artist bill lockhart, and was influenced by his striking work. Both Lubbock residents, bill quickly became Walter's mentor and taught him how to make Rokkakus and Cody kites, and introduced Walter to quilting. Under bill's colorful spell, Walter learned to envision how layered materials look in the sky and established his personal color signature. "I'm the purple guy. I like purple. It is a nice color." Regal and bright, Walter's violet handiwork looks sharp in the big blue sky. After joining the AKA and attending the annual conventions, he got hooked on sewing for competition. "The thrill of seeing your kite in the sky and winning a trophy was a great experience" that motivated Walter.

Mastering the art of kite making, Walter decided to share the magic and found that he enjoys teaching others. Relying on a trusted sled kite pattern he discovered on the Chicago Skyliners' website, Walter uses standard ledger-sized office paper to create fun. Easy to get and perfectly sized for schoolchildren to decorate, Walter uses it to guide kids through the assembly process and quickly gets them outside flying. When visiting schools, Walter loves to wow children with his playful and oversized black and white cat kite. The mammoth kite is alluring and typically prompts everyone to gather around for a keepsake group photo. Over a period of about ten years, he developed a fondness for flying large show kites. Walter made and collected giant, crowd-drawing kites that let him share the fun and made his kiteflying even more enjoyable.

While flying on the weekends in parks, Walter met many people who wanted kites that were not available locally, so he "started selling commercial kites for all ages from a trailer." Kicking off his mobile business, High Plains Delta Kites, Walter began traveling on weekends to kite events in New Mexico, Oklahoma, and Texas. Besides "making kids and adults happy with new and pretty kites," he met many well-known kitefliers on the road who nurtured his connections to the kiting community.

Fun-loving Walter enjoys sharing the sky and believes kitefliers "need to get the word out" about the joys of kiting. Doing his part, with sponsorship from a local radio station, somewhere around 1995, Walter launched the FMX Kite Fly & Fling annual kite day in Lubbock and brought kite making, flying, and outdoor fun to his community. For about fifteen years, Walter enjoyed hooking newcomers into the growing kite circle.

In 2015, Walter developed a medical problem that sidelined him from kiting. He had to have both legs amputated, "one below the knee, and the other above." Since his operation, Walter has been recovering well and will be getting prosthetics in the near future. He looks forward to being on the flying field with a kite in the air.

Scott Spencer

Scott Spencer emerged from the playgrounds of his youth in New Jersey, perhaps a little shy and reserved, but primed for a life with a creative spirit that tugged him into the kiting world at a relatively young age. Tagged organized kiteflying's "Youngest Oldster," Scott tirelessly helped the South Jersey Kite Flyers and the AKA serve its members and reach new audiences until his untimely death from cancer in 2008.

Scott took to kite making in his young adulthood with great vigor, even though his earlier experiences gave no indication of this latent passion. In fact, Scott's childhood kite memories were rather raw. Scott recalled a breezy afternoon father-son outing that left him shaken. His dad made a paper diamond kite, tethered it to the end of an old fishing rod, sat Scott atop the backyard fence, and cast the kite into the sky. The launch frightened Scott and he remembered wailing and immediately turning to his father for comfort. Eventually the shock wore off and Scott recalls afternoons later in childhood when he, his sisters, and neighborhood friends would fly kites in a nearby field when the dairy cows roamed past. The cows must have fed on onion grass because Scott remembers that "their milk tasted funny," but unlike stinky milk, kiteflying ultimately grew on Scott and he developed an appetite for kites that sustained him through adulthood.

In 1978, shortly after Scott graduated high school, his girlfriend returned from a family vacation to Cape Cod with a gift that bit Scott's imagination and irrevocably tilted the course of his

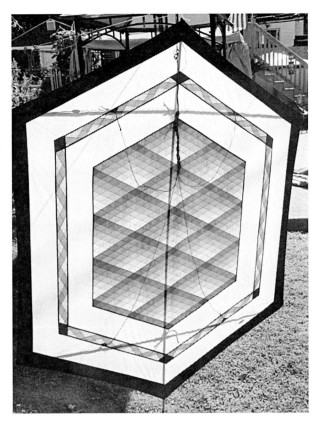

Scott Spencer wove strips of Ripstop nylon fabric into a panel and created signature designs like that on this Rokkaku (courtesy Mike Dallmer).

life, luring him into the kiting world. As he unwrapped a thirty-five-foot dragon kite, quickly christened "Charlie," Scott admired it and thought, "'This is nice. I think I can make one.'" Scott headed to the local fabric store and purchased supplies and set out, without any plans, to make a seventy-five-foot dragon kite. Working from instinct with a hunch about traditional methods, he soaked wood dowels in the bathroom shower. Over the course of a week, he bent them into a proto-skeleton for Charlie II. Flush with beginner's luck, Scott found victory with his first kite creation and looking back, Scott noted, "as for mistakes, they came later."

With the success of Charlie II, Scott started attending kite festivals, meeting fellow fliers, and borrowing kite books from the library. Shortly afterward, he discovered *Kite Lines* magazine and "joined the AKA for the newsletter." Building a kite resource network, Scott embraced kite making. At the time, Scott rented an apartment with a large attic that he turned into his kite making studio. The roof's pitch left steep ceiling slants, unusable for living space, but an ideal canopied nook to hang dragon kites that stretched hundreds of feet long. Through a friend, Scott had access to an endless supply of industrial-grade parachute fabric scraps. Most cutoffs were long and narrow, and Scott sewed end-to-end, giving rise to many dragons in the attic. Scott developed a compulsion to stretch his creations further and further, until his longest dragon peaked at 1,033½ feet. Scott thought he hit a record, but soon learned that someone in Europe flew a 1,200-foot dragon kite. He was, in a sense, devastated, but the impressive feat only propelled him further into kite making.

After mastering spindly dragon kites, Scott expanded his repertoire and began building intricate facet kites and got hooked on incorporating graphic elements into flat kites. Somewhat of an inventor, Scott created the playful transition tail that now flits about at nearly all modern kiting events. At the AKA's 1988 convention in Chicago, Scott saw Lee Toy playing with a telescopic pole that was decorated with cloth strips. Intrigued, he went home and tried to recreate it, but ended up with a "drunken mistake" that turned into his transition tail. Although his design looks rather complicated, Scott confessed, "I'm a lazy person. I wouldn't be doing it if it weren't easy." Beyond the transition tail, as Scott explored his kite making interests, he developed a technique he called weaving. Taking strips of Ripstop nylon, Scott interlaced ribbons into a panel that he joined onto the kite body. Innovative and eye-catching, Scott's woven kites are sought after today by kite collectors and demonstrate Scott's artistic talents and natural aptitude for kite making. Although Scott never considered himself an artist, preferring the label "frustrated perfectionist," Scott found happiness when others enjoyed his work.

Over the years, kiting became Scott's passport and he traveled to places he might have missed had he not been a flier. Perhaps one of the more exotic flying trips was an excursion to Colombia. In the late 1990s, this South American government adopted kites to deliver an anti-drug campaign to its youth. Scott gladly flew for this worthy cause and found the public reception to be phenomenal. In Colombia, "people are so friendly," and the fliers were revered like "sports superstars" among crowds of nearly 50,000 people. Spectators cheered on visiting fliers and asked for their autographs, while local children flew Bermuda-style eight-sided tissue and plastic bag kites. Inspired by the trip, Scott also traveled to India, England, and to all corners of the U.S. to fly kites.

Always a joiner, at conventions Scott sought out volunteer opportunities because he liked to give back while mingling with a purpose. For Scott, even small jobs, like staffing a booth or setting up for field events, "expose you more to other people" who share an interest in kites, and from "that starting point," Scott nurtured many lasting friendships and contributed to his sport. At home, Scott was instrumental in founding the South Jersey Kite Flyers club and served his club as president, vice president, director at large, and perennial workshop coordinator. Whatever post needed filling, Scott was first in line to lend a hand. Honoring his years of service and the impact he had on his club, the SJKF created an annual kite making award in Scott's honor. Close friend and fellow SJKF member Mike Dallmer suspects that if Scott knew about the award "he would be embarrassed and would give me crap for starting it," but honoring Scott is important to his friends and a touching reminder of Scott's legacy.

Debra Tumminia

Longtime friend on the organized kiting scene, Oregonian Debra "Deb" Tumminia found a career and a lot of fun designing, selling, and flying kites. Partnering her natural artistic skills with a business dream, she's made her living making kites and promoting fun for four decades. Her work is distinctive and sought after for its clean designs and masterful appliqué techniques. Yet long before making her living from kite making, Deb recalls her share of unsuccessful kite adventures during her youth when the paper kites she constructed flew only "for the afternoon" before inevitably smashing at her feet. The frustrating projects of her childhood may have been short on tails, but she remembered them fondly enough to give kiting a second chance in adulthood.

The kite making bug nipped Deb in 1979 after she came across an Eddy decorated with a Superman S. Admiring it, she thought, "'You know, that would be a really neat gift to give as Christmas presents.'" She bought a kite making book, played with designs, and made eight gift kites. Shortly after the holidays, tickled recipients approached Deb to purchase kites they could give as gifts to others, and Deb had a eureka moment where the proverbial light bulb turned on above her head. At the time, she worked at a place that made French fries and was unfulfilled. Kite making was a creative outlet, and as an artist with innate hand skills, Deb saw how kites could be more than something to giftwrap. Kite making could be her chance to chart a new career. Bold and shooting for the stars, "I cashed in my husband's and my life insurance policy, bought twenty-five yards of each color fabric that I could get and went into business." A talented sewer, making her own clothes since she was six years old, Deb had the skills needed to succeed in kite making, and coupled with her can-do ethos that "with a little practice and patience you learn to do things," she launched the Rainbow Kite Factory and hasn't looked back.

In 1980, Deb published her first catalog and started filling orders. Deb has shipped her kites, windsocks, logos, and signs around the globe, and "I even had one go out of this world." Deb sold a windsock to a doctor at an art show in Idaho, and it turned out that he was "the oldest person to go on the space shuttle." A kite lover at heart, the doctor smuggled Deb's "little wind sock in his suit and took it into space." Making history, or just flying on the ground, Deb's kites are solid fliers known for lovely nature- or mythical-themed images.

The Rainbow Kite Factory got its start through word of mouth referrals from friends and delighted customers, but not too long after starting her company, Deb looked for ways to grow the business. With a flash of inspiration, Deb thought, "'I

Debra Tumminia with her Rokkaku kite honoring her late husband Ken (photograph courtesy Debra Tumminia).

could be doing this at fairs and art shows.'" Initially, Deb brought her wares to weekly events in Portland and then stretched to shows further away to introduce people to kites all along the west coast art fair circuit. After a few years, Deb decided to tap into kite festivals where kitefliers congregate and they quickly embraced her handiwork. Traveling to kite festivals, such as the Washington State International Kite Festival, Deb did more than promote her kite business, she also met lifelong friends and a creative community that inspired her kite making. Balancing business and pleasure at kite festivals is important to Deb, and not long after setting up her sales booth, she realized that selling cut into her flying time. Thinking to herself, "'Wait a minute, I'm here to have fun, not just to make money,'" Deb does not maximize profits when pleasure is on her mind.

Armed with eleven sewing machines, Deb's cottage industry is equipped to create a range of kites. Though she's never made a parafoil, Deb bought one of her industrial-sized sewing machines from parafoil pioneer Doug Hagaman. "He was one of the first people I met in the kite world," and Doug, along with early kite making contacts Lee Toy and Margaret Greger, encouraged Deb. When Doug passed away, he had a parafoil he was making for Deb on his cutting table. Losing a friend and kiting legend is tough, but "I think of Doug every time I turn it on," and the machine continues to make kites that delight.

In addition to making kites, Deb makes time to teach kite making to others. Active with the Fort Worden Kitemakers Conference and the Oregon Kitemakers Retreat, Deb passes along pro tips to interested students, tackling everything from appliqué techniques to making banners. She even teaches a popular class she launched at the AKA convention called "Pattern Making with a Diva" where Deb teaches students how to cut sheet metal patterns that outlast conventional paper counterparts. On the Oregon Kitemakers Retreat's administrative committee, Deb is "always looking for teachers" to join her in the classroom fun.

Staying active in her local club, Associated Oregon Kiters, Deb lends a hand wherever help is needed. The longtime club president, Deb's been heading the AOK for awhile, and it keeps her in touch with kiting friends and happenings in her area. A little further out, Deb stays active in the AKA, and the national club honored her years of service, talents, and goodwill with a the Lee Toy Award in 2013. Although arriving at the convention she was somewhat suspicious that "something was going on," winning was "a good surprise" and brought back memories of Lee and meeting him during his two-year cross country motorcycle trip. Deb was one of the early stops Lee made on his *Faster than a Speeding Snail* journey, when Deb's business was just a few years old, but she was already making a name for herself as an outstanding kitemaker.

With an infectious laugh, ever ready to play and enjoy the day, Deb always keeps a "kite in the car to fly" and never goes "anywhere without a kite, even on vacation." Flying is a relaxing good time, and Deb appreciates how kites have a way of jumpstarting conversations. Deb welcomes meeting strangers who come to see what is happening at the end of her kite line. Kites bring Deb pleasure and help her share joy with others, whether it is flying side-by-side or building kites together.

In 2018, shortly before this book went to press, Debra passed away. Heartbroken friends look skyward and remember her family.

CHAPTER 3

Canvas in the Sky:
Artists and Innovators

"It came to me that anybody that does something special, no matter what it is, approaches it with a kind of insanity that somebody else isn't going to put that effort into it." John Pollock

bill lockhart

Sharing E.E. Cummings' sentiments on punctuation, art and design professor bill lockhart nurtured many young minds during his long career and later pulled kite strings into his classroom to widen his circle of students and expand creative horizons.

Born to native Texans, young bill grew up flying the Lone Star flag and dreaming big. His adolescent aspiration was to play college football. After his last tackle, he went on to teach elementary school art classes. Although this would have been a perfect opportunity to sneak kites in to his lesson plans, that assignment came many years later. With solid teaching experience under his belt, bill dove deeper in his studies and relocated to Pennsylvania for graduate school. When he tossed his tassel to the left, his Texan roots tugged and drew him home. Joining the faculty at Texas Tech University, bill shared his love of art, sculpture, and metalworking with generations of college students interested in studio arts. bill enjoyed his calling and "thought I would teach until I had to retire, but when I got involved with kites I decided to retire early." In his second act, bill did not disappear completely from campus. As emeritus faculty, bill developed the country's first graduate-level kite making studio art course and also began teaching non-credit kite making workshops. Reflecting on his early retirement, "I don't think I ever left teaching. In kiting you are still working with people, you are still sharing what you know."

Before bill brought kites into the classroom, he was inexperienced with serious kite making. As a child, bill occasionally found kite patterns in *Boys' Life* magazine and amused himself with kite building. At about age nine or ten, bill and a friend made a barn door kite complete with a long tail. Looking for excitement, they soaked the tail in kerosene and lit it just as it traveled out of reach. Spellbinding perhaps, but recalling this adventure with adult vision made bill shudder and realize the good fortune that kept his juvenile follies from getting out of hand.

Escaping childhood unscathed, bill tucked kite memories away in a sweet place and forgot about kites for many years until his granddaughter was born. After two generations of Lockhart men, proud grandparent bill bought her a kite to broaden her playtime adventures. They enjoyed flying together and soon the teacher in bill pulled out the craft supplies for an impromptu kite-building lesson. While she enjoyed their kiting romps, kites lured bill beyond recreational enjoyment. After a visit to a professional kite shop in Houston, bill was windswept and blown away by technological advancements he saw in modern kite building. Fiberglass rods and Ripstop nylon boggled bill and set his design wheels in motion. Excitedly, bill set out to learn all he could about modern kite making. Initially, bill budgeted six months to learn everything there was to know about kites. From the outset of his research, he knew he would not invent a new kite form, but as a veteran artist, bill stumbled upon a new type of blank canvas.

Something about the medium suited bill, and he managed to marry his love of building and visual arts together to create attractive and well-built kites. "I want a kite that looks good, has my mark or thumbprint on it. I want a kite that flies exceptionally well and looks great in the sky. I mean that is what I try to do." As an artist bill worked to promote his work in galleries and exhibitions, but with his kites, though beautiful and interesting, bill did not try to book shows. "Unless you are hanging it in the sky and it has air in it, it's not worth a dang anywhere else. No matter how great the kites are on the wall here, they do not show like they do when they are in the sky."

The warm feelings bill kindled at AKA conventions soon encouraged him to attend international kite events and he found that he greatly enjoyed meeting fliers from around the world. "People I consider close friends live in China. I don't speak their language and they don't speak mine. The only language we talk is kites and we can appreciate each other's kites and appreciate flying together." Globetrotting expanded bill's kiting network and while on a trip to Malaysia with Betty Street, fliers approached the two Americans and asked them to teach them western kite making. With the realities of time constraints built into traveling, full workshops were impossible, so Betty suggested people visit her and bill in Junction, Texas, where they could organize comprehensive classes. The idea was a homerun. The first Junction International Kite Retreat drew about fifty people and they capped registration at 125 spots at later retreats. For a decade, bill and Betty led kite making sessions and coached attendees on ways to tap their creative cores during the Memorial Day weekend retreats. Students with 24-hour access to the art making facilities, easily lost themselves in the tranquility of life in Junction. In 1992, the AKA honored Betty and bill with the Edeiken Award, thanking them for their role in advancing kite making to an art form.

For bill, kiteflying and the outdoor serenity it provided were essential to his emotional wellbeing. "Nature became a very important part of my life in the sense that I can be locked up in concrete for so long, but I know I have to be outdoors, too. If I don't, I lose what little sanity I've got." For him, kiting was connective and transcendental. "When I fly my kite, the earth, the sky, and I are one."

bill lockhart passed away in 2009, leaving behind the legacy of the Junction Kite Retreat, a red jumpsuit, and many friends.

Tal Streeter

Accomplished artist, kinetic sculptor, and master kitemaker Tal Streeter was a Fulbright scholar and held advanced degrees in design and sculpture. He taught fine art courses at MIT, among other universities; yet, his legacy endures beyond the classroom, largely in the sky, in his body of work.

Growing up in Manhattan, Kansas, where skies are infinite and naturally pull one's eyes outward, expansive vistas inspired and shaped Tal, and sky art themes play out frequently in his work. For Tal, "the sky begins at our feet" and his artwork launched from there. His nearly seventy-foot groundbreaking sculpture *Endless Column* was the first large public work displayed in New York City, and it begs viewers to look up and integrate the sky into their thoughts. Known for large-scale sculptures, his art is exhibited at prestigious museums around the country such as the Museum of Modern Art, the Whitney Museum of American Art, and the San Francisco Museum of Modern Art.

Tal bumped into the kite world through his installation work. "I came to kites out of sculpture because sculpture is so hard-edged and heavy. I couldn't make things more gentle. Later when I did large environments inside, I often had unstructured cloth with fans blowing it very lightly" to lighten the feel of a piece. His artwork reminded him of kites and inspired him to learn more about the form. Inadvertently, his quest for kite knowledge set him on an odyssey, which resulted in travels to exotic locations, the publication of several kite books, and a deeper understanding and appreciation of the kite as an artistic medium.

Aesthetics and visual grandeur aside, Tal also recognized the pure fun in kites. Recalling when he first got involved with organized kiting, "The word 'kite' had an aura about it that people associated with childhood and play. I think that association is still there." Tapping into this pleasure, and finding rejuvenation in its lightness, was essential to Tal. "Playfulness is very hard for us to do … we are so concerned with doing the right thing and being serious and certainly kites are connected to

Tal Streeter flying *Red Line* in Kansas, ca. 1972 (courtesy Lissa Streeter).

play and they relax that element of seriousness." For Tal, the goal was "to have a rich, full life that is meaningful to yourself and helpful to others, and somewhere, strangely enough, kites can play a very big role in that." In 1999, the AKA recognized Tal's immense contributions to kite making, awarding him the Lee Toy Award in honor of his exquisite portfolio of kite art and as an equal tribute to the friendly spirit he cultivated in the kiting community.

As an artist, Tal recognized that "invention in art is very, very important," yet groundbreakers are rare. Very few will come up with revolutionary ideas, and "the rest of us may add a little." These second steps, for Tal, are paces on the road of artistic evolution and are most interesting when they showcase an inner aspect of the creator's individuality. In kite terms, Tal got excited when kitemakers "allow their personalities to enter their kite making." Tal believed people could create extraordinary forms when "you look to yourself to make something personal." For Tal, "kites are the tip of the iceberg. They are the small point of everything that you are. They are a piece of what you are, and these other pieces are the things that are underneath that pyramid. Art is the thing that finally gives these kites their real qualities."

Well-traveled, especially throughout Asia, Tal's highly respected book, *The Art of the Japanese Kite,* is a seminal work celebrating Japan's most honored and aged kite traditions. Considered a classic, the book widened western knowledge of kiting beyond a leisure pursuit and introduced the sport to artists, historians, and culture seekers. Equally lauded, Tal's books *Art That Flies* and *A Kite Journey Through India* are celebrated texts that further examine the artistry of kites and eastern popular art. At his death, Tal was working on a biography of kiting pioneer Domina Jalbert, and had finished a manuscript entitled *In the Rose Colored Light: Portrait of an Indian Circus* that details his fifteen years performing as a circus clown with the Gupta family.

Late in life, Tal suffered a debilitating stroke in 2011. The following year, to preserve his artistic vision, Tal and his inner circle established the Friends of the Sky Foundation in Santa Fe with hopes that the organization will provide inspiring living and working space for artists, writers, and kitemakers, while preserving Tal's art, writings, and Japanese kite collection. In 2014, Tal passed away and is survived by his wife Romig, daughter Lissa, brother Ronald, artistic collaborator Bruce George, and beloved Santa Fe family David, Fiona, and Tiger Wong, who keep Tal's artistic vision alive and make his teachings and work accessible to other sky seekers.

John Pollock

Growing up in Big Sky Country, John Pollock was primed to love the sky even if his youthful Montana springs carried only the occasional kite. John, like others, bought his annual paper diamond kite from the local hardware store, but the kiting bug didn't bite until his children left home for college. Said partly in jest, "I didn't have anyone to play with anymore so I started making kites." Filling his empty nest with fun, John developed an interest in kite making and approached his new hobby as a serious art form.

Inherently creative and visual to the core, John is an artist and spent his career as a professor of art at Montana State University Billings from 1974 until he retired in 2010. A noted fine artist, working primarily in watercolors and lithography, John's work is held in private collections and has been published in *American Artist* magazine and in the books *Painting Composition* and *The Best of Watercolor 2.* Interestingly, before John took a serious look at kiting, he created a few eye-catching kites and hung them, unflown, in his art studio. As a playful nod to things to come, they decorated his walls for about ten years until his kite making interests grew.

Pinpointing the shift that brought kites to the forefront, John recalls a trip when he was in Boulder, Colorado exhibiting his artwork. During his downtime he wandered into a kite store. "I

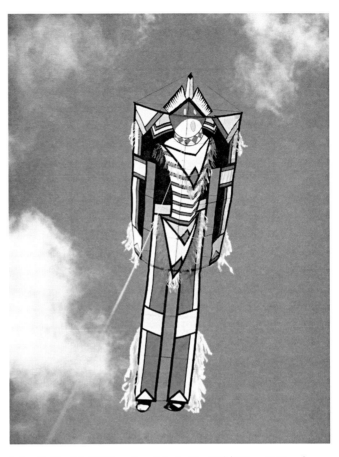

John Pollock's *UFO*, nylon fabric 4' × 15' (122 × 457 cm) (courtesy John Pollock).

thought it was pretty ridiculous to spend $50 on a kite," but he did. He purchased a stunt kite "that got me hooked." From there, John discovered the AKA, combed through Kite Builders International's plan files, turned the pages of *Kite Lines,* and "was fortunate to meet very giving people like Ron Gibian, Jon Burkhardt, and Scott Skinner," who encouraged his early kiting exploration and taught him practical flying tips that kept him aloft.

As an artist, ever on the lookout for new modes of expression, kiting opened creative doors for John. Enjoying the engineering aspect of building nimble fliers, creating a stable flying canvas became a new challenge that added to John's artistic process. Translating the lessons of his art career to kite making, John tinkered with colors and techniques until he found combinations that popped more than framed art on an easel. "Although I am not the only one who paints on kites, developing a method that I could use to paint images on kite material that resembled the way that I have worked for years with watercolor on paper has been one of my proudest achievements." Curious about fabrics, John spent a year on sabbatical researching kite making materials. His experiments blossomed and in 2004, he won his first of four AKA Grand National Champion kitemaker's awards for his silkscreen on nylon design. Attracted to the play between color and light, John enjoys using translucent colors that take on new light in sunny skies.

Many appreciate John's kite art and over the years, his creations have won several honors, including the AKA's People's Choice and Lee Toy Awards. Particularly meaningful, for John "winning the Lee Toy Award was an acknowledgement that what I was doing with kiting was more then making a kite." As an aspiration, "I try as much as possible to refer to my kites as paintings that fly, instead of painted kites" because "they are artworks and that is what I intended when I was making them." To illustrate his philosophy, "when I have exhibitions of my art works that include both framed paintings and my painted kites, I try to hang the kites more

John Pollock's *Lily Study*, acrylic on nylon, 20" × 20" (50 × 50 cm) (courtesy John Pollock).

like one would hang paintings, flat and against the wall instead of how kites fly." With an art-first focus, John elevates kite making and introduces kites to the art world.

Creative beyond the brush and canvas, John also writes short stories, and some writings inspire his kite making. His story "The Legend of the Raven and the Day Lilly" is a yin yang fable of how the Raven desires the Lily's stability, while the Lily envies the Raven's mobility and John translated the written story through his kite making, letting his artwork narrate his tale. John uses "the painting process to create images that tell that story visually in paintings that fly." No stranger to interpretive storytelling, exhibition organizers at the Logan International Airport in Billings, Montana selected John to participate in a Lewis and Clark group show. Artists told the explorers' story through kites and John, demonstrating his exceptional representational

John Pollock's *The Great Bear Hug,* acrylic on nylon, 40' × 5' (12 m × 1.5 m) (photograph courtesy of John Pollock).

art abilities, captured Clark's harried return trip on his kite panel. Whether with words or kite graphics, John weaves captivating tales.

John finds that kiting opens hearts and extends friendly handshakes, and he and his wife revel in the friendships they have built around the world and in their own backyard through kiting. As an invited guest, "I have in recent years been able to travel and meet other kite artists in other countries. This has been a wonderful experience to share ideas and to fly kites with them." Fortunate to travel extensively with his kites, "I have flown kites in the middle of an elk herd near Yellowstone Park, from the top of a ship going down the Yangzi River in China, over Stonehenge in England, and from a Mayan Pyramid in Mexico." Through kiting, John enjoys meeting fliers who push their craft to the limits. In admiration of outstanding kiters, John reflects, "It came to me that anybody that does something special, no matter what it is, approaches it with a kind of insanity that somebody else isn't going to put that effort into it. It's that kind of insanity allows them to do something special." Enamored by the magic that creative folks make, John applauds their persistence and sometimes madness, noting that moxie and talent combine spectacularly. Similar to catch and release fishing, kiting itself "doesn't necessarily have much of a practical purpose, but it has *value.*" For John, "value comes from what we are as a person, and what we share with people in different cultures," rather than what we take out of kiting. John adds, "flying kites and the aspect that kites are something beyond what we have to do" make it worthwhile.

Steve Brockett

Internationally known visual artist Steve Brockett's creative experimentations and affinity for flight drew him into kiting in the 1980s. Exchanging easels for kite-lines, he relocated the artist's studio skyward and forged the early years of his career in a somewhat untraditional path. Making a name for himself as an accomplished kite artist, Steve explored kiting and integrated kites into his work for nearly two decades before taking to the sky himself to experiment with aerial photography. Steve's art colors the kiting world and his kite art is a beautiful part of his life's larger body of work. Born on the ground, but with his soul in the sky, Steve's work blends the earth and the air.

Like many people, Steve first encountered kites in his youth. Born in the United Kingdom at the dawn of the 1960s, Steve recalls being six years old and greeted after school by his Canadian uncle and a green and yellow diamond kite with a blue bow tail. They flew the primary-colored kite at the park and it captivated Steve. "I remember nipping into a corner store to buy extra rolls of cotton string to add on to it" and then watching "the line go higher and higher until the string broke." Desperate, he hopped "around people's back gardens trying to get the kite." The joys of the outing were fleeting but deep-rooted memories endured.

Steve didn't reconnect with kiting until his early adulthood, but when he did, kiting came to him gift-wrapped. Shortly after leaving art school in the early 1980s, his girlfriend gave him David Pelham's *The Penguin Book of Kites.* Leafing through it, he was awed by the diversity of kites, and particularly taken by delicate Chinese and Japanese kite designs. As an artist, Steve painted for a number of years and had become restless. Looking for a new creative medium, and titillated by fresh ideas, Steve saw endless creative potential in kite making. Pelham book in hand, kite making was the next step in Steve's artistic career. As a person who enjoys building things, kite making was a pull rather than a push for Steve.

The sky has long tugged at Steve and kiting was, "a natural progression from pretty much a lifelong interest in flying things." In his art, even before kiting, windswept themes and imagery played important roles in his work. For Steve, metaphorically, wind is a statement of change, a symbol of chance, and an emblem of fate. Adopting kites into his artwork allowed him to interact directly with the wind and connected him with an environment that was *felt* rather than simply viewed. At the core, his kites are interactive pieces of art that he puts in the sky to be seen in motion rather than regarded by gallery goers on flat walls. "Kites are structural forms, surfaces that you can decorate, but they are also moving, living things when they are flying. I never wanted to separate any of those out." As with all exacting makers, pride in the overall product

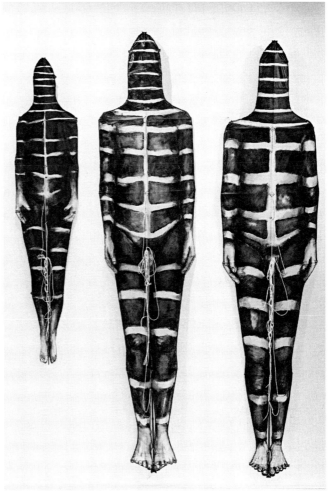

Artist Steve Brockett's human-sized kites soar in the sky (courtesy Steve Brockett).

and underlying form are inseparable and Steve devoted himself to learning the exacting craft of kite making.

Steve tinkered with kite making on his own for about five years before meeting other kitemakers and went from being self-taught to tapping into an international do-it-yourself knowledge base. Early on, Steve super-sized his kites and crafted massive twenty-five-foot fliers. Strongly influenced by Chinese kite making traditions, Steve silk-screened and painted images on bamboo-framed cotton kites. Although magnificent, large kites didn't ship well and as he began to travel, smaller kite styles caught his eye. Practicality prompted Steve to adjust his scale and as he focused on creating steadier fliers, he swapped traditional materials like bamboo reeds for modern parts such as carbon spars. Later, in his second act, Steve's designs focused on paper collage-inspired kites that delighted the eye and framed the sky.

Ever-evolving and never static, around 2006 Steve began a stringless period

Steve Brockett hiding among his screen ink and carbon fiber kite collection (courtesy Steve Brockett).

and set kiting aside for painting, paragliding, and aerial photography. "Life gets in the way of some things, and a ten year period living in Spain with no studio and kite materials resulted in my creativity flying in other directions." As a veteran paragliding pilot, Steve took to the air and reversed his perspective. "Like many, I had a wish to be with the kite when I was flying, to feel what the kite felt." Now aloft in his glider, Steve works from above to photograph beauty as seen from the sky. With the "luxury of being able to really focus on the landscape underneath my feet," Steve's photography captures patterned lines, earthy dimples, and long-drawn shadows that catch his eye. "I am constantly surprised by what I see from the air— the textures, forms, patterns and the ways we mark and draw the surface of our world are a rich resource. Most of my best images are just that, a complete surprise, a confluence of place, timing, light and planning." Responding to sensations, Steve snatches photos of sights that evoke feedback on the emotional and visual levels.

Documenting some of his finest aerial portraits, Steve's book, *Drawn Earth,* is a phantasmagoria of aerial textures and colors, all taken from the stripped-down, open-air seat of his powered paraglider. Using a reflex paragliding wing, designed specifically for motorized flight and powered by "basically a giant fan," Steve faces the risks of open-air flight in such a minimalist vehicle because "it's a perfect platform for aerial photography" where "there is nothing between you and the subject." Flying for up to three hours, and at relatively slow speeds, his aerial perch allows him the time and height to compose images, yet, sensibly, "I also carry a parachute in the event of a disaster!"

Finding success in the sky, Steve recently "returned to making kites once again alongside my photography with a new inspiration and vision." Playing with air and playing in the air both come naturally to Steve, and influence his art. Revisiting kite making after an intense study of aerial photography seems inevitable, and one can only speculate what will emerge during this new artistic chapter of Steve's life.

Jose Sainz

Born under vibrant Mexican skies, master kite artist Jose Sainz looks back at childhood, remembering the series of "one-day kites" he and his siblings built with their grandmother. "We knew we were going to trash those kites." Rough-and-tumble ephemeral child's play petered out before middle school, but his kiting "passion reawakened" in his 30s and tugged his creative life skyward as he splashed headlong onto the kite making scene in the late 1980s and early 1990s.

Now newly retired, former science-minded planner with the San Diego Gas & Electric Company Jose recalls how kites found him when he abandoned his lunch to see what a coworker did when he mysteriously slipped away on breaks. Tagging along, Jose returned with an appetite for stunt kites. "I was hooked by the end of the week." Squeezing fun in between shifts became routine as Jose journeyed into his second career in kiting.

Fate met karma and Jose's soon-to-be mentor entered the picture. During a casual fly at a San Diego park, Jose met Randy Tom, master appliqué kitemaker and founder of the legendary Hyperkites. The two became friends and Randy's audacious kites inspired Jose to dream big about kite making. Conveniently, Jose worked only a few minutes away from Randy's shop and he could dash there on his breaks. Aspiring to make beautiful

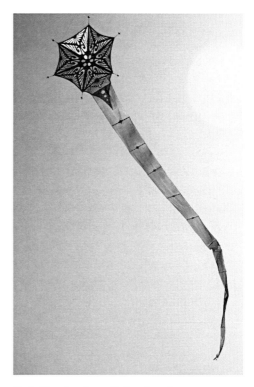

Red Star by Jose Sainz is a hexagon-shaped kite with a seven-foot diameter and a 35' (10.5 m) tail, made with Ripstop and Organza over fiberglass tubing, 2013 (courtesy Jose Sainz).

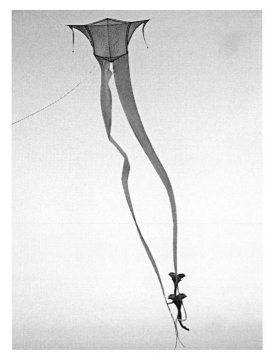 

Left: Jose Sainz made his *Wind Spirit* kite in 2008 for his first trip to the Burning Man festival and it has returned with him on every trip. The kites in the background were built by DOTA (Department of Tethered Aviation) campmates Ruth Whiting and Tim Elverston. *Right:* Jose Sainz flying *Wind Spirit* in the late afternoon over Antelope Island in Salt Lake City, Utah, 2012 (both photographs courtesy Jose Sainz).

kites of his own, Jose asked Randy for help. Not wanting to stifle the wishful kitemaker's individuality, Randy said, "'If you have questions, ask.'" But he never said, "'Do this, do that.'" Eager to learn and full of questions, this teaching model was a perfect fit. Jose recalls, "it was obvious from day one that he was allowing me to be part of his life and learn from it, rather than him telling me how to do it." Jose remembers how, in his informal apprenticeship, Randy pushed and guided him to find his own style and visual voice. "He wasn't easy on me, which is good ... he picked out things I didn't even notice." To make better kites, Randy pointed out subtle irregularities in his stitches and suggested that Jose carve out a larger sewing area because choppy lines often indicate starts and stops associated with adjusting fabric in a cramped workspace. The problem identified and easily solved, Randy's quick insight helped Jose take his handiwork to the next level.

Initially needing a push to try his hand at sewing, with practice, encouragement, and guidance, Jose eventually settled in comfortably at the pedal of a sewing machine. Coming from a family of accomplished tailors, Jose's mother was an expert seamstress who worked for a suit maker and, as a freelancer, created closets full of eveningwear. Throughout his childhood, Jose casually watched his mother fashion intricate gowns, and unknowingly the admiring son tucked away valuable sewing tips for his future kite making projects.

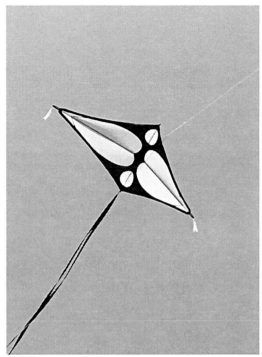

Left: **Jose Sainz flying a small kite he made with paper and bamboo framing over London's Millennium Bridge, 2015.** *Right:* **In 2006, Jose Sainz made** *Noname* **from Ripstop and fiberglass tubing. It is 3' tall (1 m) and 6' (2 m) wide (both photographs courtesy Jose Sainz).**

Known for his eye-catching graphics and splashy color combinations, Jose's style developed over the years and won many prizes. Initially, "I wanted to find something that was both new to the kiting community and yet bold and striking so that it can be recognized as my work." In 1989, Jose sought out a project for his first kite making competition and focused on a palette of vivid Aztec and Mayan designs that he always admired. As a relative newcomer, Jose conquered colossal projects and confirmed his place in competitive kite making circles, winning the coveted AKA Grand National Championships in 1992, 1994, and again in 2005. His impressive winning streak turned heads and Jose quickly made a name for himself in the kite making community.

Never resting on comfortable laurels, Jose continues to adapt and explore his craft. "I'm evolving in different ways" and open to experimenting with different forms of kite making, materials, and traditions. "I try to keep myself moving" and work with the intent of "making myself happy, and then someone else might too." Spoken like a true artist, but ironically, it is only through kiting that Jose finally realized he is an artist, and in some ways, took on the responsibility of being an artist through kite making. "For many years, I never considered myself an artist until I was recognized through the Lee Toy Award." The win in 2006 opened him up. He began to appreciate his unusual skill, and to acknowledge that his visual work is noteworthy. Having served for years on the Lee Toy Award Committee, the

Above: Rachel Ward flew Jose Sainz's *Wind Spirit* over *Wing,* an art installation, at Burning Man in 2008. *Right:* Jose Sainz's *Wind Spirit* flying at Utah's Antelope Island, 2012 (both photographs courtesy Jose Sainz).

accolade was even more meaningful for Jose because the honor not only applauded his contributions, but is also an official nod from the AKA "recognizing kites as works of art."

Celebrating kite artistry outside the kiting world, Jose is a kite ambassador and artist at the Burning Man festival. An active member of the festival's growing camp DOTA—Department of Tethered Aviation—Jose shares kites and wind-driven kinetic art displays with the 50,000 itinerant art lovers who gather annually in the Nevada desert for the weeklong art festival. Kites, banners, streamers, and flowing fabric sculptures are all tools for "wind worshiping" and color the sky. Air-dancing DOTA members lure people with their beautiful wind-filled art pieces and "are becoming well-known in the community and making a name for kites." Jose notes that beyond the nudity and festival frivolity, "there's a lot of artistic innovation" happening in the skies of Burning Man and "it is the art itself that holds things together." He started attending in 2008, and recalls, "I didn't know what to expect. I went open-minded with a case full of kites" and was surprised to find a new audience appreciative of kites. For most at Burning Man, kites are holdovers from childhood and the receptive crowds are delighted and awed by the magic kites add to

 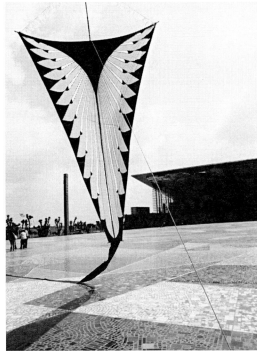

Left: Jose Sainz's three-stick paper and bamboo shield-type kite, with an ink sketch by Japanese kite artist Yoshisumi, 2017. *Right:* Jose Sainz's pointer kite at the Gota de Plata kite festival in Pachuca, Mexico, 2009 (both photographs courtesy Jose Sainz).

the festival. As a creator, the work Jose builds for Burning Man influences the type and design of his kites and has "made me look more at colors and shapes." In the desert, the sky is huge and "you need to work at being seen, one kite gets lost," and as Jose experiments, he collaborates and harmonizes with the windswept installations his DOTA friends contribute.

Just as tight friendships invariably form in organized kiting circles, relationships forged through Burning Man are strong and based in mutual interests and appreciation. For DOTA members, waiting a full year for a get together is too long, and now they sneak back to Black Rock Desert between festivals to create wind installations "and live within them for a week." Inevitably, random travelers passing through happen upon the enchanted camp and are awed by the mirage of magic. They stop to appreciate the "beauty of the wind" with the DOTA camp. For Jose, the only thing better than being with old friends is sharing art with new folks.

In addition to bridging art circles and the kite world, Jose also connects himself to the international kiting community through his work on the Drachen Foundation's board of directors. Established in the early 1990s, Drachen is a nonprofit organization founded to disseminate kite-related information and collect kite resources. With the advent of digitization, and upon reflection, the foundation realized "they aren't a museum" and decided to steer themselves to a digital future where virtual content is shared broadly. They partnered with a newly forming kite museum in Korea to transfer the physical collections and have it be seen and enjoyed by the world. "The museum is not built yet, but everything is there and ready." For Jose, his voice on the board helps Drachen envision a future that supports kiting in a meaningful way. "Being asked to be on the board of directors at Drachen is a milestone of my life" and an opportunity that allows Jose to influence kiting from another direction. "Friends and fellow kite artists in Europe *drachensyndikat* and around the world have inspired my creative freedom and unlimited imagination to the future."

Robert Trépanier

Canadian Robert Trépanier grew up the youngest of four in a small town outside of Montreal. His father, a veterinarian, college instructor, and at one point caretaker of the municipal zoo, helped instill a lifelong appreciation for magnificent wildlife creatures, but did not dictate Robert's career path. When Robert went off to college, he gravitated to industrial design. Although he never pursued a nine-to-five routine at a design firm, Robert's creative skills found an outlet building theater sets as an independent designer for many years.

Since childhood, Robert has loved kites and "all things relating to air." When he was about eight years old, his older brother made a simple kraft paper three-stick kite and flew it after dinner. Young Robert, attempting to keep up with his brother, tagged along and watched curiously until he finally got an opportunity to tug the line. And with the first pull, nothing could get him to let go. When his mother ordered the boys to come inside for the evening, Robert, not wanting the fun to end, tied the kite line to a fence. To everyone's amazement, it was soaring in the morning. Enchanted by this feat, Robert took pride in telling the grown ups about his achievement and remembers the event as "the first really big thing I had done. Older people talked about it." Later the next summer, Robert's brother went away to work at their uncle's general store. His brother and uncle made kites after closing time and his brother gave Robert a massive six-foot Eddy he made. This prized gift hooked Robert, and when it later crashed, Robert moved on to deltas and any other kite he could find.

Robert's interest in kiteflying continued into young adulthood. As a teen in college in Montreal, Robert became a frequent shopper at his local kite store. Daily visits, frequent questions, and an encyclopedic familiarity with the shop's inventory eventually landed him a part-time job. The owners hired him mainly because he was always there and they were looking for someone knowledgeable to work sum-

Artistic and haunting, Robert Trépanier's face kites look at you from above (courtesy Robert Trépanier).

mer hours. In hindsight, his summer job was something of an internship that allowed him to discover stunt kites, read *Kite Lines* magazine, and meet others "with the disease."

Inquisitive and active, kites were just one thing that captivated young Robert. Equally interested in aeronautics, bicycle racing, and art, Robert cultivated an expertise of each alongside kiting. In college, Robert studied design, delved into artistic pursuits, and learned ways to express himself visually. Nurturing his passion for bicycles, Robert became a professional cyclist and later patented an auxiliary handlebar to improve long distance cycling.

Somewhere in adulthood, his prime interests merged. As Robert remembers, "kites and art came together" and he began making artistic kites rather than plain, all-purpose kites. Developing his style, Robert is known for his sophisticated graphics that are both playful and haunting. For Robert, "My thing is to express myself with kites." This marriage of form and function is solid and Robert never ceases to turn out unique kites that captivate viewers. Well known for his caricature kites, Robert reports that he finds inspiration in the nameless faces he encounters everyday. "I make faces, often sad faces, that are of troubled people. I think it is to make those people fly or be lighter, to lighten their lives." Robert enjoys giving struggling people at least a symbolic freedom, and as a liberator, he uses brush strokes to free them from melancholy and the rigmarole of living on the ground. Always armed with a sketchbook, Robert is ready when interesting visages present themselves.

Perhaps the only thing that Robert enjoys more than the creative process of designing a kite, is "sharing friendships around the world. Even if you do not speak the same language," pleasurable camaraderie is an easy reality through the kite's common ground. Robert notes, "The people you meet flying kites are different than the rest of the people. I think they still have something of their childhood. They want to play and are people who like to play and they like to have a smile on their face. This is common worldwide."

Honoring his commitment to advancing beauty in kite making, Robert won the American Kitefliers Association's Lee Toy Award in 2004 and continues to share his signature playful dark humor in his kite graphics.

Sandra and Ron Gibian

In the 1980s, Sandra and Ron Gibian were on vacation and shuffling along the boardwalk in Moro Bay, California when they found themselves in a kite shop. Flipping through magazines and then soon out on the beach test flying their new kite, one wind led to another and Sandra and Ron's chance encounter at a kite shop changed the course of their lives. After the vacation, the couple dove head first into organized kiting, stitching countless eye-popping kites along the way.

Native to the Empire State, Sandra recalls flying homespun kites with her sisters around Buffalo before the family relocated to California. Further south along the Pacific coast in Santiago, Chile, young Ron's formative years were peppered with memories of kite fighting. Much like traditional kite fighting in India, Chilean children look forward to annual kite battles and slash jaunty tissue paper kites with glass encrusted kite lines. Ron enjoyed kite fighting season and Sandra enjoyed her youthful spring kite flies, but it wasn't until years later when kiting resurfaced in adulthood that the couple felt the true pull of kites and rode the winds into a new direction that shaped their leisure and professional lives.

During their early days in kiting, Sandra and Ron found themselves in Monterey at Windborne Kites. There they met Corey Jensen. Dazzled by Corey's love of kiting and finding that "his enthusiasm was contagious," Ron, Sandra, and Corey became fast friends. Always looking for more kids to play in his sandbox, Corey struck up conversations with the couple and asked Ron what he did for a living. Ron said he was a designer and Corey then pointed out the obvious, remarking, "'Well, then

Left: Ron Gibian with *Jango* the seahorse and *Lescargo* the snail. *Above:* Two kites from Ron Gibian's *Archirhythm* series (both photographs courtesy Sandra and Ron Gibian).

you should design kites.'" Ron did, and on a return trip, he showed Corey some kite design ideas. Corey continued to encourage Ron's creative pursuits, saying, "'I will lose you as a kite customer, but we will gain a new kitemaker.'"

Ron's background in graphic arts and visual design is immediately evident in the couple's work. Crisp, modern designs, with simple color patterns and balanced compositions all flow naturally. His signature look and hallmark artistic flare "was always there, since the beginning," on their kites. Instead of first working on simple kites, Ron was drawn to complex show ponies and mechanical wonders from the get-go. "Some of them flew marginally, but after awhile I decided I need to learn a little more about dynamics and making a flying platform." Ron recalls that he had "an endless pool" of graphic ideas to dress up the kites, but at the time, the Gibians didn't understand the fundamentals of building solid kite frames. Self-motivated and eager to learn, they read books and started attending workshops. At Fort Worden, "I finally found myself in the company of all the people I have read about so it was great to be there." Ron confesses, "I didn't go there to build kites. I wanted to meet people, talk to people, pick brains." The strategy worked. The Gibians

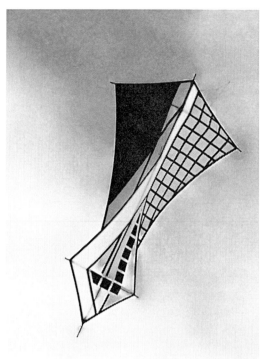

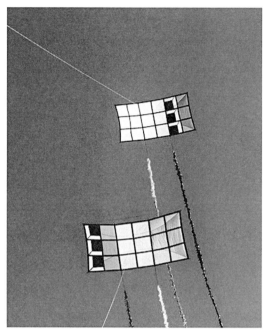

Left: **His most noted shape, Ron Gibian's** *Astralglide* **is a great performing kite.** *Right:* **Two kites from Ron Gibian's** *Archirhythm* **series (both photographs courtesy Sandra and Ron Gibian).**

collected the knowledge they needed and figured out ways to stabilize their kites so their art could steal the show.

Back in the early days, Ron did the designing and sewing, and Sandra helped out here and there. "I would cut things or try to be helpful. Eventually I wanted to get more involved with it so I said, 'Teach me what you are doing and how you do it and how you want it done.'" Ron taught Sandra the ropes and she, too, started building kites from the ground up. The couple took Sandra's first solo kite production to a party. Impressed guests said, "'Nice job Ron.'" Ron blushed and came clean, explaining, "'I didn't make that kite. Sandy made that kite.'" Victorious and proud, Sandra recalls her gratification when she realized friends "couldn't tell the difference between our work. So I think I succeed perfecting the technique that he wanted."

Left: **Ron Gibian's** *Moving Parts* **(courtesy Sandra and Ron Gibian).**

Over time, Sandra and Ron found pleasure and profit in custom kite making. Though now essentially retired from kite making, the duo once sold countless kites annually and today field only select orders for custom-designed art kites. Looking back, when asked to ponder the effect that outsourcing manufacturing jobs overseas had on the kite industry, the Gibians see both sides of the coin. On the one hand, Ron says "I am a culprit," but on the other, moving production away from home allowed them to get kites "into the hands of hundreds upon hundreds of people at a price that people could afford." Recognizing two distinct kite markets—the mass market and the custom-design market—Sandra knows people who are "looking for a special signature kite, maybe even something they want to hang in their home as wall décor" will seek out those kites regardless of where they are made. Fortunate in business, the Gibians help color the sky with striking kites. Among their best and most sought after work are the custom kites they make for Revolution Kites. In 2005, the AKA asked the Gibians to make a special design for the auction on a Revolution sail. What they came up with was wildly popular, and is now known as the Masterpiece Series. With a very limited run, Sandra and Ron's showstoppers accentuate their kite making mastery.

Harlequin, **one of Ron Gibian's first cellular kites, early–1990s (courtesy Sandra and Ron Gibian).**

Long active with the AKA, Ron chaired the Art Kite Committee for four years, and had the pleasure of presenting the club's prestigious Lee Toy Award to five highly accomplished artists. In 2007, after stepping back from the committee, Ron was "blown away" when he landed the lifetime achievement honor. Ron recalls, "It was a huge surprise for me" and a "big win because it is not an award for one kite, it is for a whole body of work." Touched and thrilled by the recognition, the award held deeper meaning for Ron because Lee Toy was a friend and mentor. The two met in Reno around 1985, and Lee encouraged and influenced Ron's kite making. On awards night, Ron stood stunned at the podium, without a prepared speech, but with a heart full of joyful memories of a dear and influential supporter.

Today, knowing firsthand the importance of mentoring, Ron feels an obligation to pay it forward by taking an active interest in the work of aspiring kitemakers. For Ron, much of the future success of organized kiting rests with veteran members' ability to reach out and "pass it on to new people." An advocate of his three Rs, Ron chants "recruit, recruit, recruit" and believes members need to do more than hand out brochures to get people actively involved in kiting and engaged with the AKA at a level that will sustain the club and the sport. Ron himself enjoys getting on the phone and talking at length with new members about their kiting. For him, a conversation is a way to connect and share his enthusiasm and wisdom with someone new.

Outside of kiting, Ron enjoys a long and thriving career as a percussionist. A longtime member of the successful jazz-fusion band ZZah, Ron has been happily drumming, recording, and touring with them to spaces ranging from intimate 300-person venues to giant 25,000-seat stadiums. Jamming with his musical family, "that's the other half of my life." No stranger to performance, before taking a seat in the music world, Ron dabbled with acting, stunt work, and reenacting cowboy westerns. For Sandra, too, kiting is just one of her interests and talents. Professionally, Sandra is a highly successful real estate agent, and Ron regards her as the "greater woman behind that dude." Lovebirds from the start, the couple ironically met at a boxing school run by Ray Notaro—the trainer who readied Sylvester Stallone for *Rocky*. Ron dropped in to visit his friend Ray and met Sandra who "was doing Ray's bookkeeping at the time." Leaving punches in the ring, Sandra and Ron enjoy the life they have created together that accommodates a range of interesting pastimes and careers.

Mikio Toki

Well-traveled kite globetrotter Mikio Toki brings the secrets of Japanese kite making to flying fields from Iowa to India and many stops along the way. The expert Edo-maker traces his love of kites back to childhood in Tokyo, where crowded urban life made little room for kiting.

In the 1950s, as a young boy, Mikio bought his kites from a local toy store, but around age ten, he set out to make his own kite to fly during the annual Boy's Day festivities in May. Determined and resourceful, he splintered bamboo rods from a broom handle, found washi paper, and decorated his handiwork with a brightly painted tiger. Proud and ready for flight, Mikio held his kite up and waited for a breeze. Outside, the overweight kite would not fly, but looking back, the enterprise hinted at Mikio's natural curiosity in kite making and his budding interest in art.

Temporarily shelving kite projects, Mikio enrolled at the University of Design in Tokyo and studied graphic design and illustration. In art school, Mikio developed the skills he would use to build both his professional life and his informal kiting career. From graphic designer to after-hours kitemaker, Mikio's creative talents keep his mind, hands, and heart busy.

Mikio rediscovered kites when he was twenty-three. He met Japan's premier Edo-maker Katsuhisa Ota and learned the proper way to make traditional Japanese kites from him. Smoking bamboo by hand and delicately melding fine artisan paper, Mikio discovered a passion and studied the art of Japanese kite making from the ground up.

Shortly after meeting Mr. Ota, Mikio joined the Edo Kite Preservation Society where he met fellow kite enthusiasts who encouraged and mentored the young kitemaker. Since those days, Mikio has joined other kiting clubs, including the American Kitefliers Association and the Japan Kite Association, but remains loyally committed, with the other fourteen members of the Edo Kite Preservation Society, to producing exactly exquisite kites and keeping Japanese kite making traditions alive.

In Japan, kiteflying is largely seasonal, with people typically flying during New Year's festivities, Boy's Day celebrations, and symbolic crop-blessing festivals like those at Hamamatsu and Shirone. Not satisfied by Japan's limited holiday flying calendar, Mikio's appetite for kiting grew quickly and he began traveling to faraway locations to fly, teach Edo kite making classes, and to exhibit his kites. Kiting is Mikio's passport, and he travels the globe, spreading Japanese traditions and sharing universal kiting winds with likeminded fliers.

As a fine craftsman, kitefliers and art collectors seek out Mikio's kites. His kite work is in the permanent collections at the Smithsonian, Haifa Museum of Art, and several kite and art museums in Japan. Inspired by the illustrative works of master kite artist Teizo Hashimoto, Mikio creates his kites using the same traditional Japanese kite making techniques passed down to him many years ago. To

Mikio Toki in his studio in Chiba, Japan (courtesy Mikio Toki).

this day, Mikio specializes in *Edo-kaku-dako*, a Tokyo-style kite, known for its characteristic rectangular shape, long bridle lines, and hummer. Mikio selects strong washi paper and bamboo for the kite body and decorates the skins using sumi-e—a dense black calligraphy ink—and a palette of colorful dyes that create an outlined, stained glass look that often depict scenes from Japanese storybooks.

As a kitemaker, Mikio receives about 300 commission orders a year. His wife and friends help him meet the demands of his challenging kite making schedule in the late fall, but even after New Year's kite festivities pass, Mikio is busy at his work bench filling custom orders. Living near the ocean in Chiba, Japan, Mikio test flies each of his kites at the beach before shipping them to customers. His kite making work keeps him active and connected to his country's customs, and his love of kiting fuels him to share these time honored kite traditions with the world.

In 2011, the American Kitefliers Association looked abroad and astutely selected Mikio for the club's Lee Toy Award. Internationally known and respected for his artistic talents, and generously committed to sharing kite knowledge through teaching, Mikio embodies the true spirit of the Toy award and is a global kite ambassador dedicated to keeping traditional Japanese kite making alive.

Anne Harris

An internationally known British kite artist, recognized for her playful and towering inflatable kites, Anne Harris discovered kiting during a family outing and set down roots in a community that nurtures her creativity and helps support the philanthropic charity she founded later in life.

Born to English parents in St. Andrews, Scotland, Anne's family relocated to eastern Africa when she was a toddler. Living mainly in Kenya, Anne grew up amid stunning wildlife and boundless savannahs in the foothills of the Great Rift Valley.

Anne's family returned to England when she was a young adult, and, in college, Anne initially studied zoology but later switched to business administration. "I had a career in various things over the years, including running a bed and breakfast and being a company director." When her daughters were young she "was fortunate not to work" and later, when they were in school, Anne volunteered "at what was called an Opportunity Group for physically and mentally disabled children under five to give their parents some respite. This was to have a big influence on me" and the experience shaped Anne's future pursuits.

By the beginning of the '90s Anne was skillfully balancing work and family life. In 1991, the Harris family attended the Bristol International Kite Festival. Looking up, Anne was astonished and purchased "some books on single line kites" to try her hand at kite

Anne Harris' inflatable *Kimberly the Kangaroo*, Washington State International Kite Festival, Long Beach, Washington, 1996 (author's collection).

Anne Harris and her inflatable *Spike the Echidna,* **Washington State International Kite Festival, Long Beach, Washington, 1996 (author's collection).**

making. Charmed by kites, later that month the family "went to another festival," and that event "was all about buggying." Her eleven-year-old son Jonathan was captivated and plunged himself into kite buggying. Jonathan went on to gain a bit of celebrity through the sport, setting a kite-duration Guinness Book record and making appearances as a flier on British television. Anne remarks, "In those earlier years I was known as 'Jonathan's mum.'"

Inspired by flying sensations created by George Peters and Peter Lynn, Anne wanted to make mammoth sky creations, but she did not know where to start. Independent and resourceful, Anne realized she needed "to dream up my own design." Intuitively, Anne sketched ideas "on graph paper and then just drew them with chalk onto Ripstop." Thanks in part to the popularity of *Jurassic Park,* her children were keenly interested in dinosaurs, and Anne thought it would be fun for them if she made "a life-size T Rex." Anne bought a bag of red triangular-shaped Ripstop cut offs from a local hot air balloon manufacturer and experimented. Improvising, she built *Dino,* her first jumbo creation that inspired her to play.

Anne continued creating inflatable characters and when *Bronty* made his festival debut on a low wind day, a quick-thinking Anne borrowed a motorized blower from a fellow flier. "Two minutes later we had about a hundred children" wide-eyed around them. Since then, Anne notes, "I have adapted everything, in an emergency, to be inflated by a blower." Enjoying forms that bounce around at eye level, Anne recognizes the price of high-strata real estate, especially in Europe, where "we are very limited for space, and there are plenty of people that want to fly. Anne creations "will never fly way up in the sky. I will take over that bottom and middle space in the kiting world," and her domination of the lower regions brings color closer to festival attendees and allows others to soar.

Anne's early studies in zoology and lifelong interest in animals comes through in her kites. "Peter Lynn was doing fish and sea-themed kites," so Anne decided she would create an animal-inspired line of kites. A conservationist at heart, Anne enjoys "supporting endangered species," and modeling kites after land creatures. This is a natural fit for her and as Anne traveled, she began taking additional inspiration from the animals native to her destinations. Anne created *Kimberly the Kangaroo* and *Spike the Echidna* for trips to Australia, *Ally* the pink alligator for adventures in Miami, and *Madiba,* a bird creation, for a festival in Cape Town. In 2004, after undergoing successful treatment for cancer, Anne started her magnum opus, a coral reef of giant inflatable sea creatures. The project helped see Anne through a personal crisis and proceeds benefited her Anne Harris Children's Fund. Anne's playful inflatable menagerie aids her charitable partnerships and help her share smiles.

Over her years in kiting, Anne discovered creative and social outlets through kiting that she had not planned on finding. For Anne, kiting "has been a marvelous way of meeting people and having something in common. I have made some fantastic friends, and since I have had my first invitation abroad, I have had the experience of a lifetime due to kiting." Anne's travels widened over the years and wherever she finds herself, Anne notes that "enjoyment is very much related to the people" she and her family have met in the kiting world.

Wolfgang Bieck

Sometimes kiting is a pure passion all on its own, but other times, without kiting another passion wouldn't even be possible. Such is the case with master kite aerial photographer Wolfgang Bieck. His spectacular airborne photos resonate in large part for their lofty vantage points and signature windborne perspectives. Over the years, Wolfgang has grown to rely on his kite as much as he has his camera to document the world around him.

Born in 1951, during the early days of the cold war in East Germany near the East Sea, Wolfgang and his family fled to West Germany when he was four years old to reunite with his father who had slipped under the Iron Curtain earlier. Wolfgang flourished in his new homeland and set deep roots, studying biology and

Wolfgang Bieck taking a selfie from his kite during a crop-circle KAP outing (courtesy Wolfgang Bieck).

chemistry, along with sports and education, for six years in Hamburg, and remaining in Bad Bevensen through adulthood. Wolfgang and his family enjoy life in Lower Saxony, and during his career as a science teacher, he often called upon its natural terrain to enhance his classroom lessons until he retired in 2013.

Before Wolfgang became an educator, he got interested in photography. Wolfgang remembers buying his first camera, a Minolta SR-T 101 reflex, when he was seventeen years old. The camera still works and Wolfgang continues to use it along with other trusted film and digital cameras. Inspired by the work of Ansel Adams and the beauty he caught in his artwork, Wolfgang enjoys photography as a way to study nature. While his dual interests in camerawork and the natural sciences grew, he began teaching himself photography and focused on taking pictures of animals and plants as a way to document the splendor of the natural world.

Over time, Wolfgang's interests escalated and he looked to kites to advance his scientific research. For a project, Wolfgang prepared soil samples of ice age till taken from sandy holes in an open field, and he cleverly looked to aerial photography as a way to capture images that would help him better visualize his rather abstract data. Not having access to an aircraft, Wolfgang began exploring ways kites could help him eek up and above the ground to document his soil sampling studies. Wolfgang taught himself to fly and in the 1980s, he tapped into the kiteflying community for flight advice and inspiration. Kiting started as something to aid his photography, but "grew from small parts into a big, big hobby." Ironically, Wolfgang logged many

An aerial zoo as seen from photographs Wolfgang Bieck snapped from his kite (courtesy Wolfgang Bieck).

flying hours over the span of a decade before he actually took a picture of the sandy holes that initially inspired him to explore kite aerial photography. Sidetracked perhaps, his roving kite and camera snapped many lovely images while simultaneously supporting two lifelong pastimes.

As an adult, Wolfgang didn't have much childhood kiteflying experience to draw from, but, just as he has done with other hobbies, such as gardening, beekeeping, and sailing, he taught himself everything he needed to learn to get started through books, conversations with fellow enthusiasts, and by trial and error. As a kitemaker, for Wolfgang, "the main point for me is to use the kite as a tool," and this tool needed to be reliable in order to safely transport his prized camera. One false move or sewing imperfection could cause his camera to tumble from the sky and crash into useless bits of metal and glass. Knowing the stakes, Wolfgang researched kite books and scouted for images in magazines, seeking a stable and reliable kite. He decided on a Rokkaku for his first project, but about five years later, he discovered that tailed Multiflares flew even better for his purposes and adopted those for his work. Always anxious about his handicraft, Wolfgang tests his kites before sending his valuable cameras up into the sky by seating water bottles in the rigging net during each test drive. Recalling a disastrous first flight and his

Decommissioned 1200-ton brown coal excavator, now part of the Ferropolis Museum in Germany, as seen by kite aerial photographer Wolfgang Bieck (courtesy Wolfgang Bieck).

panic watching tumbling bottles, Wolfgang learned "to be patient and try it again." For Wolfgang, new hobbyists on the road to mastery of any pursuit must first conquer failure. As a novice, "You will pass the valley of tears. Somewhere the valley ends and the success begins." Now an accomplished flier, Wolfgang happily remarks that, "I only need a little wind, the sun, and then I can document all that I need to."

Around 1987, Wolfgang began meeting other kitefliers and participating in events sponsored by the Kite Aerial Photographers Worldwide Association. Through KAPWA connections, he plugged into a network of fellow enthusiasts and began picking up technical tips that helped his progression in kite making, kiteflying, and photography. The spirit of camaraderie and openness in the group greatly impressed him, and Wolfgang freely shares his kiting innovations with the larger

Douaumont Ossuary near Verdun, France, where the bones of more than 130,000 soldiers from World War I rest, documented by kite aerial photographer Wolfgang Bieck (courtesy Wolfgang Bieck).

community in return. In 1993, Wolfgang designed a camera assembly called the HoVer-Rig that orients images from horizontal, to vertical, and can reverse during flight, which allows fliers to manipulate their cameras just as well remotely in the air as if by hand. Wolfgang's innovation significantly improves a flier's chance at catching outstanding shots and he intentionally didn't seek a patent on his invention because he wanted to contribute to the collective open knowledge available to kite aerial photographers, inspired by Arthur Batut from Labrugiere, France who abandoned his patent claims when he published his method of kite aerial photography in 1888.

In 1993, Wolfgang began publishing articles in the German magazine *Sport und Design Drachen* chronicling his kiting experiences and highlighting laws affecting kitefliers. He enjoyed sharing his knowledge with German fliers because such information was scarce and sharing details on kite-related ordinances helped others avoid legal troubles. During this era, aerial photography and kiteflying were tightly controlled. Before the reunification of Germany, people were prohibited from taking photographs from airplane windows and kites were classified as an aircraft. Kitefliers were required to obtain permission from the government to fly kites with kite lines longer than 100 meters, and those interested in aerial photography needed to obtain a license to capture images, and written approval to publish aerial photographs.

These tight restrictions came to an end when the Berlin Wall fell in 1989, and Wolfgang celebrated by spending the next day at the newly expired borderline documenting a reunited Germany with his kite aerial photography. "After reunification, you no longer needed to ask permission for aerial photography," and Wolfgang was perhaps the first person to take advantage of this restored freedom. In 1995, Wolfgang was "the lucky grand prize winner of the Centennial Kite Aerial Photography Contest" sponsored by the World Kite Museum and was invited to attend Washington State International Kite Festival that year. While visiting Long Beach, he generously donated prints from his reunification kite aerial photography series to the museum.

In 1997, while at the Berck-sur-Mer Kite Festival in northern France, Wolfgang met the Indonesian Kite Delegation with Sari Madjid from Jakarta, and was later invited, in 2000, to the International Kite Festival in Jakarta. There, he heard "a rumor about a cave painting" of a kite on Muna Island, located in a remote part of Indonesia's Sulawesi province. While it is commonly thought that the kite originated in China 2,400 years ago, some historians disagree and place its roots in Oceania, where indigenous people have a long tradition of building fishing kites from leaves, and argue that these kites may be older than those documented in China. Curious to see the painting himself, Wolfgang and his wife Mong-Hie made the difficult trip to the Kabori Cave in Muna in 2002. Adept and physical, the Biecks pushed through heavy vegetation and scaled a seventy-meter limestone tower to reach the secluded entrance. With the help of "La Hadha—the cave keeper and discoverer of the cave painting, La Sima—one of the best leaf kite builders of Muna, and Suarnadi Makuta—the chief of the local tourist office of Raha," the Biecks ventured inside and were delighted to see a well-aged painting of a human figure flying a typical Indonesian-variety double-bridled *Kaghati-style* leaf kite. The date of the painting goes unconfirmed, but Wolfgang resolutely believes that it is a prehistoric relic and the image inspired him to conduct personal research that he details in his book *Muna—Island of "The First Kiteman."* Island folklore considers the cave the meditation spot for the son of the island's first king. In Muna, the aboriginal people attribute religious meaning to kites and view them as connections between the earth and the sun, as well as a symbolic link between the living and the dead. With deep meanings as liminal tools, it would be very easy to understand why kites would be the subject of prehistoric cave art. Though definitive scientific tests, which require destructive sampling, have not been performed to confirm La Handa's archeological findings, Wolfgang is awed when he considers the exceptionally long reach kites have in human history.

Craig Wilson

Finding art at the end of a kite line, kite aerial photographer Craig Wilson dabbled with kites and photography until he perfected both. Self-taught, self-mastered, Craig's work impresses the kiting community and the world at large, and he freely shares the joys of kiting in his stunning books, gallery shows, and in the kite events he organizes.

Wisconsin native Craig grew up down the street from a large public golf course. "Golf in the early '60s wasn't quite as posular as it is today, so you could easily sneak out there" and the Wilson brothers adopted the course as their flying field for model airplanes and paper Hi-Fliers. Recalling a tantalizing promotion marketed on the side of frozen vegetables, the Wilson boys united and "ate our peas and sent away" for a jumbo Jolly Green Giant kite. A few weeks later, the four-foot-tall diamond arrived and they headed to the golf course. Flying victoriously, suddenly the line snapped. Determined to salvage the fun, the boys "got on our bicycles and chased that kite" until it crossed the highway and disappeared.

Choice Seats, kite aerial photographer Craig Wilson catches a unique glimpse of thousands of concertgoers who turn out with picnics, blankets and lawn chairs to see the Madison Opera perform at Garner Park, 2011 (courtesy Craig Wilson).

Craig Wilson's selfie/test shot taken with his 1970 Classic Mini as he was preparing aerial photographs of a beautiful rural property in Cross Plains, Wisconsin, for a real estate developer, 2011 (courtesy Craig Wilson).

Kites adrift, but fond memories remained; Craig left kites behind until his wife Betsy gave him a Skynasaur "for my birthday just a few months before we got married." Looking back, Craig points out that she "had no idea what she initiated, but she started something pretty big." Loving that kite, Craig started making his own, "mostly because I didn't have money to buy kites." In 1984, Craig finished building a handsome delta, and "I wanted a picture of it before it broke away like the Green Giant kite." While twisting to position himself for the shot, Craig had an epiphany, realizing "the pull on this kite is easily enough to lift my big old heavy 35 mm camera." The idea "came to me as an original thought," but he had a hunch others may have tried taking photos from the end of a kite line and decided to do some research. With an affinity for photography, Craig notes, "I have always had a camera since I was very young" and connecting "photography to my kite line was just another way to play with kites."

A new subscriber to *Kite Lines*, Craig backordered issues with kite aerial photography stories to learn the how-tos of KAP. Craig gathered information for a few years before mustering the courage to try it himself. On his first roll, Craig got shots of himself sitting at his backyard picnic table looking up at the camera. The unusual viewpoint "really ignited me," but he saw that the images could have been better. For Craig, his KAP journey began as he "started to sort out what was wrong and how I could make that right." He studied his film, improved his camerawork, and sought out technical improvements. Over time, Craig upgraded his camera and built gear that could rotate and get 360-views and was able to snap shots in a 400th of a second. "I took a huge leap not just in image quality but in number of photos." Improving as he dabbled, Craig went out flying more frequently and "suddenly the scrapbook of the *good ones* is starting to build."

Immersed in fun, Craig wanted to be around others who shared his growing interests. "I'm sort of feeling like I'm the only guy within a huge range that flies kites." Though he had a friend who flew with him regularly, Craig's world opened up at the 1988 AKA convention in Chicago. "My mind is numb by what I am seeing" in the air and, on the ground he "got turned on to this national community of people who were out there" flying. Shortly after the convention, he met other kite aerial photographers through the European Kite Aerial Photography Worldwide Association. KAPWA "was a complete and utter resource" and through the club's journal, Craig read firsthand stories on how seasoned fliers solved the technical problems that he struggled with. Looking back to the days before he found his tribe, Craig remarks that being isolated "in some ways was good because it forced me to think things through as how it would be best for me to do it," but tapping into this network gave him access to answers and new friends.

Gaining experience and learning his craft, Craig reached out and started documenting his surroundings. With his first real rig, Craig worked up the confidence to shoot over the University of Wisconsin's football stadium on game day. Snapping away, Craig rushed his film "to the one hour processor, and before the game is over and I have the film in my hand, and I am going 'Just wow, this is really good stuff!'" He got four shots published, and the vibrant images became "the best selling postcard in Madison." Inspired, "I knew I had done something right," and from there, "everywhere I went I was looking at it in terms of what is its aerial potential." Growing his portfolio, Craig went on to publish over a thousand shots, publish two books of photography, and display his work in numerous gallery shows and exhibitions.

Although he is a kiteflier, with his photography Craig gravitates away from typical flying grounds because those places aren't "necessarily where the pictures are at." Seeking opportunities to showcase the beauty and rhythms of his everyday surroundings, Craig explores offbeat places like farmer's markets, lawn concerts, and canoe rental lots, and he has amassed a striking collection of cityscapes, neighborhood shots, and lakefront scenes. Craig found that while "people are lost in the traditional aerial photos" from aircraft, with KAP he is able to direct his camera to places people gather to get low altitude shots with a perspective that retains interesting details. "You can read their t-shirts." Captivated by beauty in plain sight, Craig's work is about "people as art." Watching crowds cluster and pull apart, Craig highlights patterns that emerge organically. "People dress colorfully, and the elements of color come into play," adding lovely serendipitous hints of charm to his shots. Years into his craft, Craig is a world leader in KAP, known for his unique visual voice.

As Craig immersed himself deeper and deeper in kiting, he began traveling. "I just feel that you can't experience the world in any better way than dragging a bag of kites." An overseas trip to the RICV International Kite Festival in Berck-sur-Mer, France inspired him to create an event near home that would draw fliers from afar. Noting that real estate in Madison is largely punctuated by water, Craig embraced the idea to fly in the winter on ice. Craig himself frequently captured in his photography the doings of ice fishermen, ice boaters, and cross-country skiers, and thought a kite festival on the ice would "be different" and highlight a unique side of Madison while contributing to organized kiting fun in a new way. For seven years, *Kites on Ice* delighted people.

Francis Rogallo

Francis Rogallo, born in 1912 at his parents' hotel in Sanger, California, was one of four sons of Polish and French immigrants. The May–September couple met in San Francisco, married, and opened a hotel near Fresno. Francis' father passed away when he was twelve and his mother married a veterinarian with two children. The family, strong advocates of education, sent the four eldest children to boarding schools. Francis journeyed to Montezuma Mountain School for Boys in the Santa Cruz Mountains and then to a military academy in San Marcos, Texas, before returning to Sanger. After high school, Francis was encouraged to continue his studies. For about two years, he commuted twenty miles a day to study engineering at Fresno State College, before transferring to Stanford University to complete his degree in mechanical engineering. Diploma in hand, yet still curious, he stayed at Stanford to receive his graduate degree in 1935 from its Guggenheim School of Aeronautics, with the help of faculty who secured grants for Francis.

Ready for work, but limited by the economic realities of the Great Depression, Francis remembered, "The only job I could find was as a mechanical engineer with the Shell Chemical Company." Although grateful to find a work as an engineer, this position was not the type of work flight-lusting Rogallo was after. As a long shot, he took the civil service examination, in hopes of landing an aeronautic research position at the Langley Research Center. "There were so many papers that it took eight months to get the papers corrected." Rogallo's dream of joining this top aeronautic research team seemed nearly impossible, but despite over 2,000 applicants, "I got an offer to come to Langley. They were going to hire seven people from the whole United States, and I was lucky enough to be one of those, the top seven that took this examination." In 1936, Francis headed east to work in this elite hands-on think tank, where he logged countless hours of tests in government research wind tunnels. He finally retired in 1970 and relocated with his wife Gertrude to their summer home near Kitty Hawk, North Carolina.

Reflecting on childhood influences, interests, and hobbies, Francis recalled, "I liked anything that flew." Although kites were uncommon when and where he grew up, Rogallo remembers flying handmade Eddys and three-stick kites in the spring while away at school. "In my hometown, I never saw a kite fly until I flew one there myself." Young Francis found fun challenging classmates to heated glider contests.

His schoolyard, wedged into a mountain bluff, was a perfect location for long-distance glider competitions. Interestingly, one of his top performing designs was his paper glider "with the flex wing. It was pointed in the front and had two lobes in it, and the keel was the same length as the leading edges."

Throughout the years, Francis' lifelong interest in aviation research endured through his many experiments for work and for pleasure. Rogallo's flexible wing is perhaps his best-known invention, yet it was only one of his twenty-one patented creations, and its adaptation as a kite was a byproduct of his aviation experiments. Known in the kite community by many names, the *Rogallo Wing* or the *Flexikite* or the *Flexible Wing,* is a stick-less flier that can use two lines for directional flight control. Rogallo toyed with a three-line version where you "could do both directional and pitch control, but we decided that two lines was really all you need, and it is simpler." Although dual line control is not unique to Rogallo's kite, his version is said to have inspired many modern dual line kite designs.

Motivation to develop a flexible wing hit Rogallo in 1945, but colleagues in Virginia were initially unreceptive to its possible practical applications. "Gertrude and I just did it as a home project and we made small kites and gliders for a few years until 1958 after Sputnik was launched, and the United States decided to get into the space business." Fueled by the space race's momentum, Francis convinced government officials "that the flexible wing might be a useful thing in landing capsules and boosters, and so they allowed me to start testing in a wind tunnel that I was in charge of there." What started as a small kite grew through the experimental trials to about, "4,000 square-feet of cloth area and we carried or tested them with payloads of 4,000 and 6,000 pounds." His experiments on his soft wing recovery device continued until 1970 "when space shuttles started being operated and they decided that that would be more desirable than landing things with a flexible wing."

During his years of design development, Francis' flexible wing caught the attention of others outside Langley. The U.S. Army looked into his glider as a way to land cargo. "They did a lot of tests and showed that was feasible," but they ultimately did not widely adopt the wing. The Ryan Aircraft Company also experimented with his wing and integrated it into their *Fleep*—a quirky and not too successful military-style cargo plane, named as a contraction of flying Jeep. Developed in 1961 as a "platform with a pilot seat on the front end of it and a pushed engine with a push propeller on the rear back edge of it, and a space for quite a bit of cargo." The contraption "was mounted on wheels for take off and landing." Not many *Fleeps* rolled off the assembly line, but Gertrude and Francis journeyed near San Diego to see the *Fleep* fly, and, Rogallo recalled that "it flew very well."

With Army brass and aircraft companies investigating uses for Francis' brainchild, it was not surprising that creative thinkers from other fields soon got interested in adapting the design for their uses, too. The Golden Knights parachute team "invited me to go down to Fort Bragg and give a talk and demonstration, and they dropped some of the flexible wings of the size that would then open up and glide instead of just opening up and coming straight down like a parachute." Shortly after, the Pioneer Parachute and the Urban Parachute companies caught heard about his innovation and "they started making paragliders suitable for people to jump out of airplanes and open up and glide with, and of course people have been doing that sort of thing ever since."

In the 1950s, before the aeronautic research community took Rogallo's design seriously, Rogallo tested his plans at home and took his kite to the commercial world to generate revenue to support his homegrown research. "We thought, well maybe the kites that we made in the development might be salable, and we might make a little money to keep on with the work, and also to publicize the idea of them as kites, so we went to New York and we sold them" to the B. Altman department store in Manhattan, the FAO Schwartz toy company, and a gift shop in a nearby hotel. Marketing his design as a kite opened the door to the commercial world and helped him gain exposure to other helpful people.

At about the same time, a Langley coworker introduced the Rogallos to his relative, Will Yolen, who "was the publicity man for the American Toy Manufacturer's Association," in hopes of fostering a partnership that would promote Rogallo's kite to the wider commercial market. Many now regard Yolen's book, *The Complete Book of Kites and Kiteflying*, as a classic, but back then, Yolen "had never flown a kite." The Rogallos "went to his house and took him out in Central Park and taught him how to fly a kite and he got interested in it and thought he could help publicize it. I think he did."

Following Yolen's arrival came a brief venture with a businessman from New Haven, Connecticut. The man who "made a business of selling Silly Putty put up in plastic eggs" was now courting the Rogallos. The Rogallos were eager and "made a contract with him" but the venture floundered. "We really want to get into business, but I had a job as a research scientist that I didn't want to leave, and Gertrude didn't want to run a business either on her own, so we broke the contract."

Although his design idea eventually fell to NASA's cutting room floor, his time at the drawing board was not in vain. Rogallo's work pioneered a new dimension in the world of kiteflying and gave rise to the sports of hang gliding and paragliding. "Well I don't know whether I revolutionized" recreational flying sports or not, "but I guess we did make a dent in it or have some influence on it, and I think it is a satisfaction to know that you helped to create something new that many people find of value for one reason or another."

Francis Rogallo (1912–2009) and his flexible wing advanced science and leisure.

Peter Lynn

"My memory doesn't go far enough back to know when I first flew kites," and luckily for the kite world, Peter Lynn's love of kites stretched into adulthood, when he innovated show-stopping colossal kites and pioneered the world of kite buggying and expanded traction kiting across snow and water.

Born in 1946 in New Zealand, Peter's kite making credentials began humbly with homemade brown paper diamond kites that he sometimes flew off the roof of his two-story childhood home. "I used to relentlessly pester my mother to cook up flour and water paste" and by age seven or eight, kiting had become a major interest, especially during the August kite-flying season. Thrill seeking Peter and his friends enjoyed a game where they tied a slip knot in the bridle and let out quite a bit of line before releasing their handmade kite and chasing it "across the town." Kites were ubiquitous during childhood. Once, in the schoolyard, Peter was riding his bicycle and crossed paths with a kite line. The accident was significant and left a scar across his neck that took decades to fade but did not diminish his interest in kiting.

A few years later, around age eleven or twelve, Peter built his first jumbo kite. "My father had a joinery manufacturing business so we had no shortage in availability of kite sticks." Peter built a giant diamond kite from heavy grade packing paper that stretched seven-and-a-half feet to the cross member and punctuated it with a tail he made from eight coal sacks. Borrowing flying line from the family's "kon-tiki" fishing raft, Peter lugged his creation to the schoolyard. Sadly, its

Peter Lynn's designer Simon Chisnall created this playful crab, flying here in Kaikoura, New Zealand, 27′ × 25′ (8.2 × 7.5 m) (courtesy Peter Lynn Kites).

With some kites over 100 feet long (30 m), Peter Lynn brings color and whimsy to the sky, 2015 (courtesy Peter Lynn Kites).

tail got caught in an oak tree and snapped off a sizable branch. With the score at kite 1, tree 0, this was "a promising start, but unfortunately, in later years the trees have generally won." From an early age, Peter learned firsthand the kite's quiet power and witnessed its strength.

Later, as a teenager, kiting became decidedly "uncool" and Peter "didn't fly kites much" until he was out of college and married to Elwyn. Landing his first job as a professional engineer, Peter worked for an American company in Sydney. At the time he nearly relocated to Portland but, as a new father, got cold feet and returned to New Zealand to set down roots and welcome four more children into his family. With the joys of parenthood, Peter decided to make his daughter a kite, but "thought I'm not going to make a traditional kite, I'm going to really make something different." His valentine didn't fly and "I was really annoyed about it." From that moment, Peter began studying "kite behavior, trying to find out why and what. It just became an obsession." During the next few years, Peter was also involved in motocross and then yacht racing. Looking back, Peter recognizes being "very intense about" his hobbies. Acknowledging that "competitive sports are really all the same," through motocross and yachting, Peter learned to race strategically and picked up lessons and techniques that later became very useful in kite buggy racing.

As an adult, Peter initially made polystyrene kites that he shaped with hot wires, glued together and reinforced with wood. Liking these "hard" kites because they kept their shape in flight and, unlike soft fabric surfaces, allowed Peter to study and quantify "various attributes that define lift, drag, and stability" easily. In 1973, Peter and Elwyn sold their first kite, and by 1975, the couple launched their Craft

Peter Lynn's *Humpback Whale* overseeing a proposal in Singapore, 2017 (courtesy Peter Lynn Kites).

Kite Company. As entrepreneurs, early on, "we had other businesses, but the kite business started to consume us more and more." In 1976, Peter attended an international wood collector's meeting in Portland with his father, largely because he heard there was "a shop there dedicated to kites." Slipping away from the convention to look for the rumored kite shop, without an address, Peter asked taxi drivers for help locating the store, Windplay. "I finally found it, walked in, met John Waters and Grant Raddon, caught up with what was happening then in the U.S. and left in a highly excited state with kite books, issues of *Kite Tales*, and various kites." Back in New Zealand, business duties were beginning to detract from the pleasures that drew them to the hobby, and Peter and Elwyn sold the company to their doctor "who had some children he wanted a business for." The deal freed up time to play with kites and the sale paid for Peter's return trip to the U.S. to attend the AKA's inaugural convention in Ocean City, Maryland in 1978. Regrettably, "the doctor had the misfortune to die soon after this," and by 1979 Peter and Elwyn were back in the kite business.

About a decade later, "kites had lost some of their challenge and excitement" when John Waters of Catch the Wind gave Peter a "sky-diving foil re-rigged as a two-line steerable kite," and put him on course to explore what is now known as kite traction. Back in New Zealand, Peter first used John's "sluggish monster kite" for water skiing and then for kite sailing. Pulled into a new part of kiting, Peter

A pod of Peter Lynn's *Humpback Whales*, Thailand (courtesy Peter Lynn Kites).

began "intensively developing new kites and equipment for kite traction." Building several prototype boards, boats, and kites, Peter tested his experimental gear at an alpine lake where winds are frequently quite ferocious. Wrestling with power, Peter recalls "quite a few near death experiences for me and the various crash test dummies who had been roped in," and began building in safety features to minimize danger. Early traction kites were pulled by oversized deltas but soon Peter developed his 'Peel' two-line ram-air design, which included an ingenious quick-release handle system that could detached the kite in emergencies without sending bars or handles flying through the air.

Experiments continued, and in 1989, Peter fabricated a craft with a seat and three water skis that riders could steer from the front. "It was a complete failure on the water," but after Peter swapped the skis with wheels, he hit the mark and developed the "first practical modern kite buggy." The buggy debuted at the Pattaya Kite Festival in Thailand in 1990 and is now retired and on display at the World Kite Museum in Long Beach, Washington. Kite buggying quickly became an international sport, and beyond the buggy, Peter pushed that idea and innovated new generations of traction fun, developing kite surfing and snow kiting. Looking back, Peter takes pride in his inventions and says it is "good to be part of that history."

Tearing up land and sea, Peter's imagination also colors the sky. An innovator of giant inflatable kites, Peter's whimsical school of towering sea creature kites has become the iconic emblem of kite celebrations around the world. Testing the aerodynamic principles parafoil pioneer Domina Jalbert tapped into, Peter began developing stickless ram-air show kites in 1994 that preserved their form without a rigid skeleton. Seeing "so many possibilities in terms of shape," in the middle 1990s, Peter

Peter Lynn's 130-foot (40 m) *Octopus* **dangles its tentacles teasingly (courtesy Peter Lynn Kites).**

developed a system he calls "Super-Ripstop" that uses a grid work of sewn-on reinforcing cords to strengthen fabric structures. His innovation effectively removes dimension caps, allowing for an exceptionally large canvas where "maximum size limits have not yet been approached." Designing for the boundless sky, Peter's line of fantastically playful maxi kites, like the Octopus, Ray, and Trilobite are exclamation points at kite festivals around the globe. In 1997, Guinness Book took note of Peter's 635-square-meter Megabite kite and within ten years, he smashed that record with his 1,000-square-meter Kuwait flag kite. Expanding dimensions further to 1,250-square-meters, Peter's Ray kite became the world's largest kite in 2014.

Off the flying fields, Peter shares his kiting knowledge and has written a number of technical papers documenting kite aerodynamics and has his name on many patents in the traction kite trade, yet Peter's inventive mind stretches outside of kiting where he has made contributions to a range of industries. Peter designed a widely used portable circular sawmill system with a single circular blade that tips and rotates 90 degrees to produce rectangular lumber, and has recently developed down force wings that prevent wind damage to large irrigators. Whether inventing for leisure or utility, Peter dissects problems and devises improvements for all varieties of tools.

Peter Lynn's *Pegasus* shimmering at sunset (courtesy Peter Lynn Kites).

Filling the sky with oversized fun, Peter Lynn's inflatable creatures delight onlookers, 2015 (courtesy Peter Lynn Kites).

Peter Lynn's *Humpback Whale,* designed by Simon Chisnall, weighs in at about 20 pounds (9 kg) (courtesy Peter Lynn Kites).

The sun sets behind Peter Lynn's *Humpback Whales* as these giant kites swim through the sky (courtesy Peter Lynn Kites).

Wolfgang Bieck's kite aerial photograph rig allows for interesting bird's-eye glimpses (courtesy Wolfgang Bieck).

Wolfgang Bieck's kite aerial photographs are eye level with jumbo kites (courtesy Wolfgang Bieck).

Jose Sainz's *Wind Spirit* flying into the sunset over Antelope Island, Utah, 2012 (courtesy Jose Sainz).

A trio of deltas in formation as captured by aerial photographer Wolfgang Bieck (courtesy Wolfgang Bieck).

C11

One of six in a series of block-printed bamboo and paper kites called *Monkeying Around* that Jose Sainz made for a cooperative kite exhibition that featured kites by graphic artists from the U.S., Mexico, Japan, and Europe, 2010 (courtesy Jose Sainz).

Inspired by Leong Chee Wan's design, Jose Sainz made this 18' (5.5 m) pointer kite with a 20' (6 m) tail from Ripstop and fiberglass tube framing and personalized it with an appliqué feather design, 2013 (courtesy Jose Sainz).

Jose Sainz's pointer kite flying over the *Wind Labyrinth* art installation at the DOTA (Department of Tethered Aviation) Burning Man camp, 2013 (courtesy Jose Sainz).

Aztec Calendar is a Bermuda-style hexagonal kite Jose Sainz made from appliquéd Ripstop with fiberglass tubing (courtesy Jose Sainz).

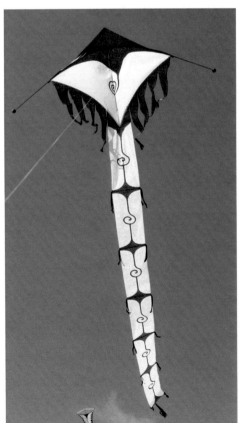

Jose Sainz's *Wind Spirit* flying over an art installation at the Burning Man festival (courtesy Jose Sainz).

Jose Sainz's *Fire Dragon* kite is a Hata-style kite spanning 4' (1.2 m) with a 35' (10.7m) tail that he built for the Artevento Kite Festival in Cervia, Italy, 2012 (courtesy Jose Sainz).

C13

Ken Conrad and a 150-disk traditional silk dragon kite from Weifang, China, at the Washington State International Kite Festival in Long Beach, Washington, in the late–1990s (courtesy Suzanne Sadow and Ken Conrad).

Pete Dolphin at Jacob Riis Park, Rockaway, New York, 2004 (photograph by Mike Carroll, courtesy Pete Dolphin).

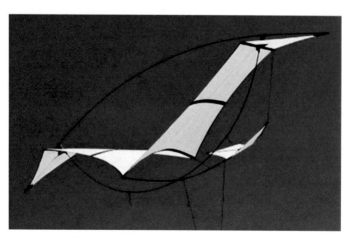

Ron Gibian's incredible flying machine *Celeste II* (courtesy Sandra and Ron Gibian).

C14

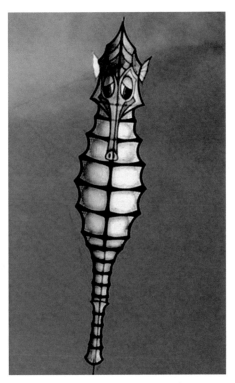

Ron Gibian's *Kiko Sr.*, Cervia, Italy, 2014 (photograph by Malcolm Goodman, courtesy Sandra and Ron Gibian).

Ron Gibian's seahorse *Jango* flying in Cervia, Italy (courtesy Sandra and Ron Gibian).

Ron Gibian's *Lescargo*, 2007 (photograph by René Maier, photograph courtesy Sandra and Ron Gibian).

Sharing the fun, Suzanne Sadow and Ken Conrad bring *Fly Me Paper Bag Kite Kits* to Seattle's Family Fourth celebrations at Gasworks Park, 2011 (photograph by Chris Nelson, courtesy Suzanne Sadow and Ken Conrad).

Suzanne Sadow (center, front) helping children make *Frustrationless Flyers* at a kite festival in Seattle's Gaswork Park in the early 1990s (courtesy Suzanne Sadow and Ken Conrad).

CHAPTER 4

Club Business:
The Business of Doing Business

"Although I'd rather be out on the field flying kites, the business of the business is important." Jon Burkhardt

Bob Ingraham

The roots of the American Kitefliers Association trace back to member number one, Bob Ingraham, who ran with his idea to gather a few adult fliers and ended up creating the AKA in 1964. Over the years, he nurtured the club, promoted membership, and kept the cross-country dialog flowing. His recreational forum grew into an international brotherhood with membership thousands strong, and shortly before his death in 1995, Bob looked back proudly on his role in kiting, happy with all the strings he pulled.

At the heart of it, Bob loved the sky. With equal interest in aerodynamics and aircraft, kites bridged his need for fun and aerial experimentation nicely. In his youth, Bob sold rides for a barnstorming group. Outfitted in a white jumpsuit lined with deep pockets, young Bob hawked rides and "turned over $800 to $1,000 in ten and twenty dollar bills for the rides I sold each day." Yet despite his love of flying, he didn't pursue a career in aviation. Entering adulthood at the cusp of the Great Depression, fate dashed his hopes of becoming a pilot or studying aerodynamics. "You want to raise a family and become an adult and you have to give up some of the things that you always thought you wanted to do." When the Depression ended, Bob was a little too old to start anew and he had already found his way into a journalism career, yet the sky never left him. Bob's involvement in kiting connected him to his skyward interests, even if this avocation didn't present itself in a nine-to-five paycheck kind of way, Bob pulled pleasure from the sky.

Fully of age, Bob felt self-conscious about kiteflying. "I begun to wonder why, as an adult with two grown children, was I flying kites, when that normally was supposed to be a child's endeavor. For many years kiteflying was not considered an

In his youth, Bob Ingraham worked from a barnstorming group and earned free rides on this Curtiss-J-1-718 (courtesy Bob Ingraham).

adult sport, and if you were seen flying a kite as an adult they'd question your man-liness." Some wounds never heal, and in his twilight years Bob vividly recalled the afternoon when he was flying in the park and two teenaged girls walked up to him and pointedly asked, "'What do you do that for?'" Flabbergasted and answerless Bob felt embarrassed and alone about his kiting interests until he read a feel-good piece in the newspaper about Edward Aff, vice president of the Federal Reserve Bank of Philadelphia and an avid kiteflier who gave kite making lessons at his local Kiwanis and Rotary meetings. In that short article, Bob found permission to enjoy kiting without apologies. "I thought, 'Gee wiz if the vice president of the Federal Reserve Bank can go fly kites, why should I be bashful about it?'"

Encouraged and excited to find a kindred spirit, Bob reached out to Aff. The banker gave Bob the names of seven men he had met with mutual kite interests and Bob wrote to each suggesting that they start a kiting organization. And there, with a few letters exchanged by mail, the AKA was born.

The AKA "started with nine members and it just took off. I mean way beyond what we thought it would." Looking back, Bob credits word of mouth promotion as the key element to this club's grassroots growth. As a journalist, Bob had expe-rience in public relations and "would plant little things that developed into stories" in major newspapers. The Wall Street Journal picked up on the AKA's activities and the Detroit Free Press called him every spring for a kiting story. Ever the cheer-leader, Bob promoted the club because he enjoyed "letting people know what this was all about." His advertising reached a wide audience. Even celebrities, including Charles Schulz, Jimmy Stewart, and Paul Harvey, joined the AKA, and President Hoover's adult grandson came to visit Bob and his wife Hazel in pursuit of his kiting interests. "We used to have to push ourselves into it and now we have had no end of visitors here in the last twenty years."

Second only to perhaps Bob's leadership in influencing the young club's success, the newsletter kept members in touch and spread the word. Bob sent out the first issue of *Kite Tales* in 1964 and ran the publication for fourteen years before Valerie Govig took the helm and adopted the name *Kite Lines.* Bob remembers, "from the time I started the magazine I was a busy boy. I did everything on that magazine except the actual printing. I made all of the layouts. I did most of the writing. It got to be quite a job. Even with Hazel taking care of the business end of the association, I still had an awful lot to do." With the first issue, "I didn't dare do a whole lot because I didn't know whether I'd have money enough to pay for the damn thing or not." But after about three months, "the advertising money began coming in and new memberships" increased and things started looking up. Thankfully, Bob didn't tire with nitty-gritty publication details and each issue delivered kite news and stories to an ever-widening audience.

Bob's behind the scenes involvement set the stage for the AKA's growing success, yet he still found time to fly for fun. Bob, a devoted single line flier, loved his trusted deltas and had fun pushing the limits with parafoils. Somewhat of a rascal, Bob enjoyed dropping things from his kites using mounted releases he fashioned from the works of old alarm clocks and mousetraps. Bricks, jugs of water, bags of sand, Coke bottles, and even man-sized dummies with helmets and parachute back-

Before founding the American Kitefliers Association, a young Bob Ingraham recruited riders for a barnstorming group (courtesy Bob Ingraham).

packs were dropped from high above for Bob's amusement and curiosity. He recognized in hindsight that "there was a danger, fooling around like I did," but he enjoyed the splendor of each drop with childlike wonderment.

In addition to a lifelong fascination with kiting and things that flew, Bob was outdoorsy, enjoying rabbit hunting, camping, hiking, and, his son Bob recalls that "dad became a very amateur archeologist soon after we moved to New Mexico, and used to take me out on 'digs,' which today would be frowned upon and might even be illegal." Looking back, "dad was quite adventurous" and once accompanied horseback forest rangers on a multi-day supply run to Mogollon Baldy, the highest peak in the Gila Wilderness Area. "Dad had never before been on a horse. He was so sore when he got home that he could hardly move … but I don't think he regretted a moment of the ordeal." Bob also enjoyed raising chickens, and put his woodworking skills to use, making a lovely coop for his bantams. But perhaps his most beloved pastime was the violin. For seventy years, Bob played, and did so well. Son Bob notes, "I believe dad could have become a professional violinist. He seemed to have a natural talent, which may have been genetic, from his mother" who played the piano in a movie theatre during the days of silent films. Bob played first chair with the Western New Mexico University Orchestra and was their concertmaster for three years.

A man of many talents, the kiting world is forever indebted to him for nurturing his interests in kiting. As club ambassador Bob enjoyed spreading the word and watching people enjoy kites. Reflecting on the folks he crossed paths with he remembers that "the most remarkable thing, of the thousands of people we have met in all these years, hardly a one was somebody we didn't like. All pretty high class people, and that says something for kitefliers." Enjoying the company he kept and acknowledging the importance of the AKA never escaped Bob. Getting straight to the heart of his legacy, "I'm just selfish enough that I don't want to see all this die and be forgotten, you know. I don't expect that you are going to maybe remember me, but keep this kite interest alive."

Robert "Bob" Ingraham, 1911–1995, flew countless kites, met many people, and helped us all find our space in the sky.

Bob Price

Legendary kite enthusiast and former AKA president and archivist Bob Price was born in 1922 in Evanston, Illinois, and remained in Chicago's suburban north shore until he journeyed east to study at the Michigan College of Mining and Tech-

Bob and Jewell Price in front of their *Mobo* (courtesy Marae Price).

nology. In 1943, Bob graduated and embarked on a scientific career at an underwater explosions research laboratory in Massachusetts before taking up a rather exciting post at Maryland's Naval Ordinance Laboratory. Summing up his duties, Bob said, "My work was doing underwater explosions. I was taking photographs of them, making pressure time measurements, and things of that sort. Anything from small detonators up to atomic bombs."

Looking back, Bob remembers a couple commonplace kite making experiments in his childhood, but kiting as a passion came later in life. In the early 1960s, Bob made kites with his daughter, Marae, and flew them near their Maryland home. "Across the road, this field that had been mowed for collecting hay was on sort of a ridge that ran down in the northwest—beautiful. Wind would come up that thing just as smooth as glass. We'd fly our kites over the field." Over the years, their kite making techniques evolved from loose-paneled Eddies to more sophisticated tetrahedrals with Bob's handmade cast fittings. Although Marae eventually moved away, as well as on to other things, their hay field experiments hooked Bob into the world of adult kiteflying.

As the 1970s approached, Bob investigated the art of kite aerial photography and began attending the early Smithsonian festivals. One of his earliest fans and guides into the kiting community was Valerie Govig. Marveling at his box kite, Valerie encouraged Bob and invited him to join the Maryland Kite Society. He did, and was pleased "to learn that there were other people that were interested in kites. I didn't know that they existed until that time."

As Bob's kite curiosity grew, so did his involvement with organized kiting. While the AKA expanded, new offices were created to address issues facing the growing club. The membership elected him to the new office of archivist. He took the position seriously and, as a person of foresight, he enlarged the scope of the group's collection focus. He accumulated "the minutes of all the meetings and all that sort of stuff, and the financial records," in addition to several thousand snapshots, clippings, mailing lists, and articles relating to the kiting world. The trove survives today and records the history of the club and is an anthropological record of the evolution of modern kiteflying.

With a successful track record as archivist and increasing involvement in the AKA leadership circle, his election to club president was a logical progression. President Price took on the task of growing the then 850-member group and pulling them across their early period of financial thin ice. At one point when the bank account fell below the minimum $1,000 safe line, Bob took action by streamlining operations and beefing up the auction as a viable revenue source. He recalls, "the philosophy was that we would need to have enough money in the bank if we said we were going to close the AKA to pay back the people who had just paid their dues." His strategies worked, but he recalled that during the club's early days, "we were never sure from one moment to the next whether we'd have to close or not."

Committed to organized kiting and helping keep the club in the black, Bob sacrificed his signature hobbyhorse to the AKA's auction block to raise funds. Over the years, he had created an unusual kite anchor from a bicycle frame that he salvaged from the city dump and weighed down with a coin-op appliance he harvested from a target practice gadget. For fun, Bob gussied up the anchor with the head of his daughter's outgrown hobbyhorse, which he created for her earlier. Curious and eye-catching, Bob's seated anchor made a steady and reliable base for his aerial kite photography that allowed him to pedal line in and out quickly. Bob generously parted with his Frankenstein to support the club. Equally altruistic, Bob gave his time to his local club and for decades was on the Maryland Kite Society's board of directors. In 2001, the AKA honored Bob's years of service to organized kiting and awarded him its Robert M. Ingraham Award.

Adept with his hands and blessed with a double dose of ingenuity, Bob created some of the most intricate kites in the sky. "Nine out of ten times I will be flying a kite, it will be a box kite. I built large box kites and you could get inside of them." Box kites, especially large rhomboids, were Bob's favorites because they were stable fliers that made "good photo platforms" for his kite aerial photography pursuits.

Forever nurturing a scientific bent, Bob tested the flying performance of kites and painstakingly recorded his data in volume after volume of research notebooks. "You have to measure the wind velocity and the forces on the kite in the air—where it is, and this is not wind tunnel stuff, or theoretical, it is actual measurements." When explaining the inspiration for his fieldwork, Bob simply stated, "It occurred to me that there aren't any very good measurements on kites, on how well they were doing, and so I started working on that." Incorporating his fieldwork, Bob improved kite designs and shared his findings.

In 2006, organized kiting lost a kingpin when Bob succumbed to pancreatic cancer, but his lifelong contributions to the AKA ensured the club's longevity and ability to service current and future members.

Tom Sisson

A founding father of the Washington Kitefliers Association, an early recipient of the Edeiken Award, and someone festival promoters billed as "the man who could fly any kite," Seattle's Tom Sisson contributed more than just a helpful hand and friendly smile to the kite world. Tom's legacy as a brick-and-mortar kiter helped lay the foundation for the modern era of organized kiting, and his infectious interest in people kept him engaged in kiting throughout his life.

Growing up in the Rainier Valley in Washington State, looking back, Tom quickly linked his father's interest in kites to his own. His father was an avid recreational flier who frequently made towering box kites, cross-braced and fortified with string and quarter-inch rods, which he dressed up with Christmas wrapping paper. His flair and clever repurposing of holiday paper impressed Tom and smiles were quick whenever Tom recalled the colorful kites he made with his father. Green before the modern reuse movement, his dad's penchant to give materials a second life impressed Tom, and later it became commonplace for Tom to incorporate found material, like plastic shopping bags and stockpiles of discarded misprinted stickers into his kite making. For Tom, childhood kiting "was great fun." Even when those kites "crashed and burned," he enjoyed the kites and lessons of his father.

Beyond the twilight of youth, Tom managed to keep tugging on kite strings straight through to adulthood. During a tour of duty in World War II, in the Merchant Marines his superiors selected him to fly target kites off the ship. Tom flew these early dual-line maneuverable kites on deck, sharpening his kiteflying skills as he dodged bullets his shipmates fired toward the image of a plane painted on his kite to keep their shooting skills nimble between combat missions. Being the ship's official kiteflier, Tom would occasionally set aside his government-issued Eddy kite and pop up kites he made aboard the ship "without much being said, except when we were in war waters." Kite at the ready, Tom showed his mates that kites were both tools and toys.

Once he returned stateside, Tom settled into a domestic world complete with Boy Scout badge-worthy kites and plenty of, "Chubby and Tubby" dime store kites that entertained both him and his children. Weekdays, Tom dutifully worked for the Engineering Department for the City of Seattle for thirty-three years, but left

Always embellishing his handiwork, even the tails on Tom Sisson's hexagonal *Flexagon* kite have pizzazz (courtesy Jean Sisson).

time on the weekend for kiteflying, lawn bowling, gardening, cards, camping, movies, and wine tasting.

In the early 1970s, with his kids grown and leaving home, Tom had more free time and kites took on a larger role in his life. During a fortuitous trip to Fort Worden, Tom and his wife Jean were visiting on an afternoon when a small group happened to be flying kites on the grounds. The Sissons struck up a conversation and met area kiting enthusiasts Dave Checkley, Tony Toledo, and Ken Conrad. Sharing an interest in kites, the fliers became fast friends. About a month later, Tom joined them at an informal fly on the grounds of a nearby college. Interest in flying together grew and the group soon became the Washington Kitefliers Association and started holding monthly club meetings at the Seattle Science Center. Finding fellow enthusiasts with whom he could share his interests in kites, Tom "got hooked" into kiting, witnessed the WKA's growth, and assumed leadership roles in the club. Tom served three years as president, including one where he wrote the club's constitution to help the fledgling organization gain its legal nonprofit status. Over the years, the WKA attracted members young and old with a variety of events such as their annual *Protest the Bowls* fly on New Year's Day, *Fly Every Week* events, and the springtime *Cherry Blossom Festival*. The club remains active today, thanks in part to the groundwork Tom and fellow founders laid and the fun they enthusiastically promoted.

With an eye on ways to impress others with kites, Tom and fellow WKA club members Carl Brewer and Bob McCort set an aviation record for the longest indoor kite fly in 1980. The trio captured the indoor duration record at the old Seattle Kingdome sports arena. Using two thirds of the stadium's floor space, they flew continually for 39 hours and 57 minutes—just three minutes shy of their personal 40-hour goal, which was dashed when one of the Seattle Super Sonics' bouncing basketballs trampled the kite line as the group victoriously walked their kite onto the court. A minor disappointment perhaps, but even clipped a few minutes shy of their goal, their effort was good enough to set a record and land their kite in the Smithsonian's permanent collection.

As life and leisure evolved, Tom inadvertently took up the role of teacher after he was asked to demonstrate kite making. One thing led to the next, and Tom set off on a lifetime of kite making instruction, sharing the fun with over a quarter of a million people. Along the way, Tom perfected his trademark assembly line set-up that positioned young kitemakers and adult helpers along a circular or triangular workspace where the kids proceed to progressive workstations to complete various components of their kites. Tom's workshops were extremely popular and kite festival organizers well beyond his home state club copied its format endlessly. To help spread the joy, Tom instructed adults to lead workshops, often coaching his volunteers with pep talks. "If the kids for some reason get to you, go back to the hospitality room, have a cup of coffee, gorge on doughnuts, do anything you want, have a cigarette, but please come back." And back they came. Throughout the years Tom perfected ways to train the trainer and ultimately planted the seeds to his kiting legacy.

Tom's wife Jean recalls, "Tom was always interested in meeting new people and the new kite designs by younger flyers … keeping the interest alive." Sadly, Tom died in 1999 of pancreatic cancer but was involved in kite projects until three days before he passed. Friends still feel the loss, but remember fondly the sight of their pal in his signature flight gear—straw hat, one orange sock, one green sock, wildly happy-colored pants, and an inviting smile that he flashed frequently while on the lookout to help folks fly.

David and Dorothea Checkley

Late Seattle architect, painter, inventor, and designer Dave Checkley didn't have a childhood history of kiteflying, but later in life he immersed himself in the international and cultural aspects of the sport, making connections and friendships in the United States and overseas that helped people around the globe learn about the world of kites.

David's wife Dorothea recalled, "It was my husband of course who was the kite enthusiast, but I accompanied him when we took trips to the orient. I don't really have that much kite experience," yet together the couple became part of the backbone of the organized kiteflying movement in the 1970s and 1980s. Thinking about how kiting entered their life, Dorothea notes that things started as "just as an idea" that evolved into a passion. "No specific thing I ever heard of" sparked David's interest in kites. "He was a kiteflier, but not a great flier compared to some people, and somehow or another he just started enjoying kites and went at it with great enthusiasm when we moved to the west coast from Connecticut." His daughter Leslie remembers him more as an artist, with watercolors being his specialty, than a sportsman. He liked solitary, contemplative activities and was inclined to quiet pursuits like sailing and flying kites rather than spectator- or motor-sports.

Checkley's interest in kites was ignited when he and his family settled in Seattle in 1964. Dave was recruited there to manage an architectural firm and he involved himself in various civic activities. Through the Seattle Rotary, he met Japanese Rotarian Masakatsu "Henri" Kato who was involved with the long-running Japanese Hamamatsu Kite Festival and in charge of foreign guests. David wrote Kato-san a letter and made arrangements for a visit. Dorothea traces David's serious interest in kiting to his first visit to Hamamatsu where it "sort of ballooned" into a grand interest, and he and Mr. Kato "developed a deep and lasting friendship that continued until David died." In addition to their shared interest in kiting, Mr. Kato was also a watercolorist and introduced David to kite historians who helped him understand the kite's cultural significance. Kite history fascinated David and he greatly enjoyed sharing what he learned with fellow western fliers. "Eventually it worked out that David was responsible for having a cover story in National Geographic about the Hamamatsu Festival" and he arranged for PBS to create an hour-long documentary about the festival that was distributed nationally. For David, exploring kite history helped him promote worldwide kiting.

Equally fascinated with Chinese kites and kite making traditions, David toured China extensively. "He went to China with the Japanese before Americans were allowed to go, but somehow they always put him through" and David expanded his kite network through travel. In 1984, David founded the now renowned Weifang International Kite Festival, and Dorothea recalled that his colleagues in China "were proud to have David" because "they hadn't had international recognition before" and David helped them "bring in the outside world" and that "was a whole new thing." Fascinated by his travels, David pioneered kite tourism to Asia in the early 1970s. The Checkleys organized and led tours, usually of about twenty people, first to Japan and, later, to China as well. Dorothea recalled that "David acted as an ambassador, and only kite enthusiasts went with us" on trips that typically lasted two weeks, but some years they organized two-month-long excursions. Although some repeated the trips, Dorothea recalled that the guest list varied greatly from year to year. "David, I think, sort of became the number one international kite man because when he started taking people" to China and Japan, "people from other parts of the world would join the groups, it wasn't just Americans." Back at home in Seattle, the Checkleys had an enormous basement and dedicated the space to kites, outfitting the room with large tables. Dorothea remembered that, "kitefliers would come and stay with us from various parts of the world and never really wanted to leave that basement area. They enjoyed it thoroughly." David naturally played the role of ambassador, whether he was traveling or hosting friends from afar.

Although David is largely remembered for his international contributions to kiting, at home he was in on the ground floor of the budding kiting renaissance and was a founding member of the Washington Kitefliers Association. Dorothea cannot recall how plans for the WKA took shape, noting, "those things just start and you don't really get a beginning … people who were interested in kites just got together." With a small core of enthusiasts, the group grew into a club and started local traditions that still run today, like the annual New Years Day Kite Fly (aka *Protest the Bowls* fly) and the beloved cherry blossom-themed kite programming at the Seattle Science Center. While some events interested children, most of the club's outreach was for adults. "I think it was terribly important when he started flying kites the whole feeling was that it was for children and he soon developed and promoted the idea that this was very much an adult hobby, or occupation, and changed it from being just for children." David and the WKA helped welcome the young at heart back to kiting and spurred a resurgence in organized kiteflying.

In retirement, kiting became an unofficial second career and Dorothea recalled that David "was busy, if not busier, than when he was on a regular working program." With unstoppable energy, David started his Kite Factory business, in addition to continuing his kite tours and club activities. Copyrighting eight kite designs, for about fifteen years "he had a bit of a cottage industry for the parafoils and larger, costly kites" and employed a group of fine tailors in Seattle to fulfill wholesale orders for retailers such as FAO Schwarz, Neiman Marcus, and Abercrombie & Fitch. David also held a patent for his *Fly Me Paper Bag Kite Kit* that was mass-produced and sold as a beginner's sled kite that delighted groups of schoolchildren. Ken Conrad took over that product and continues manufacturing the perennial favorite. Bringing kites to the general public, David worked with corporate clients to print DIY kites onto their retail bags that customers could cut out and make from their empty shopping bags. Through various commercial streams, David helped kites proliferate and assisted the budding kite trade.

Through their extensive travels, the Checkleys amassed a large collection of beautiful kites, particularly strong in Asian kites. "When you go to the Orient, it is inevitable, people give you things. You bring over gifts and they load you down with kites they've made, which are usually marvelous," and over time, the Checkleys "started buying some too, very special ones, primarily in China." Shortly after David passed away in 1988, Dorothea donated his kites and their library of kite books and video footage they shot from kite festivals they attended around the world to the newly forming World Kite Museum in Long Beach, Washington. The Checkley Collection is the basis of the museum. "The Kite Museum, that was a very good thing that happened. I think they are doing a very good job." Decades later, the museum continues to showcase the Checkley collection, and generations of visitors are charmed and inspired by their exquisite kites.

Kites were "a passport to meeting interesting people" and though Dorothea personally did not "have this great feeling for kites as some people do," she recognized how valuable her hospitality was to their enduring success promoting kiting.

Top: The World Kite Museum, founded in 1989, is the only museum dedicated exclusively to kiting in the United States. *Bottom:* World Kite Museum packs a lot of kite history and fun in its two-story home in Long Beach, Washington (both photographs, author's collection).

Dorothea recalled that David "was fascinated by kiting and finding people who were involved in kites themselves, always searching for people who were really above the pack, so to speak. I think he had an affinity for making friends with people who were interested in kiting, so they kept coming from all over." The Checkleys met thousands of people through kiting and, "it was very rewarding."

Dorothea passed away in 2006.

Masaaki Modegi

Out of admiration and shared curiosities, Japan's Masaaki Modegi continues the work of his famous kite collecting father, the late Shingo Modegi, and has accomplished an impressive body of work of his own. President of the Japan Kite Association, Kite Museum director, and good spirited friend of all kitefliers, Masaaki Modegi proudly holds the strings that his father passed on to him many years ago.

As a child, Masaaki flew kites only during the traditional Japanese kiteflying season. To ring in the New Year, Japanese children take to their rooftops and fill the sky with small kites during the holiday. Masaaki remembers his father waking him on a cold night from his cozy bed to fly a Rokkaku from their roof. Good times were had during the cool night and dreams of kite fun started to seep in.

Throughout his lifetime, Masaaki's father Shingo amassed an impressive kite collection. In kite circles, Shingo Modegi was famous for *not* making kites, and revered for his curatorial knack of collecting fine samples of original, well-made, and beautiful kite work that caught his eye. As Shingo often quipped, "'Babe Ruth never made any bat,'" and he cherry-picked fine art without apologies.

When Masaaki was a child, he was unaware of the extent of his father's interest in kites until one day when he noticed that his dad's restaurant was literally wall-papered floor to ceiling with kites. In that moment, Masaaki realize his father was a kite fanatic. Open and alert, Masaaki began observing ways kites circled around his father and he began developing his own appreciation of kites.

In the early 1970s, Shingo and fourteen others, got together and formed the Japan Kite Association. The popular club rapidly grew its membership to over 500 members within its first year. Masaaki believes his father got involved in kiting simply for enjoyment and always managed to have fun when he was around kites and fellow fliers. Now as an adult, at the helm of the JKA, Masaaki honors his father's attachment to the club and enjoys promoting the pleasures of kiting.

Masaaki grew up witness to the JKA's growth and looking back, he remembers when the club expanded to the point that it needed to turn inward and reorganize.

During this coming of age, the club elected official officers, scheduled regular monthly meetings, and published official rulebooks for competitions. Yet even today, the crown jewels of the group's event calendar remain the same—the well-celebrated New Year festival, an international fly in May, and an end of year autumn gathering, designed in part to tide members over to the next year.

As president of the Japan Kite Association, Masaaki works tirelessly and keeps a bustling event calendar that finds him at two or three kite events a week. Joking that he finds it easier to rest at a kite event abroad than it is for him to find quiet time on Japanese flying fields, Masaaki takes his travel duties seriously and chronicles trips in the association's newsletters to keep members informed. He also shares photos and stories with staff at his local newspaper. Being everywhere and handling everything himself, some mistake him as a professional photojournalist rather than a talented club envoy.

Knowing firsthand the benefits and joys of traveling to festivals, Masaaki is committed to promoting conference attendance and has developed a reputation as a patron of kiting. In the spirit of international exchange, Masaaki underwrites travel, sending Japanese kitemakers to important international kiting events and he singlehandedly ensures that delegations of Japanese kitefliers make it to the AKA's annual conventions.

At home, Masaaki is equally busy running the world's oldest kite museum, *Tako no hakubutsakan.* Established in Tokyo in 1977 by his father after he met a child who had never seen a kite, Masaaki says you have to be determined when building a museum to keep its focus solely on kite-related items. Masaaki takes great pride in maintaining a narrow collection focus and selectively adding to his father's exquisite treasures. The museum showcases outstanding pieces by kite artists, flawless examples of traditional Japanese kites, along with samples of international kites that tell the stories of foreign lands. As the museum's director, Masaaki displays two main exhibitions a year. During summer months, he puts on a kid-focused exhibition and highlights cartoon kites from the collection. In the wintertime, Masaaki selects "happy" kites to help celebrate the seasons. He often juggles the bi-annual schedule a bit to squeeze in astonishing new arrivals from his international travels.

Masaaki recognizes the difficulties in keeping his doors open and has politely declined offers from Tokyo's mayor to transfer control of the museum to the municipality. As many non-profit museum directors know, it is hard to keep private museums solvent, especially during unsteady economic times. Masaaki's commitment to retaining the reigns has tightened his partnership with his father's restaurant, Taimeiken. The family's thriving upscale restaurant subsidizes the museum and helps cover the gaps in the organization's operating budget. Together, business and culture thrive and keep a father's dream alive.

Committed to promoting international kite relations, preserving kite history, keeping organized kiting afloat in Japan, and growing his father's impressive kite collection, the AKA honored Masaaki Modegi with the 2001 Lee Toy Award. A well deserved accolade, and one he continues to build upon. In 2007 he wrote the book *The Making of Japanese Kites: Tradition, Beauty and Creation* and continues to keep a full schedule promoting kiting.

Jim Miller

Jim Miller took to organized kiting rapidly in the 1980s and swiftly found himself in the AKA president's chair. His administration sowed many seeds, and his legacies continue to support organized kiteflying, however, his love of kites does not reach back to childhood. "I, like most other people of my generation, probably flew a simple Eddy kite with kraft paper and balsa sticks when I was seven or eight or nine, I would guess. I don't remember flying or not flying."

Jim spent his early childhood in Milwaukee, where Wisconsin weather limited flying time, but in adolescence his family moved to sunny southern California where kiteflying happened year-round. Not too long afterwards, Jim remembers flying kites at the beach in his late teens. "I guess this is when I really started flying kites. I liked to go down to the beach to fly a kite. In fact I flew kites even before I met my wife." For the most part, Jim flew "different kinds of traditional things, maybe delta kites and box kites," until he discovered the controllable kites that fueled his fun. "I certainly had a Peter Powell. I still have a set of Rainbows that was made in 1977, which I still fly."

Corey Jensen in his trademark cartoon-clad MC suit and Jim Miller at an AKA convention on auction night (courtesy Jim Miller).

Although a leisure flier, Jim's interest in kites did not bear fruit or command his full attention until later in life. He spent his twenties tapping into career niches and settling into family life. Living in perhaps the most urbane city in the nation, Los Angeles, Jim had few ties to the agricultural sector when he sat down to plan his vocational path, but he ultimately found success in the cattle industry. "I had a succession of executive positions, interestingly enough, in the meat packing and cattle feeding industries, which is sort of funny because I have always been a big city boy and not agriculturally oriented." His introduction to the industry came through "an uncle of a roommate who owned a meat packing plant in Los Angeles. He asked me to come to work for him and I sort of ended up as his right-hand man." Jim embraced the seemingly curious opportunity and went far in that unfamiliar world. Jim managed cattle feeding and ranching operations for over a decade and then realized "that in that business, market price is really more important than anything else. No matter how effi-

WINDY CITY '88
THE GANG FROM
CHICAGO SAYS,
"YOU BETTER BE DERE."

Gangsters pose along Chicago's lakefront to promote the 1988 AKA convention (courtesy Jim Miller).

cient a producer you are, whether you make money or not, success is dependent on the fluctuations of the market." Jim saw the forest through the trees and decided to "concentrate on just trading cattle futures." He knew learning those ropes meant that he "needed to go to Chicago where it was really done." So, the young Miller family moved and life in Illinois set the stage for Jim's entrance into organized kite-flying.

"We lived a block from the lake and one day I was riding my bike with my wife and I saw this guy flying what looked to me like an air mattress with two lines on it. He was doing dives and swoops and it was really going fast. It was amazing!" Jim's first experience with a Flexifoil stopped him in his tracks and the anonymous flier tipped him off to the Chicago Skyliners kite club. Jim investigated the lead and soon began attending club events. The Chicago kite scene in the early 1980s lit Jim's imagination and offered him many pleasurable experiences.

A natural leader and a consummate can-do man, Jim's trajectory in kiting administration was swift. Soon after joining his local club in the early- to mid–1980s, members elected him vice president and left him to organize their annual *Sky Circus* event. With that feather in his cap, Miller went national and "got involved and immersed in the AKA," volunteering at first on the annual meeting committee.

Welcoming Masato to Chicago at the airport (left to right) Charlie Sotich, Lu Fyler, Elmer Wharton, Masato Horikiri, Jim Miller, Felix Cartagena and Pat Daly as Madame Booga Booga (courtesy Jim Miller).

Jim's interests focused on streamlining convention operations and documenting his findings for future conventioneers. He envisioned creating a manual to help the next person put on a smoother, more enjoyable event. Written guidelines and tips did not exist and Jim recognized the void. "I thought that this was a silly and dumb way to run a railroad." His dream of documenting the behind the scenes procedures was bigger than he imagined, and he sent out questionnaires and letters of inquiry to AKA "elders who had been involved" in past conventions. Jim remembers plenty of one-sided correspondence. "It was letters going out and nothing coming back. I got frustrated," but he pulled together sage advice that he later augmented with insights from his own convention planning experiences.

Jim kept up volunteer administrative posts and gained experience with club management. When the Skyliners decided to host the AKA annual convention in Chicago, they elected Jim as their convention chairman. Looking back, he recalls that the club's aims were sharply focused. Put simply, the club "wanted to put on the *best* convention that the AKA had ever seen." Topping the past would be difficult but not impossible. Jim decided to pre-promote the 1988 convention and the Skyliners made a splash at the 1986 auction when he, Elmer Wharton, and Al Hargus dressed as mobsters to auction off a pair of cement boot kite anchors. The Caponeites, complete with faux machine guns, stormed the staged to recite their message: "'Windy City '88. The Chicago mob says you better be dere!'" Miller believes promoting the convention two years in advance helped boost the attendance, and under his leadership, he encouraged brainstorming that identified fun and playful ways the Skyliners could welcome guests to their convention. Looking back thirty years later, the 1988 convention was the high point of his kiting career and Jim remains "proud of our whole crew" for pulling off what many still praise as the *best* convention in AKA history.

In 1989, people recognized Jim's leadership qualities and elected him president of the AKA. He arrived in office with a set of objectives. He wanted to increase membership, standardize flying rules, and position the AKA as "a central focal point" of kite information. Jim promoted kiting nationally, by encouraging kiteflying at local events. This small-scale participation helped "spread the word" and boosted membership. Jim took his post and promises seriously, and he charged vice president Eric Wolff with putting together a rulebook, which became the worldwide standard for sport kite competitions. Also, during his tenure, he recognized the need for an executive director to support the overall club. "Brooks Leffler was of course the first executive director, and I think that was an important step in the AKA's growth."

After Jim left office, he returned to managing conventions. In the early 1990s, when the AKA grew enough to outsource the convention manager position, Jim bid on the job and saw to it that fliers would have hassle-free flying time and many laughs at AKA conventions throughout that entire decade. "My intention is the nuts and bolts of the convention should be something that should not be primary in anybody's mind. They should be able to come into registration and pick up their packet and go on their way." Jim's hard work and attention to detail meant that "people who can come have more fun doing what they came to do: attend the workshops, participate in the competitions, fly kites, and enjoy the good fellowship of the AKA. That's what it is all about." Perhaps a thankless job, but one Jim did outstandingly well.

Now retired and living in Palm Springs, Jim likes to hike and be outdoors, but he finds his desert home is not the best place for kiteflying. He typically flies only when he travels on vacation. Looking back, "Kiting was my principle hobby outside of work for many, many years" and allowed Jim to make cherished friendships, and his leaderships roles within organized kiting put Jim in a position to leave a lasting stamp on its framework. Reflecting on his years of club service, a proud Jim sees that he "really accomplished a lot of the goals" he set for himself and contributed to the long-term success of the AKA.

Jon Burkhardt

Jon Burkhardt's avocation in organized kiting is testament to his commitment and genuine love of kiting. With an impressive kite resume that includes dual terms as AKA vice president and treasurer, multiple terms as a regional director and member of the board of directors, along with noteworthy contributions launching and chairing the AKA's international committee and being the chief author of the organization's competitive scoring guidelines, Jon has proven his tireless commitment to the club and to the advancement of kiting as a sport.

Born in Wisconsin, Jon moved with his family to Massachusetts and New York before setting down roots in Indiana. Later, Jon turned east again, when it was time for him to go off to college. With his sights set on a corner office at an architectural firm, Jon enrolled at the Massachusetts Institute of Technology, but he found after four years, "I was beating my head against the brick wall and that architecture wasn't any fun. I decided that I really wanted to be a city planner." Jon fine-tuned his dreams, earned a master's degree in city planning, and got involved with courses that "had to do with transportation and economics and architecture and planning and political science and all these things." This interdisciplinary, renaissance-man approach to planning "sounded like a lot of fun and I eventually decided that was more fun than what city planners usually do." After graduation, the well-trained Jon moved down the eastern seaboard to the D.C. metro area and made a successful career researching and planning the specialized transportation needs of seniors, the poor, rural communities, and persons with disabilities. Jon's career was rewarding professionally, but didn't provide a venue for his interests in graphics and design. Through the years, kite making "became my outlet for graphic and artistic expressions" and helped satisfy Jon's creative urges.

Although Jon's adulthood is defined by his kite involvement, ironically, as a child, he doesn't recall kiteflying, even though he was later told that one of his grandfathers made and sold kites. "I heard stories abut him flying the kites through the streets of Milwaukee." Kites had to wait until Jon's adulthood and "came into my life as an activity to do with my children." On a business trip to San Francisco, "I stopped into the Come Fly a Kite store and got myself

Master kite designer Jon Burkhardt enjoys the breeze (courtesy Jon Burkhardt).

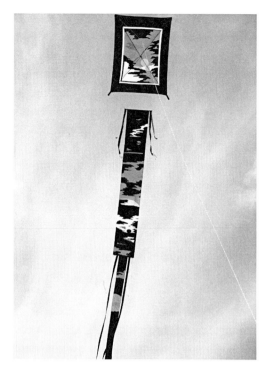

Left: *South China Seas*, **Jon Burkhardt, 2014.** *Right: We Become Birds C*, **Jon Burkhardt, 2015 (both photographs courtesy Jon Burkhardt).**

a parafoil." Shortly after that trip, Jon visited another store and bought a White Bird kite. "I thought it was absolutely beautiful.... The kite cost $50 and every woman in my family, except my daughter, said that was outrageous! My daughter said, 'Let him spend his own money." The sticker shock eventually wore off and Jon proved kiting's unequivocal value and worth.

Intrigued and hooked by kite making, Jon continued to discover beautiful kites and his family supported his new pursuit. "My parents said to me, 'If you are going to be serious about this, you need to meet this old man who lives by us." While on a trip to visit family in Indiana, Jon had the honor of meeting the kite legend Ansel Toney. At the time, "he was 89 years old and he could run circles around any ten of us, and I looked at him, and I looked at his kites and said, 'This man has found the fountain of youth.' The ideas that he could create when he was in his 90s were astounding." Inspired, Jon explored kite making and found his visual voice. In the early days, "I was really learning about color" and saw "how much punch you could get with the other colors by using black." Controlling hues and shades were all part of the early days, and as Jon recalls, "It's not magic, it was a lot of experimentation." Through the years, his enthusiasm and perseverance soon led to mastery and he became an influential and accomplished kitemaker. Jon's kite designs are an obvious marriage of his innate visual talents and distinctive graphic style.

In the late 1970s, Jon purchased kite books and casually dabbled in kite making. Some successes were followed by failures, but never discouraged, Jon overcame his learning curve follies and kept an eye out for new kite experiences. While flying stunt kites with friends on a beach in Virginia, he noticed a newspaper article about a convention in Manassas held by "something called the American Kitefliers Association." He attended, recalling, "I went out there with a friend on a Friday night and saw this very strange auction going on. We came back the next day for more," and so began Jon's long involvement with the AKA.

Attuned to details in the sky and on the field, over the years, Jon sacrificed precious flying time to help the club. "Although I'd rather be out on the field flying kites, the business of the business is important." Jon has worn multiple hats in organized kiting, from editor to club officer, and has taken each seriously. In addition to governance, in the late 1980s, Jon collaborated with a committee of fliers to create a unified set of competition scoring guidelines. "Judging criteria was more loose and open early on," and codifying the scoring system gave "people a way to rate their performances on more specific factors" and was a significant contribution to competitive kiteflying. Jon's work endures and modern kitefliers on flying fields across the nation can tip their hats to expertise he brought to the field.

Not all of Jon's kiting forays deal with organizational details. In fact, he prefers to "leave the trouble of the world behind" when he picks up a kite. "I think of kites as a celebration. And it's my goal to share the happiness and share the enjoyment with other people." As an artist and design buff, "I love the color of it all, skies full of kites, it is something that really makes my heart jump." But along with the fun and beauty, kiting provides Jon with the opportunity to travel internationally and to publicize kiting, including an interview on National Public Radio and a kite making segment on Martha Stewart's television program and magazine. But perhaps the greatest joy Jon has found through kiting have been the friendships he's made throughout the years and around the world. "I enjoy seeing the creativity of other people. To me, kitefliers have always been very appreciative of the creativity of other kitefliers, unlike the business world, where when someone has created a new idea, they'd be damned if they'd tell you how to do it. I think the openness and the enjoyment of others' work is what brings me back again and again to kiting."

Lois and Dave DeBolt

First Lady of Kiting Lois DeBolt remembers trying her hand at kiteflying at a time when most folks her age were picking up pension checks, doting on grandchildren, and beginning to ease into their golden years. Although being 60-year-old newcomers to the flying field is a little unusual, Lois and Dave DeBolt's

Dave and Lois DeBolt with their nearly human-sized delta, Provo, Utah, 1984 (courtesy Mindy Hogg).

involvement in organized kiteflying quickly made a significant impact on the kiting community in their home state of Indiana, and as they met other fliers, their reach made a splash in the national organized kiting scene too.

Making their home in Winchester, Indiana, Lois spent her career in the medical field as a nurse's aide and as a ward secretary at her nearby county hospital and Dave was a laboratory technician at Overmyer Mould Company, specialists in the glass mold making industry. In the early 1980s, with retirements approaching, perhaps the couple was open to leisure, that was when Dave learned of legendary kitemaker Ansel Toney's handiwork and realized he lived only about ten miles away. Becoming fast friends, Lois recalled that Ansel, too, was a latecomer to the kiting world. "He started making kites when he was eighty-seven years old" after his wife passed away. Kind to a fault, Lois remembered Ansel fondly as a generous flier and friend who opened doors for the DeBolts and helped them learn kiting fundamentals.

Looking back on her life in modern kiting, she notes that she did not have any interest in kiting as a child, and only developed an appreciation for kites after Dave got hooked on kiteflying. Dave made her a large, eight-foot delta and put her name on it. "That was my first real kite," Lois remembered. Although Lois initially got involved in kiting "just to keep up with my husband," she found joy meeting people

Left: **Dave DeBolt flying his train of 101 rainbow Eddy kites, 1988.** *Right:* **Lois DeBolt, Summit Lake 4th DeBolt Fly, 1991 (both photographs courtesy Mindy Hogg).**

and formed treasured friendships that remained years after her husband passed away suddenly in 1987.

The kiting bug bit Lois and Dave hard, and as they mastered the art of fun-filled backyard flying, they searched for other fliers in their area and started meeting fellow enthusiasts at regional and national events. Somewhere down the line, Lois recalled kiteflier David Berndtson suggesting "that we try to organize a group in the state of Indiana. In October 1986, we organized our first Indiana club and as far as I know it is the only club in Indiana." Lois and Dave, along with Ansel Toney, Mike and Pat Bragg, David Berndtson, and a few others came together to write bylaws for the Hoosier Kitefliers Society. Lois recalled, "We had, I think, twelve people there at our first meeting, which was kind of good for a first meeting. We were rained out the first meeting so we got a lot of talking done and not much flying, but we were still getting things organized and it worked out fine." Active and flourishing to the present, today's Hoosier Kitefliers Society members are grateful to the legacy these charter members built.

Early in their history, the Hoosier Kitefliers Society joined forces with the Academy of Model Aeronautics hobbyist group and established an annual fun fly for both model airplane and kiteflying enthusiasts. As Lois recalled, the Academy of

Model Aeronautics would "have us over to help them celebrate and bring people in and have kites in the air." This interesting marriage continues today and air chasers of all kinds enjoy an afternoon of playing in the air and learning about another aspect of flight.

Throughout her history with the Hoosier Kitefliers Society, Lois donned many official and unofficial hats. She was elected as the membership chairwoman by popular vote and saw that "every membership that I get, I make sure that they get an application for the AKA." Lois' personal efforts expanded her local club while simultaneously helping grow the national association, and Lois' foresight strengthened the structures of organized kiteflying.

In addition to membership and club cultivation, Lois also wore the editor's cap and ensured that the Hoosier Kitefliers Society newsletter came out every two months with plenty of personal tidbits, information on upcoming flies, and, of course, pictures. Lois' entry into the kiting world uncovered her budding photographic talents. Before kiting, "the only photography that I ever did much was just family pictures, but when Dave got into kiting, I started taking snapshots of kites." As her skills improved, she "got a better camera" and got more involved with kiting by using her picture taking as a way to break the ice. "Photography was a way of communicating with people. My husband was really the kiteflier and the kitemaker, and when he was busy flying kites and when I didn't have to go fetch something for him, I would take pictures and make a new friend." For some, a picture is worth a thousand words. For Lois, a picture was the key to a thousand friends.

Lois remained active in kiting and promoting the Hoosier Kitefliers Society until her illness took away her ability to participate. She passed away at age 89 in March 2013.

Mel Hickman

With his trademark brand of dry humor, Mel Hickman looks back at his childhood years, and says, "I started out as a child." Born in Indiana, Mel recalls making kites from newspapers that he was careful not to use "before dad had a chance to read it." Kiddy kite building aside, it was not until he was fully grown that kiting entered his life in a meaningful way. In 1987, Mel was living in the Portland area and saw a newspaper ad for the Washington State International Kite Festival. Intrigued, and without weekend plans, Mel drove over to Long Beach to check out the kite scene, and "got hooked immediately."

Jumping straight into the deep end, Mel started making his own kites right from the start. Mel credits veteran kitemaker Kathy Goodwind for teaching him how to use a sewing machine at the Fort Worden Kitemakers Conference. Learning on slick, synthetic materials like Ripstop, Mel somewhere down the line switched over to plusher cotton fabrics, and eventually began quilting kites in denim. A long-time resident of Walla Walla, Washington, Mel quips that the town is "the garage sale capital of the world where you can get a lot of denim." With ready access to a surfeit of sturdy blues, Mel incorporated secondhand jeans into his kite making. Enjoying the durability, feel, and range of colors, Mel took a shine to patchwork quilting in denim and the Levi's look became his hallmark in the kiting skies.

In the late 1980s, Mel's wife's uncle passed away and left the family property along the Oregon coast. Mel and Annie relocated to Seaside and Mel found work at the thriving Catch the Wind kite store chain. Snatching up this avid kiter, Mel joined the Catch the Wind family and immersed himself in the world of kite retail during "a boom time for kiting and for the whole kite industry." Landing in the perfect place, Catch the Wind nurtured their employees and actively supported their professional development. Mel learned the ins and outs of kiting on their retail floor and through their travel support, he attended AKA conventions, the Washington State International Kite Festival, and manager trips to Lincoln City, where he test-drove the industry's latest kites.

Loving his time on the sales floor, Mel learned how to get a kite in people's hands and get them out flying, yet in 1991 the winds switched and his career flew in another direction. AKA president-elect David Gomberg approached Mel with a proposition to become the AKA treasurer. Mel accepted his offer, but soon learned he would have to actually join the AKA to take up the post. Writing his first dues check, Mel entered into what became a long and fruitful marriage with the AKA. For about three decades, Mel conquered club logistics, and in retrospect takes "great pride in the fact that I was a good ambassador for kiting and the AKA" for so many years.

Enjoying his time in the AKA clubhouse, Mel increased his responsibilities and, in 1995, he transitioned to the executive director's office. Continuing in that same role for over twenty-five years, Mel's astounding service record directly helped keep the club running smoothly. In 2010, the AKA officially honored Mel's unparalleled contributions to organized kiting with the Robert M. Ingraham Award. Having tended to everything from processing memberships, tallying up auction receipts, to billing venders for advertising space, Mel's work kept the kiting community organized and alive. Sadly, in 2014 Mel's wife Annie passed away and her death set in motion Mel's retirement from the AKA. Time will tell what direction Mel takes now that he has left the business of club work behind. But for Mel, kiting is his second family, and he cherishes the friendships he made through kiting. "I met a lot of great people." Typically things started with a phone call, then people become acquaintances, and then over time "they become family."

Throughout his AKA career, when Mel was busy minding club duties and details during the annual conventions, his absence at the end of a kite line created a wedge-driving rumor that Mel does not actually fly kites. Though it is true that Mel only flew twice at the past twenty-six conventions, rest assured, Mel flies and is a kiteflier. However, attempting to shatter prevailing misconceptions, at the 2001 Billings convention, Marti Dermer impishly asked Mel to hold her kite line while she hopped back to snap photographic evidence. A black cat must have been nearby, and just as she was getting the shot in focus, the kite swooped, bottomed out, and flopped to the ground within seconds. Laughing at fate, Mel walked away with a heightened air of mystery.

Outside of kiting, and often running concurrent with kiting posts, Mel has mastered several interesting careers. At seventeen, Mel landed a journalism job in Chicago with British Reuters News, a break that "helped me grow up and warped my accent." Learning his way around the newsroom, Mel later landed a job as a sports editor in Walla Walla before moving to Portland. There, expanding his journalism work into public speaking, Mel took a job with the health department speaking about human sexuality, VD, birth control, and homosexuality at high schools. Unflappable while disseminating important but supremely awkward health messages to the world's toughest known audience, Mel was unstoppable. "I thoroughly enjoyed that job ... it was performance with a message." After his gig informing high school hecklers, Mel also championed public service announcements for national neighborhood watch programs, and was a crime prevention officer, editing the Scruff McGrath "Take a Bite Out of Crime" books. When not spreading helpful PSAs, Mel helped people sort out their financials. For twenty years, Mel worked for H & R Block as a senior tax advisor. Recently, Mel began volunteering his time with the Living Hope program that provides breakfast service for homeless people in his community. For Mel, public service can mean improving the lives of others through social programs or through the leisure pursuits that bring joy and fun.

Don Jaspers

Never keeping kites too far away, longtime flier Don Jaspers has tugged countless lines and found pleasure teaching others how to let some line out and pull a little happiness from above. With an eye to the sky, but with his feet planted firmly on the ground, Jaspers has enjoyed kiting through a lifetime of flying seasons.

A Minnesota native, Don grew up in the small town of Shakopee during the early days of the Great Depression. The son of a blacksmith and wheelwright, Don had access to his father's tools and his mother's household recycling bin to build kites from the odds-and-ends he found around his home. In the Jaspers household, kite making was a fun family event and Don's parents enjoyed teaching him how to make kites. Clearing the kitchen table, the Jaspers assembled butcher paper and grocer's twine, along with rags and sawed off pieces of wood. Flying mainly in March, the Minnesota winds were strong and the excitement of spring fueled their spirits after long snowy winters.

Young Don greatly enjoyed kites, as did his friends. While they dabbled in making the occasional barn door and box kites, the Eddy was their go-to

Minnesota Kite Doctor **Don Jaspers founded the Solid Kite Flying Club and always makes time to help fliers repair battered kites (courtesy Don Jaspers).**

kite that stormed through winds ranging from puffy breezes to strong, tugging gusts. Kiteflying was a crowd favorite and the kids of Shakopee would fly whenever and wherever they could. Don remembers flying a kite with friends on their walk to school. Not wanting to end the fun when the school bell rang, they tied the line to a light pole and headed to class. Inside absorbing arithmetic and grammar, they focused on the lessons while their kite soared outside all day. When school let out, the kids untied their kite and had fun flying it on their walk home.

As time passed and friends scattered from the playgrounds of his youth and abandoned kites on their paths later in life, Don recalls, "I never forgot kiting, even while I was a young man during high school. Whenever I could, I would fly." After graduation, Don entered the military and made a career in the U.S. Air Force. He served in Japan and Korea and flew kites every chance he got. Throughout adulthood, when the Jaspers siblings got together, they would often fly kites and rekindle the childhood joy they shared flying in their youth.

Don retired from the Air Force in the early 1970s, and set out on a civilian career at UNIVAC in St. Paul making computers in the experimental days before the tech field was industrialized. At about this time, Don learned of the AKA and began meeting members who shared his passion for kites. Doors opened, Don met kindred spirits, and began experimenting with new types of kites and learned about kiting innovations from the stories he read in the AKA's newsletter *Kite Tales*. In the 1980s, Don began attending the national AKA conventions and met many of his kiting coconspirators in person and forged friendships with kindred kite enthusiasts.

Although a longtime and early member of the AKA, staunch individualist Don found organized kiting to be "riddled with politics" and eventually let his membership lapse. Not liking the group dynamics that crop up in any organization, when

Don decided to start a kite club he made sure it was without the formalities that tired him. In 1993, Don founded the Solid Kite Flying Club and it flourished for decades, with members meeting monthly from spring through fall. "We don't have officers, we don't have dues, and there's no structure." To stay on the mailing list, one just needed to show up to one of the past three flies. The group took to the air on Schaar's Bluff overlooking the Mississippi River in Spring Lake Park Reserve in Dakota County, Minnesota. With generous but hands-off municipal support, the group had exclusive use of the field for their flies and the county insured the events and handled the group's advertising. With declining health and a drop in attendance, Don recently dissolved the club, but throughout the years he maintained an active hand and focused his energies on helping newcomers enjoy their days.

Known as the *Minnesota Kite Doctor*, Don planted his Kite Doctor flagpole to claim the spot at the monthly Solid Kite Flying Club flies where he manned his kite repair station. Sporting a pith helmet and aviator glasses, Don, a natural troubleshooter, found great pleasure in helping people mend and adjust their kites so they could enjoy kiteflying. While easy to approach, Don left solicitation up to people wanting help. "I don't want to barge in" and hover around troubled fliers. If people sought assistance, Don was more than glad to lend a hand. Don began fixing kites formally in the early 1970s, and his original repair cart had retractable wheels that he could extend to roll over summer terrain and retract to sled his rig over snow. Year-round, the Kite Doctor came to the rescue.

In addition to helping fliers repair bruised kites, Don freely shares his knowledge to improve kiting experiences whenever he can. In 1992, Don published detailed plans for his Deep Space Winder—the heavy duty rig he created to hold over 3,000 feet of line and to pull it in 56 inches of line per revolution. With a strong base, his winder is a workhorse and helps fliers manage long lines. For highfliers, his device is a must have, and Don generously shared his designs so others can lighten their loads and focus on enjoying flights rather than fighting to manage kite lines.

Forever active and in love with kites, even in the twilight of his retirement, kites continue to fuel his heart and imagination. In 2010, Don wrote a novel, *String Walking*, that prompts readers to imagine themselves time traveling with the help of a kite. As an author, Don followed this project with another book, *Exotic Adventures: Narrative of the 20 Years That I Spent in the United States Military*, in 2016. Whether thinking about the past or the future, Don does so with a kite at his side and he has spent a lifetime helping others embrace kiting.

Barbara Meyer

Expert kitemaker, international kiting representative, and former AKA president Barbara Meyer carries a particularly bucolic childhood memory of running through a Kansan wheat field with her dad and a paper diamond kite. "I don't even remember if it flew, I just remember that sense of exhilaration of running and playing with the wind." Childhood kites may have lost wind and stalled in those fields, but Barbara remembers the joy of that outing affectionately and often replays it in her adult life.

Fast forward to the late 1970s, and Barbara's fiancé Alex surprised her with a bright orange two-line French military kite. "We really had a good time flying," and the kite became a gift they both enjoyed. Not too long afterward, they happened upon a kite in a Lands' End catalog. Now clothing-focused, the company once sold six-foot deltas, and the Meyers "ordered several of those." In those days, the young couple lived in an apartment in Minneapolis and flew kites from their building's rooftop nearly year-round. Alex traveled regionally for work, and the couple learned to piggyback out of town kiting events onto his business trips. The getaways gave them time together and allowed them to widen their network of kiting friends. Looking back, kiting quickly gained a toehold in their lives, and Barbara pinpoints the tipping point when she realized kiting had went beyond a mere pastime when she told coworkers, "'I really need a winter coat, but we bought a kite instead.'" With that purchase, kiting officially became something they did with purpose.

With kite fever rising, Barbara grew curious about different types of kites and looked for kite making patterns. "Since I was little I have always sewn, but for some reason I thought kites were too difficult," so she turned to her mother-in-law to take the lead on her first project. Without experience, no one knew that the material they selected was too heavy, but they learned by trial and error and the challenges prompted Barbara to explore kite making herself. Dabbling with plans she and Alex found in *Popular Mechanics* and *Kite Lines,* these new AKA members went from bed sheet Edos to colorful Ripstop parafoils quickly and, somewhere in the '80s, Barbara married American patchwork techniques with modern materials and began producing colorful and unexpected kites. "Having been a math teacher, I like geometrics" and Barbara's signature style pairs shapes with bursts of strong color that help her kites stand out. For her, the secret to kite design is to drop inhibitions. When giving kite making advice, she always instructs people to "be adventurous … because designs need to be effective 300 feet away" and "what is going to look good in the sky" is not the same color or pattern combinations you would wear. Sagely put, "If you are going to do all that work, make people notice it."

Around 1986–87, Barbara's kite making took a quantum leap "when we adopted our son and I decided to stay home." In 1991, her daughter rounded out the brood, and Barbara recalls those years fondly. Dedicating space and time for family fun alongside household chores, Barbara made sure kiting was always on her to-do list.

"My kite room is my laundry room" and multitasking Barbara would toss in a load, set a kid on her lap, and together they would make kites. "That was our time" and everyone was happy.

As Barbara took up kite making, the young family set down roots in Minnesota and the Meyers were invited to become members of the newly forming Minnesota Kite Society. Meeting kitefliers in her backyard was surprising. Thinking, "'Where have you been?'" Barbara was thrilled to meet kite neighbors and got involved with the emerging club to strengthen ties and help expand the organization. Putting her new Apple II computer to use, she agreed to make mailing labels for the club newsletter. Having fun, she kept volunteering and worked her way through every office from treasurer to club president. As her kite resume lengthened, she gathered experience that uniquely qualified her for national leadership roles and in 2001, she was appointed to the American Kitefliers Association's annual meeting and kitemakers committees. From there, she joined the AKA's board of directors before taking up office as a regional director. In 2010, she took on the top leadership role in the AKA and began her three-year tenure as president. Looking back, Barbara's road to the top seat in the AKA was a "great journey." She met "lots of interesting people along the way" and was able to give back to organized kiting while helping the sport forge ahead.

Making an impact with her clubs locally and nationally, Barbara reached further to promote kiting internationally. While president of the AKA, Barbara was invited to serve as a vice president of the International Kite Federation. IKF organizes the annual five-day international kite festival in Weifang, China in April. Working with well-known international colleagues such as New Zealander Peter Lynn, German Hans Boehmer, Australian Steve Donovan, Macanese Su Hung, Belgian Johan Van Eeckhout, and Andreas Agren of Sweden and Bali, Barbara represents the American Kitefliers Association at this very prominent foreign kiting festival. "We meet once a year and then have the opportunity to encourage openness and cooperation between China and the world" and Barbara enjoys helping share "the long history of kites in China" while promoting kite tourism.

Outside of organized kiting's boardrooms, the teacher in Barbara prevails and since the early '90s she has shared the joys of kite making in classrooms. "One of my favorites to do is team building workshops for companies providing some supplies and acting as coach for them to build a kite without using any prepared plans." In addition to teaching newcomers, Barbara has become a go-to instructor for serious kitemakers at the Upper Midwest Area Kitemaking Event (U-MAKE), the Midwest Area Kitemakers Retreat (MAKR), the Oregon Kitemakers Retreat, and Fort Worden Kitemakers Conference. Whether it is teaching adults or children, Barbara actively seeks out ways to share her kite making knowledge. "I think at heart people still love that feeling when the kite takes to the air. They are still kids. It is that joy and wonder ... that never gets old" that Barbara enjoys sharing with fellow kitefliers.

Ralf and Eva Dietrich

Founding organizers of the legendary Fanø Classics, now the three-day event Fanø Kitemakers held within the Fanø International Kitefliers Meeting, Ralf and Eva Dietrich, were thunderstruck the first time they stood under a mesmerizing Peter Powell stunt kite in the mid–1980s. Left chanting, "Amazing! Amazing!" the couple was hooked instantly into a new world of modern kiteflying. Deciding on the spot to try their hands at flying, Ralf recalls how later that day "I came out of the mall with four kites." Captivated from the first launch, their new interest reshaped their professional lives, impelled them to relocate to a new country, and prompted them to learn Danish.

In childhood, Eva and Ralf both experimented with kites, but their youthful flies only hinted at the pull kites would later have on their lives. Eva's father kept

Ralf and Eva Dietrich flying their *Fischbach XL Manta* at one of their favorite flying spots on the beach in Blokhus, Denmark. *Right:* Ralf Dietrich keeping cool in Kuwait while he tries to get as much as possible of the Dietrich's *Fischbach XL Manta* in the desert air (both photographs courtesy Ralf and Eva Dietrich).

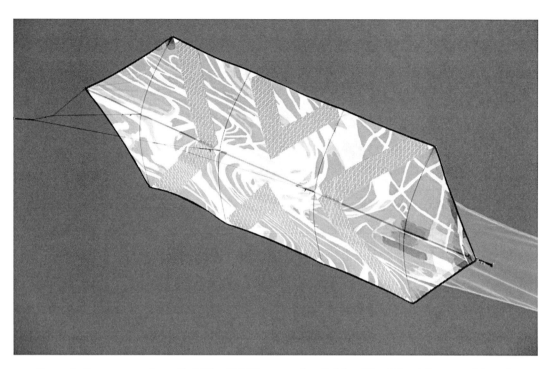

Part of a four-part series called *The 4(5) Elements* that Ralf and Eva Dietrich created for a kite making competition in Dieppe, France, 2012. A Frenchman declared space as the fifth natural element, and for the contest, Ralf decided to use transparent parts that infuse color into kites and honor their place in space (courtesy Ralf and Eva Dietrich).

kites and she recalls pleasant times sharing his kites with her sister. Growing up in Germany when it was illegal to fly kites beyond 100 meters, Ralf, unaware of these rules as a boy, reveled in sending his kite out until it was just a "small point in the sky." Ever fascinated with the air, young Ralf also enjoyed building radio-controlled glider models with his father, and for the most part, kiting fell a distant second to motorized aircraft until he eventually lost interest in it altogether.

As adults, Ralf and Eva explored kiting with wonderment. Denting a few early kites after flimsy kite string snapped, Ralf headed to a kite store in search of heftier gear. Tough line in hand, an aisle over he discovered a large and irresistible stack of Hawaiian stunt kites that, with its price tag of 350 German Mark, "cost a lot of talks with my wife." A few short years later and newly enrolled in law school, Ralf found it hard to justify kite purchases on their lean student budget, so he turned to kite making rather than sacrifice fun. Wanting a Revolution, he got measurements from a friend and Ralf set out to build his own. There was a hitch. "The problem was, I was not used to the sewing machine." Eva gave Ralf pointers, but she forgot to teach him how to load a bobbin. Out of thread, later that night Ralf woke Eva up for help. Bleary-eyed she gave him a lesson and returned to sleep. When she woke again, the Revolution was finished. It flew wonderfully and kick-started the couple's kite making journey.

Their interest in making kites progressed into entering competitions. Winning

Ralf and Eva Dietrich's 897-piece star kite named *Hang Bao Singh* flying in San Vito, Sicily (courtesy Ralf and Eva Dietrich).

several German championships, the couple was encouraged and entered contests around the globe. In the U.S., Ralf earned the "Grandmaster" title, and in 2007, they won the World Championships in Weifang with their 897-piece cellular star kite Hang Bao Singh. Reaching the "top of the line" in competitive kite making, Ralf and Eva retired from the circuit and turned their attention to learning about historic kites, a subject that has interested Ralf since 1990. The couple cannot pinpoint exactly when they got involved with vintage designs, but taking long looks at historical models fueled and informed their renewed interest in kite making, and Ralf notes that "all kite builders take ideas from the past" because these proven styles are time-tested and reliable.

Over the years, traveling became a higher priority for Ralf and Eva, as their interest in learning "how other cultures work with kites" grew. Enjoying travels and kite tourism, when Eva's parents passed the loss prompted the couple to question their lifestyle and ask themselves, "'What now?'" Serendipitously, right at that time they were approached with an opportunity to buy a kite shop in Copenhagen, Denmark. Even though they did not speak Danish, the couple decided to follow the stars and moved from Germany. For over two years, they ran the shop during the day and took language classes at night, and when they decided to shutter the store and return to their earlier professions, the travel-loving couple opted to stay in their new city and get active in international kiting.

In the late 1990s, while looking upward at the beach, Ralf was curiously pleased to see a sky dotted with Bell tetrahedral kites, and he got an idea to organize a meeting for box kite enthusiasts. Tapping his global kiting connections and advertising on the burgeoning web, he put out a call for the first international tetrahedral fly. The goal of the event, held on Denmark's Fanø island in 1999, was simply to have fun and come together for the day. The turnout was larger than expected, and the couple decided to expand the program and repeat it the next year. In 2000, renamed the Fanø Classics, the event was even more successful and continued to grow in scope and popularity and became "the most important event within the classic kite scene worldwide." In 2014, the couple wanted to reach wider audiences and opened up the event beyond vintage kite themes to examine kite art, experimenting at first with variations on modern "Peter Lynn kites." Encouraged by the success and growing number of participants, Ralf and Eva "decided to move ahead with this concept" and renamed the event Fanø Kitemakers. Now focusing on exceptional kite making art and techniques from any era, the couple invites renowned kitemakers, such as Rob Gibian and Mikio Toki, to teach workshops. More than a typical flight-based festival, Fanø showcases kite exhibitions, offers daylong symposia on kite history, and gathers people together to celebrate kiting and the kite's storied history.

As kitemakers, Eva and Ralf are playful and openly share their knowledge. Easy to spot on flying fields, their energetic spiky spheres and colorful gummy bear line laundry are recognizable and have become their calling cards. Generous with their techniques, they regularly publish kite making plans, including instructions for their clever technique to color both sides of Ripstop with fabric paint markers to produce a beautiful, eye-catching effect. In 1991, Ralf first began writing for the German kite magazine *Drachen Magazin* and soon began contributing to *Sport und Design Drachen.* His involvement grew, and today he edits Germany's leading kite publication *Kite & Friends.* Online, Ralf and Eva document modern kiting through their blog and YouTube channel. Whether disseminating information on the web or in person, Ralf and Eva create fun and enjoy being part of kite history.

Scott Skinner

Long before becoming a meticulous kitemaker, discerning collector, author, and philanthropist, kiting was only a casual activity that happened infrequently for Scott Skinner. During his childhood in Raton, New Mexico, Scott recalls that "we had very few kite experiences but the one or two that I had were memorable ones" that he shared with his family and friends. A little while later, Scott attended the Air Force Academy, and as a history major, kiting was far from his mind. Looking back, "I feel badly about not knowing about kites because there were so many interesting things I could have done while there at the Air Force Academy that would have been kiting specific or kiting relevant." But the potential of those years was not lost. Later, when kites arrived in Scott's life, his aviation background helped him nurture the interest and explore the sky with knowledgeable enthusiasm.

After graduation, Scott headed to pilot training in North Dakota. "I didn't know much about North Dakota but I knew the winds blew" and en route, Scott "happened to walk into a kite store in San Francisco and just fell in love with the whole idea" of kiting on the spot. Wandering around the store agog and curious, Scott decided to buy two decidedly different kites: a traditional cloth serpent kite and a small Jalbert parafoil. Unaware of innovations Domina Jalbert spearheaded, Scott recognized that his parafoil was a "breakthrough design" that he wanted to experiment with and compare to conventional kites.

From around 1976 through 1982, while in the Air Force as a flight training instructor, Scott nurtured his budding kite hobby and tested kite designs in his off hours. For Scott, recreational kiteflying became "kind of a rebellion of the rules and regulations of real flying" that he enjoyed during his spare time. Throughout these years, Scott recalls flying "predominantly by myself," but soon, kiting became a social activity.

In 1983, Scott began an MBA program in Denver and met Reza Ragheb, a kiteflier who greatly influenced Scott's kiting and the owner of a kite store in nearby

Aurora. "When I walked into Reza's store, everything was new and different and it opened up a whole new world, at least as a customer of kites.... He really was instrumental in keeping things percolating in my mind." Although, thinking back, Scott believes he likely joined the AKA in 1982, it wasn't until Reza convinced him to attend the Nashville convention in 1984 that he found his community. The winds didn't blow much that week, but the trip "had a profound impact on me because it showed me that there were people who were really, really serious about what they were doing with kites." Impressed by others, Scott allowed himself to follow his kiting passion.

Up until Nashville, Scott "felt like every kite that could be made, was being made by someone, and so I thought, 'Why should I do that?' I felt like I could just be a discriminating buyer." However, what Scott saw in Nashville galvanized him. He returned to Colorado, bought a secondhand sewing machine, and learned to sew "with the intent of customizing the kites that I owned." Modifying gear soon led to kite making experiments and, nearly from the beginning, "I really just took a right turn and went straight to patchwork." Geometric patterns attracted Scott's eye and "I edited in my mind what I thought would work." Soon, Scott "married the idea of American patchwork quilt blocks and traditional Japanese kites." By the mid–1980s, he found his signature design style, and has "done it ever since."

In the early 1990s, Scott had an idea that later tapped his history and business degrees. "I had been around kites for many years. I wanted to do something kite-related, but not making kites for a living, not selling kites for a living, yet something complementary." After measured thought, Scott launched Drachen Design, Inc. As an incorporated entity, Drachen Design gave him the latitude to do things he could not do as an individual. As an initial project, he and Drachen head Ali Fujino decided to document the lives of contemporary kitemakers and created an exhibit of personalized cloisonné pins accompanied by kiteflier biographies. The project was successful and they underwrote pin production so kiters could build their collections and promote themselves, while also documenting the lives of influential kite personalities.

Nearly as an afterthought of the 1991 AKA convention in Jacksonville, Scott and Ali curated a pin display and were surprised to see how attentively people studied the panels, "reading every word and remembering every word." Such strong interest encouraged them to continue documenting modern kitefliers. After about two years, they realized they were doing the work of a non-profit and reorganized to form the Drachen Foundation. For nearly a quarter century, Drachen aimed to "do anything really that we could to increase knowledge about kites." Collecting widely to tell the global story of kiting, Drachen sagely decided to digitize its holdings for universal dissemination. Reevaluating their charter in 2016, Drachen focused their mission and announced their new "role as an online international kiting archive." Through its website and social media, Drachen continues its educational mission online, where it disseminates a trove of free education and historic kite information to its international audience.

Whether forging friendships on the flying field, designing marvelous kites, or spreading kite knowledge through Drachen, Scott is a longtime fixture in the international kiting community and has elevated kiting beyond a hobby. Starting from a casual interest, Scott's all-in involvement insures that people can enjoy the science and beauty of kiting today and in the future.

David Gomberg

Born in London in the early 1950s to a British mother and father in the U.S. Air Force, ten-term AKA president and four-term KTA/KTAI president David Gomberg cannot pinpoint when kites entered his life. "I feel like I have always had kites with me." Back at Albert Einstein Junior High, David's handmade Eddy won him a first place trophy, and later when he started driving, "I always had kites in the trunk of the car." Fittingly, he and his wife Susan went to the beach to fly kites on their first date. Kites have been at the ready and the Gombergs have made their life in kiting, through kite books, heading organized kiting, kite travels, and simply enjoying kites with friends around the world.

Moving around a bit in childhood, David's family settled in Sacramento and he relocated north to attend Oregon State University. Elected student body president, David found time to represent the voices of his peers as he studied political science. Staying on for a master's degree, David continued stretching his mind and earned an MBA at Willamette University. Sharp and well-prepared, David "went to work in the Oregon legislature" after graduation, helping on political campaigns and "working for our congressman." Serving the public in numerous civic capacities, in 1989, David "was offered a position in Lincoln City to run the Chamber of Commerce, and part of the job there involved organizing kite events." Helping his community from a different angle, David was paid to coordinate kite festivals, something "I had been doing for many years previous to that" in his off-hours.

Never more than an arm's reach from a kite, when David was a student he dabbled, as a spectator, in organized kiting and unknowingly began building lifelong connections into the growing kite community. One afternoon, David wandered into a kite festival where there was a high flying contest going on. Intrigued, "I went back to the car and pulled out something called a Vic's fighter kite" and joined in. Not an experienced fighter kite flier, David blindly added a tail for stability and his Hail Mary strategy was simply to keep it "moving around in the sky." When the judges called the contest, David's kite danced at 900 feet and he won. "My prize was a set of six brand new kites called Rainbow stunt kites." Repeating victory later

Under a sea of dancing sea creatures, former president of the American Kitefliers Association David Gomberg and wife Susan have traveled the world promoting kiting (courtesy David Gomberg).

in the day, David got a second set. Dual-lined and stackable, David "immediately put them all together into a twelve-pack," and looking back, he now sees that "flying stunt kites really changed my life."

Captivated by stunt kites, these revolutionary new fliers energized David, and hooked him into kiting. A few months after winning his Rainbow stacks, "the Hawaiian team kite came out and were flying things radically different than anything we were flying. Suddenly you have this hard-pulling, noisy thing that was scooting around the sky." Dazzled and entranced, "I spent years flying stunt kites" and, unknowingly, they became his gateway into organized kiteflying. Always a joiner, in the late 1970s and early 1980s, David helped "run kite festivals in Lincoln City" to promote fun in their region and to keep current with stunt kite trends. The experience opened doors and introduced him to a leisure community he would later lead.

As his kite involvement progressed, David became an unintentional author, and traces the idea for his first book back to a chance conversation he had with a fabric store clerk who asked him what he planned to do with all the Ripstop fabric he just bought. Intrigued by his kite projects, she suggested he teach a kite making class. Preparing lesson plans, David started putting together instructions and soon his notes "stretched into about fifty pages." David was later chatting with a local kite store owner about the classes who said, "'We would like a copy of your book.' I thought, 'My book?'" Starting humbly with a photocopied production, David's marketing background helped him polish and promote *Seven Kites*. Though book sales were modestly successful, more than anything, the endeavor taught the Gombergs "there are a ton of better books on how to make kites," but there was a need for sport kite book. Researching and writing drafts for six months, David solicited feedback from key people in the sport and expanded his manuscript. *Stunt Kites* came out in January 1989 and was hugely successful. It helped David and Susan learn the ins-and-outs of self-publishing. A few years later, they wrote a book about fighter kites, and in 1996 released *Sport Kite Magic*. Writing together, the Gombergs share their kite knowhow with a print audience.

Initially, David "really didn't do much with organized kiteflying" but he eventually learned about the Associated Oregon Kiters. At his first AOK meeting, "I got up to use the restroom and when I came back I had been elected president." Falling into leadership turned out to be a natural fit, bringing together David's interest in kiting and innate political skills, his accidental presidency "got me into organized kiting in a much deeper way." No longer just a flier, David began observing bureaucracy and examining the armatures that supported organized kiting. Honing his commitment to service, David's involvement insured that others could have fun. In 1988, Oregon was vying for the AKA's national convention and David "went off to my first national convention in Chicago and presented Oregon's bid." Competing with Hawaii, David took a step back and suggested that the AKA award the 1989 convention to Hawaii and give it to Oregon the following year. This was a brilliant solution, one that gave his club more time to prepare, allowing them to orchestrate "the most successful convention the AKA had ever had."

Now involved nationally, "somehow I blinked again and they convinced me to run for president of the AKA." Stepping into a role he was born to hold, "I became president of the national association and that is about the time that I stopped flying kites as much and started dealing with the politics, the personalities, the business, and everything else that makes it possible for other people to go to festivals. So I traveled, went to meetings, I gave speeches, and that was my kite life for the next four years."

As club leader, David rallied his colleagues and created an administration that pinpointed issues and solved problems. Together with new executive director Brooks Leffler, they focused on the business of running the club. "We did seemingly simple things like set up the toll-free telephone number, we got a credit card system so you could charge your membership, we asked the regional directors to participate in conference calls, and we implemented an insurance program so every kiteflier had insurance. Those were some of the administrative things we put into place and we started to notice dramatic changes." Building consensus and helping the club mature, David saw growth. During his administration, the AKA went from sanctioning about twenty-five events to over a hundred a year. Membership doubled and "when we hit 5,000, we started joking about having 6,000" people in the association. Enjoying his work and showing results, but aware that every club needs to rotate its leadership, David stepped aside in 1994 to focus on growing his kite business. At the end of the decade, David was urged to return. Voted president by a landslide, he served six more terms from 2000–2006 and skillfully guided the club through a time when the face of organized kiting was changing.

Immersed in kiting and enjoying kite life, in the 1990s, David and Susan were also "growing a business." Starting with their books, they then partnered with Greens of Burnley in England and later collaborated with Peter Lynn. Over the years, Gomberg Kite Productions has grown to feed international flying markets and is recognized as a premier designer and manufacturer of show-stopping specialty kites. Alongside these ventures, David and Susan jumped into the brick-and-mortar kite trade in 2005 and opened Northwest Winds, with stores in Lincoln City and Seaside. With his MBA background and accomplishments in the kite business, David served four terms as the president of the Kite Trade Association and lent his leadership skills to help another facet of kiting. In 2016, the Gombergs turned ownership of their stores over to their managers and refocused on their wholesale business.

Ever ready to promote kiting and share the magic with audiences outside the AKA, the Gombergs orchestrated a park-wide kite extravaganza at Disney's Epcot Center, flew kites during the Super Bowl, demonstrated kite moves at the London Millennium Celebration, and graced the silver screen in the early scenes of Cuba Gooding, Jr.'s sleeper movie *Snow Dogs*. The couple has an entry in the Guinness Book for their 10,000-square-foot kite. "We own the largest kite in the world." Three were made, allowing them to share the record with an owner in Kuwait and another in Japan.

As something of a fringe benefit to his service to kiting, David began traveling extensively. Recalling his first kite trip to Weifang, China in 1990, David notes, "It was the first time in my adult life that I had really gone overseas and it changed my life. It was just an incredible experience for me" and jumpstarted a new interest in kite travel. "It sounds corny, but there is this kite brotherhood and sisterhood where you can sit down with people you have never met before and talk about things you have in common and you are drawn to each other." Traveling mostly with their larger inflatable show kites, twenty-five years later, David and Susan have visited over forty countries and attended hundreds of international events. Finding kindred spirits in all corners of the world, the Gombergs organized kite excursions to Africa, Asia, and Europe to help others share the excitement of international kiting and cultural exchange.

In 2012, life took a dramatic turn. David was asked to run for Oregon's state legislature. "I took a deep breath and then jumped in with both feet." At one point, the local newspaper reported that David received many out-of-state financial contributions. "That's generally frowned on. But then the paper said the money had come from members of the national kite lobby and all was good again. National kite lobby—*right*." David won his race with roughly 60 percent of the vote.

Now in his third term, David is highly active and serves on numerous committees. In 2016, he was elected into the House's leadership core, where he works to strengthen public education, shore up government efficiency, address senior citizens' issues, and stimulate small business growth. When Representative Gomberg reflects on how his kiting background influenced his public service career, he notes that "kite politics was a great introduction into real politics," because "kitefliers are very passionate and in some ways very partisan." Successfully navigating the spirited terrain of organized kiting, David's years of pulling kite strings and serving the kite community now help him accomplish good for the people he represents.

CHAPTER 5

The Kite Trade

"If you want to make a small fortune in the kite industry, you start with a large fortune." David Gomberg

Dinesh Bahadur

Self-proclaimed *Master Kiteman of the World,* Dinesh Bahadur's kiting career began in childhood. Dinesh grew up in a kite making family in Rampur, India. His hometown is "world-famous for its fine arts, top musicians, craftsmen" and "the specialty of my town, and my great grandfathers, is kites." In fact, the Bahadur family "exported kites all over the country," and some members made "kites from sunrise to sunset." As children, Dinesh recalls, "We had a kite teacher, before we went to any school, and he doesn't really teach kite making, he teaches kites through lessons of patience and understanding. For three years he won't let us do anything but shape bamboo sticks because that is the basics of the frame of the kites." Gaining a solid mastery of skills might be too tedious for some, but the painstaking lessons ensured quality workmanship and instilled a lifelong reverence for the delicate paper spirits that danced about the skies in Dinesh's well-traveled life.

Dinesh honored his kite teacher and family by winning kiteflying competitions at a very young age. His family home, had a trophy room and "we could not go to that kite room and enter until we won some of the championships. I was the youngest one at the age of seven. I won the town championship." Whether it was the thrill of victory, the excellence in his training, or the desire to honor his family, young Dinesh took to kite fighting like a prodigy.

Growing up in a kiting family was both competitive and fun. Dinesh recalled childhood experiences at Rampur's annual fighting festival. "Right after the monsoon … that's where you can see over four, five million kites up in the air." His family home stretched "a whole block, with sixty rooms in the house, and we have the most popular rooftop" used during this season as a kite fighting platform. "Any kite that comes there, that's ours." During the festival season, Dinesh and his tireless relatives fought into the night slicing lines and gathering their prize kites. "We collected all of our kite inventory for the whole year because, even though the kites are very cheap, the kids generally can't afford them." Kites fell from Dinesh's youthful skies, and as he grew more savvy with glass encrusted kite lines, he began stockpiling trophies.

As the annual post-monsoon winds died down and Dinesh grew serious about his academic career, he immigrated to New York to pursue a Ph.D. in political science in the 1960s. In his spare time, Dinesh flew kites in Central Park until he was ticketed for violating an antiquated anti-kite ordinance ratified when startled working horses put carriage riders at grave risk of injury. The ticket was an injustice to Dinesh. He had trouble seeing how his meditative hobby threatened anyone and decided to dispute the matter with the park commissioner. Dinesh argued that kiting "is my childhood hobby, that's the only pastime I have. I have no friends in New York City, I go out and fly kites whenever I get a chance." The commissioner had a heart, allowed Dinesh to fly in the park, and granted him a weekend concession to teach others to fly.

In 1964, Dinesh collected kites and displayed them at an art gallery. Soon after, he turned the gallery into his first kite store and named it Go Fly A Kite. "I didn't even know the meaning. One of the girls in the park said 'Go fly a kite,' which I thought was maybe a compliment until somebody told me that's how they say get lost." When Dinesh relocated to California in 1972, he changed the store's name to Come Fly A Kite. After shuffling around a couple different locations in the San Francisco area, Dinesh settled into his Ghirardelli Square location and watched the kites fly off the shelves. Dinesh recalled, "Over 5,000 people going through the store everyday."

To meet demand, he partnered with seventeen local kite manufacturers. "I had standing orders months in advance. I could not manufacture more than those kites, but it was fun. It was never planned. I think maybe that's one of the reasons it worked." Within a few years, Dinesh's siblings joined him in the American kite retail trade. Come Fly a Kite incorporated and opened several stores "across the country, in Atlanta, Florida, New York, Texas, and all along the coast of California. We still have four stores in the family. I gave it to my brothers and sisters because I want to be free from day-to-day things to do my kiteflying." Reflecting on the unexpected business venture, Dinesh comments that the family "held a monopoly for almost ten years. We were the only people making, wholesaling, mail-ordering kites, and selling them retail. It took off."

In the 1970s, as business responsibilities switched hands, Dinesh carved out time to fly kites. Whether it was private, meditative, Zen-centering flies at his local beach or crowd-drawing shows put on to entertain the Hollywood crowd at their Malibu parties, Dinesh enjoyed looking upward for meaning. "My mission was: I make a kite, one kite a day. I am very happy. When you are flying a kite you can't be serious. You have to loosen up." Tapping into kiting's therapeutic side effects caught the attention of unlikely audiences. Corporate giant IBM hired Dinesh to demonstrate kiteflying for their employees. Dinesh wowed the techies and gained exposure. Later, Dinesh hopped the globe to showcase kiting. "I went around the world three times, traveled to about 120 countries, and I traveled across this country to almost every town in America to fly kites at the universities, colleges, all major department stores, libraries, and museums." Later, entertainment managers for the San Francisco 49ers football franchise recruited Dinesh for a halftime fly. He wowed the crowd and introduced another unlikely group to the splendor of his lifetime passion. To reach wider audiences, in 1970, Dinesh wrote the book *Come Fight a Kite,* and a few years later he made a short movie, *Master Kiteman,* where he reveals the meditative enjoyment he found through kites.

When reflecting on his time with kites, Dinesh tenderly likens kiting to "being in love." Kiting amplified Dinesh's life, defined his family business, and accompanied him throughout his travels. Comparing kiting to love is an apt description, and Dinesh explained, "When you are in love, only the lovers know. They cannot go out and tell a third person, you have to experience things to understand them. Kiting to me is like being in love."

Dinesh Bahadur passed away in 2008, but the Bahadur family carries on their kite making legacy.

Heloise and Chris Lochman

Founders of White Bird Kites, Heloise and Chris Lochman's career in the kite trade started unexpectedly when they accepted a standing invitation to fancy afternoon picnics hosted by free-spirited friends, who toted china, crystal glassware, gourmet cuisine, and handmade kites to picturesque Bay Area parks. With fine food and fun, Heloise recalls that kites were "always a part of the atmosphere" and the couple learned kite making from these friends. "We fell in with a group of people who knew how to make kites, and that was a very unusual skill in 1965."

Their early works weren't elaborate. In fact, some were just salvaged Gayla kite frames dressed in pretty tissue paper. Later, after poked fingers ruined their delicate handiwork, their preferences switched to colorful and heartier fabrics. Heloise admits, "They weren't really great technically, because I didn't have a clue what I was doing, but they did fly and they did have a lot of bright colors in them."

In the early 1970s, the Lochmans welcomed the birth of their son Sean. For the young family, money was tight and their kites made thrifty gifts. Heloise remembers, they would "make them for friends for their birthdays, or just for a little treat, instead of, say, baking cookies." Their gifts were so well received that the couple was encouraged to try to sell a few. After a little tinkering with designs, they brought

Left: **White Bird Kites founders Heloise and Chris Lochman's son Sean Christopher Lochman, with winged box kite at the Golden Gate Park crafts fair, San Francisco, 1972.** *Right:* **Heloise Lochman enjoying Hawaii's endless beaches (courtesy Heloise and Chris Lochman).**

their kaleidoscopic wares "down to the place where the cable cars turn around, down on the Fisherman's Wharf. That was the beginning of the street artist scene in the city, before you had to have a license or there were fist fights over spots."

Early inventory was mainly limited to brilliantly colored Japanese, box, and, by popular demand, classic diamond kites, but soon into their kite making journey, they abandoned the straightjacket nature of detailed kite making plans and dabbled with their own creations. Heloise reminisces, "Most of them flew." As time went on, they stabilized their shaky fliers, expanded their design repertoire, and sales flourished. They would "sell five or six of them at Golden Gate Park on the weekends." Around that time, they began a consignment relationship with an upscale craft gallery and leased booths at area art fairs. These steps gave them the opportunity to hone their techniques and offered them a glimpse into the demands of the kiteflying market.

Their big break into large-scale kite production came after Chris won the battle to introduce a television in their home, and the media-wary family saw master kite-flier Dinesh Bahadur showboating on the local news. A group of fliers organized a weekend kite festival and Dinesh's kiting captured the cameraman's attention. Heloise and Chris turned off the program, picked up their young son, grabbed a few kites, and "immediately piled into the car and ran down there to meet him." This was the beginning of a beautiful friendship.

White Bird Kites took a quantum leap with Dinesh's arrival into their world. Heloise recalls, "Dinesh was a tremendous teacher. He could just look at a kite and make ten suggestions that made it a really viable, strong flier." Along with smoothing out their rough kite making edges, Dinesh opened doors to large-scale kite production. Business at his kite store in Ghirardelli Square flourished in the early 1970s, and he looked to Chris and Heloise for inventory. Heloise remembers that "at the time we weren't packaging the kites or anything, we would just bring him down big handfuls of kites, sort of tied by the bridles." Their collaboration "was a monster success and everything we brought him ran out the door instantly."

Soon Chris and Heloise found themselves at "the point where we had to quit our jobs and make more kites." Chris reflects on their decision and admits, "You know I probably would have made more money staying at Standard Oil, where I worked at my last job, but it was good to get out of the city and into the country." Their venture ballooned and they enlisted the help of Chris's sister Laurel, her husband Steve Young, and a group of home workers, cottage-industry style, to fill orders for Dinesh and other wholesale clients. Chris recalls, "We split the business up where they made the less expensive kites" and he and Heloise "made the kites that ranged a little bit higher out of our house and back in the garage that we converted into a warehouse."

As business grew over the years, Heloise and Chris continued to push the design envelope and tinker with their products. Chris believes that they were the first company to introduce fiberglass spars to the kite skeleton. Wanting a durable, flexible, and lightweight material to improve their kites, Heloise and Chris researched companies that manufactured fiberglass at the library. They found Glass Forms, a company in San Jose that manufactured rods that housed antenna wires for remote control cars. Stripping the part, White Bird Kites adopted a new material and blazed trails in the industry.

Noted over the years for their fine quality, White Bird Kites also holds a place of honor at the Smithsonian Institution. In 1975, the

Influential White Bird Kites founder Chris Lochman (courtesy Heloise and Chris Lochman).

curatorial staff "acquired one of our fifty-five-foot dragons for a show called *Craft Multiples* at the Renwick Gallery." The show featured work "produced in quantities of less than ten, in any media," and Chris and Heloise brought the artistry of kiting to museumgoers.

Now retired and living in Hawaii, looking back on their voyage into the unknown, Heloise expresses "the gratitude that we feel for having made our living this way, and it is a wonderful thing to make your own choices, to be respected for doing something that you are going to do anyway, something that you love. I just think it's been a real gift."

Steve Lamb

Before Catch the Wind entrepreneur Steve Lamb ever dreamed of building his successful kite store empire, a young Steve dutifully delivered the news to folks in Medford, Oregon. The pinnacle of his paperboy success came when he edged out other carriers and won a trip to Disneyland where Walt himself extended a congratulatory hand. The job taught him a little about business and gave him pocket money to spend on kites, splurging in particular on Hi-Flier box kites. Yet, just as Mouseketeers inevitably outgrow their mouse ears, Steve, too, retired his newspaper sack, but luckily for the kite world, he never tired of kites.

Later, after earning a degree in English, Steve initially thought he would be suited for a career in journalism and took a job at the High Desert Museum as a writer. The term position ended and the grim employment forecast caused concern but also provided relief. Facing joblessness, in the end, gave Steve the freedom to chase a new career and actualize a budding dream of owning his own business.

Understanding his strong independent streak, Steve knew he could be "happy being relatively poor working for myself" but figuring out what type of business he wanted to start remained sketchy until about 1977 when he saw kids flying kites on the beach at sunset. The silhouettes danced and shimmied in front of Steve and he was thunderstruck by the beauty. "I caught my kite vision," and that night he set out to bring kites to his beloved Oregon coast, where splendid views draw people to the often-blustery beachfront. He knew the kiting business was suited for this geography and saw the coastal "wind as an advantage."

Although not an active flier at the time, Steve had enough exposure to see "all kinds of possibilities" associated with kites. He headed to the library to research kiting and found an early issue of *Kite Lines* magazine and a book called *Kite Craft*. Steve combed the publications for contacts and wrote to commercial kitemakers and suppliers to learn more about the business. He soon found Dinesh Bahadur at his store, Come Fly a Kite, in San Francisco's Ghirardelli Square. Dinesh's family ran Kite World and sold kites wholesale. They were able to supply Steve with a seemingly endless stock of fighter kites and other playful fliers, notably White Bird's attractive handmade kites. "I don't think I would have been as successful without White Bird's high quality products." From the get-go, Steve recognized their quality and beauty.

Steve opened his first Catch the Wind store on St. Patrick's Day 1979 in Lincoln City. Perhaps it was the luck of the Irish, but Steve sold his entire inventory within a couple of hours. At that point, "the world of business was real mysterious to me." He was amazed and even "thought it was illegal that you could buy something for $1 wholesale and sell it retail for $2." After he sold his initial $200 worth of inventory in a matter of hours, he then bought $400 more merchandise and soon watched it fly out the door. Later he purchase $800 worth of kites, and kept increasing his orders every couple of days. "If it wasn't for UPS and Kite World being able to supply so quickly, business would have fizzled."

A short while later, Kite World hit a patch of financial black ice and went out of business. A bankruptcy broker purchased their entire inventory for a fraction of its value and Steve was "heartsick that I missed out" on the opportunity and contacted the broker with an offer. The dealer, not knowing what to do with the kites, accepted Steve's offer and was amenable to installment payments. Steve is grateful that this "stroke of luck" bolstered his business and took it to the next level. As the receipt drawer filled, Steve nurtured his enterprise and eventually, in the years that followed, opened ten Catch the Wind stores along the Oregon coast and a kite making factory.

Steve remembers that in the late 1970s and early 1980s that if you were plugged into the kiting industry, "all the kite crazies eventually made it to your doorsteps." Enter John Waters—candle maker, eccentric, quiet genius, one-time record holder for indoor kiteflying, and integral character in the long-term success of Steve's Catch the Wind enterprise. Steve hired John to manage one of his kite shops in the early 1980s, and for a period of time, John also acted as the unofficial store sentry, sleeping in the backroom at night to stretch his dollars and to prevent the inventory from walking. Steve knew John brought more to his job that the average store clerk, so he presented John with a special assignment. Steve had an idea for a spinning windsock and asked John to invent an "affordable, easy spinner." After countless prototypes, John developed a winning solution. Steve listed John as the inventor on the patent, and the Spinsock became Catch the Wind's "bread and butter" item and the cornerstone of his manufacturing and wholesaling businesses. Steve takes pride in the Spinsock's success, and is pleased to see how it inspired other rotating fliers and helped "drive interest in kites all over the world."

Homerun inventions may come but every blue moon, yet Steve is ever on the lookout for opportunities. In late 1985, Steve read about Spectra—an ultra strong, weather-tough fiber developed to anchor deep-sea oilrigs to the ocean floor. He and John collaborated and contacted Allied Chemical for a sample of the raw product and worked with a braider on the East Coast to create line for kites. It was an experiment, but when the 300-foot-long prototype took its test flight, Steve immediately spotted its commercial potential and quickly began negotiations to market the line. Mere months later, in 1986, Spider Line was on the market. Later, a company in the fishing industry orchestrated an elaborate marketing campaign for their Spider Wire but did not do a trademark search before they named their product. When they did, they discovered Steve's Spider Line. Desperate for the Spider name, the company presented Steve with an irresistible deal and he relinquished his branding rights and started selling "Catch the Wind Spectra" instead. In the end, a good line is worth more than its label and Steve takes satisfaction in knowing he brought a great product to market first. Three decades later, "nothing beats it" and it is used in plenty of other sports and has allowed the sport of kiting to expand.

Astute in business, over the years Steve continually adapted and expanded his product line to grow his kite store operations. In the company's heyday, Steve employed around seventy people in his kite making factory and retail stores. Supporting recreational and competitive kiting, Catch the Wind's trajectory mirrors the rise and crest across organized kiting and wears the battle scars of the 2008 Great Recession. Today Steve runs one shop that is buoyed by occasional internet sales and custom Spinsock orders. Experienced and able to understand that "the market doesn't have the ability to take off now," Steve's labor of love may not be lucrative, but he enjoys that it gives him the opportunity to "interface with the public and be around kites."

Aside from being a leader in the kite trade, Steve has been an active flier since the early days of organized kiting and a firsthand witness to kite history. In 1983, Steve was in Long Beach, Washington flying and documenting an attempt to reclaim the largest kite flight record. Vying for victory, an eager twenty-six-member flight team hoped to fly a parafoil so large it needed two dump trucks with full payloads to tether it down. Day one was a bust and fickle winds persisted the next day as fliers struggled through several otiose efforts to fly the behemoth, but between attempts, an ill-fated gust ripped the kite aloft and startled onlookers. The merriment over the unexpected launch rapidly turned to horror as people realized the kite had snared their friend Steve Edeiken. With his leg tangled in the line, the kite skyjacked Edeiken to heights he could not survive when the snagged line unfurled and released him. At the hospital, when his wife Cindy called, the phone was given to Steve along with the task of telling her Edeiken had passed. The tragedy is unforgotten and the American Kitefliers Association memorializes the short life of Rainbow Stunt Kite founder and sport kite pioneer with its annual Steve Edeiken Award. Recipients of the club's lifetime achievement accolade embody the goodwill, sportsmanship, and benevolence that attracted both Steves to kiting and motivated them to contribute personally and professionally to the sport.

Maggie Vohs

The winds of fate put strings in the right hands, and in 1984 Maggie Vohs grabbed an opportunity that brought kites into her life and shaped her professional career. She was visiting the Oregon coast, looking to move to Lincoln City, and while driving down Highway 101 she looked up in amazement. "I'll never forget seeing a 90-foot Spinsock in the air over this hotel, and I thought 'What is that?'" Spellbound and curious, Maggie found herself inside the Catch the Wind kite store looking for answers, and left with a job that changed everything. "I actually went to work that day," and from 1984 through 1996, Maggie grew from assistant book-keeper to general manager and helped shape Catch the Wind's impressive period of growth.

Business-minded Maggie looked around the bursting Catch the Wind store, jumped in, and got to work. First tackling low hanging fruit, she straightened out the invoices and got their books up to speed before helping the company's team grow into a bona fide kiting empire. Catch the Wind's "growth was huge and quick," and in the 1980s, what started as a lone retail store budded into three corporations. In its heyday, Catch the Wind's retail arm had ten kite stores open for business. Catch the Wind Incorporated tended to the wholesaling business, supplying kite shops across the country with a variety of quality kite gear, while Catch the Wind's manufacturing division developed new kite products and cranked out kites and accessories at a breakneck pace. Maggie's talents were in management and finance, and she was promoted to general manager of the wholesaling and manufacturing divisions. At its height, the company employed seventy people and the tight-knit group felt like a family to Maggie.

Billy Jones and Maggie Vohs at an American Kitefliers Association convention in Seaside, Oregon (courtesy Billy Jones and Maggie Vohs).

Although Catch the Wind offered a range of kite products, its golden goose was the Spinsock. Owner Steve Lamb's patent blocked others from importing and selling knockoffs and the company's foothold in the market guaranteed quality workmanship. The dependable and playful spinner even appealed to buyers outside of the kite world and Maggie helped broker sales with a diverse audience of people, some interested in developing decorative lawn products and other folks who wanted to adapt the innovative spinners into novel vehicles to market corporate logos. Overall sales were phenomenal and the popular spinner, which came in about fifteen standard sizes, ranging from ornamental twelve-inch spinners up to monster pullers that took up 150 feet of air space, appealed to many. Steve's patent expired in 2004 and Maggie recognizes a loss of quality with the second-generation imitations that now crowd the shelves.

As a way to give back to organized kiting, Maggie put in overtime and sought out the AKA treasurer's post in the mid–1990s. Remembering her tenure, "the AKA was a very vocal group of people," and when dues went up from $20 to $25, "I thought they were going to throw tomatoes at us!" To date, Maggie vividly recalls the referendum and ranks that particular meeting as the most hotly contested one of her career, but the overall experience toughened Maggie and helped her learn to stay the course to effect organizational change.

In 1996, Maggie was a single mom and she was interested in bringing her office home so she could be closer to her then seven-year-old son. With an insider's perspective and a deep knowledge of the kiting industry, Maggie developed a bold idea that would galvanize both her professional and personal lives. She believed that if she could become the president of the Kite Trade Association, she could gain the ear of the board, point out the shortcomings of their current management company, and convince them to turn the reigns over to her. Up until then, the KTA was the smallest client in its management's portfolio and Maggie felt that they underrepresented the KTA and were not the group's best advocate. As a smaller organization with particular business needs, Maggie wanted more personal attention from a management company and better overall support. The current firm was not making the grade and in 1996, as the newly elected president of the KTA, Maggie rallied board support and fired the management company. In act two, she resigned from the KTA and took over the association's management as an independent contractor, launching Cameo Management Solutions Incorporated.

With undivided attention, Maggie managed the KTA as her sole client for about five years. Building slowly, Maggie reached out and took on a second client, the AKA, and began overseeing the management of the annual convention. With close attention to her clients' needs, Maggie continues to grow her business and manages a tight roster of seven well-supported clients. Reflecting back, Maggie finds the key to success and longevity in the kite business is having "a love for the industry *and* the people." With her deep connections, Maggie protects the best interests of the kiting community as a businesswoman and a longtime kite supporter.

Outside of the office, kites are an integral part of Maggie's life, and a common interest she shares with her beloved partner Billy Jones. Seasoned in every aspect of the kite trade, skilled stunt kite flier, and active all-around doer in organized kiting, Billy's involvement in kiting runs as deeply as Maggie's, and together the two ensure people can enjoy kiting as a sport and as a casual pastime.

Billy Jones

Seasoned kite merchant, agile stunt kite flier, and budding kite historian Billy Jones started tugging at kites at a young age and has long welcomed kites into his life as a source of fun. Growing up, his pilot father flew for Pan American airlines and delighted young Billy with the kites he toted home from Asia. With an eye for exotic beauties, his father gave Billy a glimpse of the kite's global reach.

As an adult and full-grown lover of the sky, avid kiteflier and daring skydiver Billy jumped swiftly into the kite trade. Studying music and forensic photography at the University of Tampa and then at Duquesne University, Billy "took a break and discovered kiting ... next thing I knew, we had sixty-five employees." Looking back, his entry into kiting seems like a flash, but it started in 1984 when became part of the crew at the Kite Loft in Ocean City, Maryland. "I came to the kite industry through distributing juggling equipment and immediately realized I liked the kite industry and wanted to get into retail." Billy set down roots and eventually became a partner in the Kite Loft of Ocean City.

In 1993, warm winds pulled Billy and he sold his Kite Loft stock and helped a friend open a new kite store in Rehoboth Beach, Delaware. With ground-floor ownership under his belt, awhile later, Billy's career branched out in a new direction. He ventured into kite manufacturing and helped the historic stunt kite manufacturer Peter Powell Kites transition into Caribbean Kites, based in Jamaica. After a few successful years, he returned to his retail roots and partnered with Key West Kites on Florida's sunny southernmost island. In recent years, Billy added to his professional portfolio and partnered up with veteran Kite Trade Association International consultant and his longtime domestic partner Maggie Vohs to help organize large-scale trade shows for the kite industry, and is now with one of his former suppliers, In the Breeze, selling a wide range of kites and outdoor, wind-related products.

With decades of kite retail and manufacturing experience, and having mastered all sides of the kite commerce, it is only fitting that the kite industry recognized Billy. In 2006 he earned the David Checkley Lifetime Achievement Award and won the Retailer of the Year trophy from the Kite Trade Association International, accolades very fitting for Billy's impressive kite resume, and ones that humbled him. "I was blown away and extremely honored" because people were impacted by things he did twenty years earlier and that his peers acknowledged and valued his personal contributions to their field.

Finding success behind the counter and in the kite warehouse, off the clock Billy recharges and delights in the outdoor pleasures of flying kites. Pulling with both arms, this veteran flier vividly remembers the splash early stunt kites made and their quick evolution. During sport kiting's toddler days, Billy witnessed a chain reaction as dual line kites improved, the industry fortified, and the flying community fine-tuned sport kite competitions and pulled in larger audi-

Billy Jones flying a dual-line stunt kite in Ocean City, Maryland, in the late 1980s (courtesy Billy Jones). *Below:* **Billy Jones' store Key West Kites in Key West, Florida, late 1990s (courtesy Billy Jones).**

ences. The evolution of the sport kite was quick and punctuated. Innovators arrived on the scene and made changes to products that "became common place in the industry." Adopting carbon spars and Ripstop polyester, for instance, were two innovations that shocked the sport into a period of quantum growth. Analyzing this history a bit, Billy points out that "the kite conventions and kite festivals and independent kitemakers, really, have been the catalyst for the changes within the industry." Chicken or the egg questions aside, Billy witnessed a fertile time that became the "creation of the modern day kite industry."

As both a customer and a merchant, Billy eagerly flew emerging kite novelties and looking back remembers how kite making pioneers and the products that sprung onto the kiting scene influenced one another like a rapid fire tennis volley in the '70s, '80s, and early '90s. "Three or four different schools kept making larger sparless kites. They brought it to the public's eye, that then helped refine it." Recalling many influential kitemakers, Billy singles out a few leaders that altered the landscape of sport kiting like Dom Jalbert who originated the stickless parafoil and kicked off an exciting period of kiting modernism that helped to reshape the kite industry. Other kite pioneers like Doug Hagaman and Dean Jordan, who advanced kite designs and created parafoils, since used to lift infinite lengths of wondrous windsocks, "line laundry," and Spinsocks that bedazzle the skies. Awed also by the work of New Zealander Peter Lynn, Billy credits Peter for populating the sky with his larger-than-life cartoon cats and octopus fliers that kicked off a subculture of large form, "jaw-dropping, show pieces," that have dominated kite festival skies since the 1990s and shown that line laundry could be more popular than kites.

Looking back, Billy notes, "I've been in every seat" of the kite trade, knowing the needs of the merchant, salesperson, supplier, and customer. Over the years, Billy has had a firsthand look at what influenced evolutions in the modern kiting landscape and is able to connect the dots of the contemporary kiting history. "I enjoyed the ability, or the opportunity, of working for years and seeing industry pioneers" leave their marks and watching others build on their work. "I've been in a position to meet, and know, and respect all of these guys ... and ask them about what they did, and ask them how they got started." Being able to talk to others about kiting and their experiences has "been a treasure" that Billy gratefully appreciates and sees as a unique opportunity that allows him to better understand the emerging trends in the industry. These days Billy is interested in the impact technology and handheld gaming has had on kiting. Compared to earlier generations of childhood fun, when kites and outdoor play prevailed, today's youth are increasingly plugged in and Billy sees new "competition for leisure time" that sidelines kiting. Always with an eye to the future, Billy recognizes that kiting needs a new pioneer, "someone who is tech savvy but who understands the fundamentals of outdoor play" to reintroduce kiting to a generation that is increasingly anchored indoors and, perhaps, less familiar with the joys of playing in the wind.

Ken Conrad and Suzanne Sadow

The long-time face on the kite trade scene, Seattle's Ken Conrad has filled his days with kites since the 1970s and by the close of that decade, he met his future wife Suzanne Sadow and cast the kiting spell over her. Together they experienced the salad days of organized kiting, met the changing retail needs of generations of customers at their store Great Winds, and continually make kiting accessible through their kite making and classes.

Initially preparing for a left-brain career somewhere in the hard sciences, in college, despite his natural aptitude, Ken found that the scientific path "didn't click with me." As the out-of-synch Ken flew kites for fun between classes, people stopped and asked him where they could buy a kite like his. Having fun and unknowingly listening to his budding entrepreneurial voice, he noticed the attention kites brought and had his first business idea—Why not leave science and sell kites?

Ken and a couple of industrious kiteflying buddies made 100 or so fabric deltas to sell at street fairs. The stockpile didn't move, so Ken and his partners decided to hitchhike down the west coast to hawk their wares. Wanting $10 a kite, they ultimately took "whatever we could get," and when sales flattened, they moved down the coast, but only sold a handful of kites. "Try hitchhiking with three people" and a pile of kites. The equation didn't work well, and his discouraged partners inevitably said, "We're out," but Ken scratched his head and kept going. In San Francisco, his luck changed when he walked into the wildly popular Come Fly a Kite

Ken Conrad flying a colorful train of 300 kites given by Eiji Ohashi in the late 1980s (courtesy Suzanne Sadow and Ken Conrad).

store. Owner Dinesh Bahadur had trouble keeping enough kites on hand and snapped up the lot for $3.95 each. Although this first big sale was at rock bottom wholesale prices, it launched Ken's business.

Shortly after making his way back home, a local junior high art teacher got a plum grant and asked Ken to teach kite making at her school. Ken assembled 800 individual kite kits for each of the kids and launched the Good Heavens Kite Company for the project. Selling the

Right: Nina Conrad anchoring her father Ken's 300-kite train made by Eiji Ohashi at the Seattle Kite Festival on Father's Day, Magnuson Park's Kite Hill, 2001. *Below:* Suzanne Sadow helping make a *Frustrationless Flyer* at a kite festival in Everett, Washington, 2001 (both photographs courtesy Suzanne Sadow and Ken Conrad).

Suzanne Sadow in front of Great Winds Kite Shop (first location) on Fat Tuesday, 1980. In one window are the kites she and Ken Conrad imported from Sri Lanka, and in the other are traditional windsocks they imported from Japan (courtesy Suzanne Sadow and Ken Conrad).

kits at a dollar a unit showed him that he could earn his rent for a stretch through kite making. Encouraged, after the gig he began selling his kits to a kite shop in Seattle.

Seattle's Air Force Kite Store opened in 1973 as an urban outpost of the original store in Bellingham. The owners, tired of the distant commute to their city store, sold the shop to a medical supply salesman who was losing his eyesight and looking to downshift into a slower-paced, zero-travel job. But shortly after successful eye surgery, the clear-sighted salesman questioned, "'Why do I have a kite store?'" and approached Ken about coming to the other side of the counter. For the price of the inventory on hand, Ken could have the business. At the time, Ken remembers, "I didn't have two nickels to rub together," but he borrowed money and "hit the ground." Great Winds kite store opened in the fall of 1976 and grew to be a leader in kite retail and a beloved institution in Seattle.

Early on, Ken crossed paths with the right folks and "these people enabled me to develop a successful business." His initial partners didn't love kites, and they came and went, but each brought skills that nurtured the budding business. One early partner, a former DJ, introduced Ken to radio PR and helped him tap into the

Ken Conrad and Suzanne Sadow tailgate flying at a Washington State International Kite Festival in the early-1990s (courtesy Suzanne Sadow and Ken Conrad).

inexpensive and ever-growing FM radio market. Another had an idea to promote kiting by capping a Seattle skyscraper with a sixteen-foot-long salmon windsock. Controversial because the fish, like tacky animated used car lot banners, was restricted under municipal code and couldn't fly, legally. But this gigantic fish developed a huge following and ultimately got flight time. Meanwhile Ken gratefully realized the media storm was free PR for the store. In the evenings, Ken took business classes and these firsthand experiences with advertising dovetailed nicely with his lessons.

Right at the critical time when the business was really coming together, Suzanne entered the store. Literally. She just walked in off the street and struck up a conversation with Ken. Sparks building, the two stepped out for a cider, kept talking, and time nearly escaped Ken until he realized he needed to leave for a very important class. He was in a bind because none of his employees could work that night and he had invested in radio ads promoting evening hours. Explaining this to his new acquaintance, Suzanne offered a simple solution. She could watch the store. Knowing it was impulsive and a gamble after chatting for only an afternoon, Ken recalled "it just seemed right" and he showed Suzanne the ropes. Suzanne minded the store as Ken went to class and, looking back, Ken notes, "it turned out great." Nearly four decades later, the couple continues working and playing together with kites.

That chance stop into a kite store and spontaneous evening shift unknowingly moored Suzanne to Seattle. Suzanne grew up in New York. "I was always a creative person" and went to art school. Majoring in drawing and focusing on textiles, Suzanne wasn't entirely sure what would come next after graduation. While at her first job at a children's library, she heard it rained frequently in Seattle and thought that it would be a lovely place where she could retreat to do studio work. She had a friend there, and knowing that one person, she switched coasts in 1978 and set out to try something new. Kite making draws, in part, on artistic skills that come naturally to Suzanne, but she recalls, "I'm sure I was far too grown up to fly kites as a kid." It wasn't until a freshman year art class that she tried her hand at kite making for a course assignment. Unknowing of the role kites would eventually play

Ken Conrad flying one of his early experiments with Tsutomu Hiroi's centipede kite body design, ca. 1975 (courtesy Suzanne Sadow and Ken Conrad).

in her life, she designed an ethereal tissue paper kite that semi-self-destructed on the way to the field. Many kites later she developed an expertise and perfected her *Nishi* sled—a playful variant of Takeshi Nishibayashi's double layer sled that she personalizes with a peephole to give viewers a glimpse of her fanciful designs.

In the tradition of classic mom-and-pop shops, Great Winds was more than a commercial enterprise. It was a headquarters for its customers and the place where Ken and Suzanne made friends as they offered a full-service kite experience. Great Winds stocked a library of kite books, windsocks, and every imaginable type of raw material for kite making alongside a line of kites they manufactured in-house, kites from independent kitemakers across the country, and imported traditional kites from Asia. Great Winds had it all.

Great Winds had a great run, but around 2000, when their landlord needed to make building improvements that would close the shop for a stretch, Ken and

Suzanne realized the gentrified post-rehab rents and the changing face of kite retail weren't a good combination. Having a sixth sense, the couple decided "it was time to hang up the retail" business and focus on just the manufacturing and creative arms of their company. Relocating to a workspace near their home, they have maintained their Tyvek kite kit production, honed the craft of digital printing on fabric for kite making, and taken on various kite-related projects over the years to continue making their career in the sky.

Kathy Goodwind

Closing in on 40 years in the kite trade, Seattle kitemaker Kathy Goodwind started out in an unlikely first career path. Professionally trained as a scientist, Kathy holds a degree in chemistry and became a medical technologist. "I did that until I went into traveling sales with chemicals. I was a single mom, and at the time that was a real difficult thing to do." After a decade of juggling career and family, Kathy happened to visit a kite festival and left captivated. Kathy quit the medical corporate world in 1976 and took up kite making. "I got involved in a local kite shop, making kites, it was just a lark, I don't know why. All I can say is that the universe must have pointed me the way and said, 'You take it from here.'" Working part-time supervising a lab "was enough money to keep me going," and Kathy dipped her toe into the kite trade before plunging into the deep end.

Taking to kite making like a natural, Kathy started a long career as a custom order kitemaker and expanded to a bricks-and-mortar retail business in 1980 "because I had made somebody a bunch of kites and he didn't pay me." In lieu of payment, she told him to send her his unsold kites and she figured she would sell them to recoup her costs. "I started in basically a little closet, and I just put stuff in the window and people started coming in." Even though it wasn't really a well traveled area, "I thought, 'Wow, I have to order some more.'" Over the years, Kathy's business name evolved and moved around Seattle a bit, starting out as Suspended Elevations and emerging later as the beloved Gasworks Park Kite Shop. Kathy hung out her shingle until 2012 when she closed the store, and in retirement joined a sculpture atelier. Kathy's business stood out among kite retailers because through it she ran her retail shop, her custom order manufacturing business, and the wholesale arm that focused on worldwide mail order and internet sales of kite repair and fabrication supplies. "I got into part building and repair supply because I realized I could make a business selling parts because there are so many people who want to realize their own creativity and they may never become a fine artist but they may

Kathy Goodwind enjoying a day at the beach in Wildwood, New Jersey, at the 2011 AKA convention (photograph by Cat Gabrel, courtesy Kathy Goodwind).

become a fairly decent craft person." Close to home, Kathy's son illustrates her point perfectly. "He is an extremely creative person" and he designed kite wrist straps. "I went out and got my son a patent, they were that cool. We sell a ton of them."

Over the years, Kathy remained active in kite making and became an instructor. Implementing her vision, she played a crucial role founding the Fort Worden Kitemakers Conference. "Doug Hagaman, myself, and Jack Van Gilder just got it all together one year, and I think Tom Sisson helped a lot, and we put it together."

With a modest start in a small church at Fort Worden in 1986, the annual instructional event attracts makers from around the globe and has set the standard for serious kite making workshops.

Beyond the classroom, Kathy's legacy in kiting is wide. On the local level, she organized the Seattle Kite Festival and shared the joys of kiting with her city for many years. To help advance her state's club, she held offices as the vice president, secretary, and treasurer in the Washington Kitefliers Association. Nationally, she served in the Kite Trade Association International administrative offices and was the AKA's first vice president. Beyond her work in the boardroom, she was "instrumental in writing the rules for AKA single line and dual line" kiting that helped codify competitive events and bring structure to them. Honoring her contributions, the KTAI presented her with the David Checkley Lifetime Achievement Award in 1996, and in 2015, the AKA honored her with its Steve Edeiken Award for her long career in kiting and the wide influence she has had on the club's reach.

Throughout her life in kiting, many have commented on the appropriateness of her last name, Goodwind. Her ex-husband's surname was Goodwin, and when "we went our separate ways," as part of the terms of the divorce, she wrote in a condition to add a D and change her name to Goodwind. "The judge said, 'Why would you want to do that?'" Explaining its connection to her career, the judge approved her petition and it "seems like second nature now." Over the years, people continually ask, "'Is that really your name?'" and Kathy keeps her driver's license nearby to quash doubters.

Brooks Leffler

Second-career kite storeowner, first executive director of the AKA, and ground floor member of the contemporary kite aerial photography movement, Brooks Leffler's association with kiting has seen him through his working days and into retirement. Fliers worldwide recognize his lasting contributions to organized kiting with gratitude.

Born in the 1930s in San Francisco, after high school Brooks relocated to Washington State to attend Whitman College and find his own path, but eventually his family circle reconnected when his minister father became dean of Saint Mark's Cathedral in Seattle and Brooks transferred to the University of Washington. As Brooks recalls, "I was sort of floundering around in a small liberal arts college and thought it was time to focus a little more." Excited about the University of Washington's new radio and television major, he moved to Seattle to explore broadcasting.

Life on a string, pioneering kite aerial photographer Brooks Leffler's self-portrait (courtesy of Brooks Leffler).

In 1956, after a few years of working and going to night school, Brooks graduated and "stepped right into a job" producing and directing educational television at Seattle's nascent public television station KCTS. This was the "beginning of a twenty five-year career in public broadcasting," one that took Brooks to cities around the country and culminated in a move to Washington, D.C., where Brooks worked for PBS, the U.S. Department of Commerce, and, eventually for the Corporation for Public Broadcasting as and administrator. During his exciting career, Brooks was put through his paces and was frazzled. "To escape from the grind of doling out money to the public television stations of the country, I would fly kites on my lunch hour." One afternoon, during the Reagan administration, Brooks was flying a few kites and eating his sandwich. Looking up, he noticed a secret serviceman on a moped heading his way. The agent "sheepishly came over and said, 'Sir would you mind taking your kites down? The President wants to leave.'" Brooks pulled his kites in and the President's helicopter flew overhead. "That is the closest touch I have had to controlling the presidency" and perhaps a rare instance of kiting interfering with government operations.

Yet beyond lunchtime flies, as work demands climbed, Brooks explored kiting afterhours and his interest expanded. Brooks began attending kite festivals and trying his hand at kite making, once winning the best box kite award at the Smithsonian's annual fly. Heavily oriented toward single line flying, Brooks dove deep into his local kite scene and found an outlet that sustained him. As work became "much too tense and much too political," Brooks eventually found that he no longer enjoyed his workdays. The realization came at a time when Kites Aweigh, his local kite shop in Annapolis, went on the market. Seeing possibilities for a different life, and with full support from his wife, "I decided to take the plunge." The Lefflers purchased the store and Brooks "became a full-time kite merchant" in 1982.

The first owners of Kites Aweigh had approached the store as a hobby, and initially the "shop was in the red," but with some heavy lifting Brooks "pulled it up by its bootstraps" and created a successful business. Expanding the retail base, Brooks became the wholesale distributor for British manufacturer Greens of Burnley and began manufacturing Brooxes Boxes, his signature line of box kites inspired largely by Bob Price's sturdy rhomboid box kite ideas. Brooks' handiwork "flew pretty well" and he tapped nicely into a pre-stunt kite retail market. A few years later, "although everything was happy for us there, and I liked the kite business a lot," Brooks' wife inherited a house in California, and "the opportunity to move was pretty persuasive." In 1987 Brooks sold his kite shop and moved to Pacific Grove the following year, but brought "the wholesale part of the business, which I had developed, with me."

With his newly streamlined business, Brooks had more time for kiting and began exploring a budding interest in kite aerial photography. Looking back, Brooks cites two motivating factors for his foray into KAP—advertising and kitchen remodeling. As the distributor for Greens' Stratoscoop kite, he thought a bird's eye photo of the kite would look great in full-page color ads in *American Kite* and *Kite Lines* magazines, and, around the same time, he was remodeling his kitchen and the plans radically altered the shape of the house. "For my own entertainment I thought it would be fun to take some pictures of it." Learning as he went, for eight months Brooks tinkered until he got his shots. The Stratoscoop photo turned out, "and the aerial photographers of the world remember it to this day, which is nice." Once he figured things out, "I think after I got into it, I wanted to perfect it."

Jumping into his new hobby, Brooks looked to meet other people interested in the craft. In Europe, the Kite Aerial Photography Worldwide Association—KAPWA—existed but, without an accessible membership directory, Brooks was stranded in his search for others. In the early 1990s, KAPWA ceased its publication, yet Brooks and mid–Atlantic AKA member Steve Eisenhauer recognized a need to keep kite aerial photographers in communication, and approached the AKA with their idea to publish the *Aerial Eye* newsletter. Working together on the venture, Steve gathered content and Brooks, having novel desktop publishing capabilities at home, put everything together. "The more that we worked on the first issue it was obvious that it was pretty hard to get it into publishable form without acting as something of an editor." Brooks took up that call and did the page layout work, and Steve stayed on as chairman, wrote articles, and maintained an editorial presence. It was a "pretty good collaboration" and for less than $100 an issue, the two met their quarterly publishing schedule, starting with their kickoff issue in the fall of 1994. Subscriptions started with around fifty people, attracting mostly kitefliers but also appealing to people new to kiting who came to the sport through their interest in aerial photography.

In the early KAP days, camera rigs were hand-built DIY creations. In the late 1990s, Brooks standardized the wheel and came up with a camera cradle kit that got cameras up and overhead, allowing even gadget-shy beginners to start taking shots. Brooks ran a KAP workshop at Fort Worden introducing his kit, and then went on to fabricate and market them. With years of cottage industry success, Brooks engaged a professional fabricator and later passed on his online KAP rig business to old friend, fellow KAP flier, and kite merchant Ken Conrad. Over the years, thousands of fliers have gotten their shots thanks in large part to Brooks' kits.

Tom McAlister

Long after graduating college at UC Berkeley in the early 1980s, it dawned on Tom McAlister that maybe he should have majored in business rather than psychology. Although commercial sensibilities come naturally to him, in the end, his chosen studies likely helped him understand his future customers better than a dollars and cents training path. The longtime kitemaker and kite merchant has made a living trusting his entrepreneurial instincts and the skies of Berkeley are forever tattooed with colorful kites due, largely, to his vision.

Tom traces his interest in kite making back to his youth, where his curiosity was influenced by his stepfather's love of flight. Naturally skilled with his hands, Tom took to kite making quickly and cultivated a life-long interest. Later, as an adult, Tom landed a job apprenticing with an antique carousel restorer and continued making kites on the side. Watching his boss transform his hobby into a livelihood, Tom remembers seeing a good man with average skills succeed at business, and thinking, "I could do that." With that realization, Tom began setting aside more time for his own kite building and started Highline Kites.

In the 1980s, the City of Berkeley began cleaning up a derelict section of its waterfront and over the years, with several steps in between, transformed the municipal trash dump into Cesar Chavez Park, the picturesque home of the Berkeley Kite Festival. With steady San Francisco Bay winds and a lovely view, early on, Tom saw a future for the park full of kites and approached the city about opening a kite shop. On public land, a brick-and-mortar retail shop was not possible, and when he asked permission to set up a concession stand, he was put off with a lukewarm, "Maybe." Somewhat of a bootlegger, Tom sold kites out of his Honda Civic hatchback for three years before he re-approached the city with his idea. The second time around, the city council asked him to submit a formal proposal and granted him a long-term lease. Light-years ahead of today's food truck movement, for three decades, Tom has operated on wheels and Highline Kites is now an eighteen-foot-long mobile kite store—impressively, one that happens to be solar powered. Focusing on service and quality, Tom drives to the Berkeley Marina and greets his loyal customers, and increasingly their grown children and occasionally grandchildren.

Creating traditions and building a scene, Tom helped make kiting ubiquitous at the park, so much so that author Dave Eggers describes the fervent foothold kite-flying has at the park in a passage in his best-selling memoir *A Heartbreaking Work of Staggering Genius.* From miniatures to giant custom kites, Highline Kites can help with everything, but if forced to pinpoint his own kite making specialty, Tom never tires of three-dimensionality. With the exception of some time-tested plans in David Pelham's seminal 1976 book *The Penguin Book of Kites,* Tom generally skips canned instructions and uses his own wits to solve kite-building puzzles. In addition to his many original designs, Tom is best known for mixing space-age framing materials with traditional, handmade papers. Perfecting the art of cellular kite making, Tom's handiwork is top-notch and hangs on Japanese museum walls and is admired by many fliers. With a delicate hand, Tom is making a name for himself as he dabbles and explores kirigami kite making. Similar to origami, kirigami relies on an intricate series of folds, but with kirigami, the paper is cut as well. Though Tom considers himself "a student of kirigami," his miniature kirigami kites are playful and eye-catching, and demonstrate his fine kite making abilities.

Always eager to share kites with others, when Tom is not helping customers find the perfect kite, he might be teaching kite making classes at Fort Worden, lecturing about kite history, or organizing the very popular Berkeley Kite Festival. Tom founded the Berkeley Kite Festival in 1986 and the two-day event is a high point of his year, when he shares the magic of kiting with tens of thousands of die-hard fliers and enamored newcomers. Strongly believing the event belongs to the community, Tom works tirelessly to organize and promote the festival and keep it admission-free. For Tom, the real magic happens when people cross over from casual volunteering and develop a personal stake in the festival's success. Creating an army of kiting devotees supports the sport and grows the community of fliers.

Making connections beyond kiting circles, Tom has been approached by Hollywood filmmakers for his kiting expertise. Tom was a prop consultant on Kevin Costner's *Waterworld* where he built a model of a self-assembling Cody kite. During the scripted chaos of a chase scene, Costner's character shot the trick kite out of a cannon mounted on the deck of his trimaran boat. Assembling in mid-air, the kite became a lifesaving accelerator that allowed his character a split-second getaway. Though film critics roasted the movie, the scene endures as a kiteflier's favorite. A few years later, in the mid–2000s, when moviemakers began adapting the acclaimed book *The Kite Runner* into a movie, they hired Tom to teach a legion of extras how to fly fighter kites for flight scenes filmed stateside. Whether on the big screen or out in the open sky, Tom's kite knowledge brings the joys of kiteflying to many.

Don Tabor

Pioneering stunt kitemaker, team flier, and businessman Don Tabor took to controlled flying early, found something he adored, created kites that influenced the sport and set the standard in the kite trade business. Rebounding and weathering the highs and lows of the kite trade, Don's Top of the Line Kites still flies and is something of a darling comeback story of kiting.

Don's post-college life found him refinishing boats in the marinas of San Diego. In 1980, he saw a man trick flying in the park and decided to get himself a kite. Don flew single line kites for a long time, and later, between boats jobs, "I had some money, so I bought some dual line kites. I fell in love with the six foot Flexifoil." Dazzled and hooked, "I was in between boats and in no hurry to start working again. I flew probably eight hours a day for six months."

Interests escalating, in 1982, "I wanted to make a kite." Don got an idea and prototyped the Hawaiian stunt kite. "That is where it started." The Hawaiian became his signature kite, and it set benchmarks for competitive kiting. A licensed pilot, intuitive designer, and active experimenter, Don made eighty-two modifications to the Hawaiian "before I said, 'This is the kite, I don't have to change it.'" For about two years, Don stuck with the Hawaiian exclusively and "couldn't make them fast enough." Working out of his living room, Don repurposed his closet door into a workbench and got to work. Scrounging cutoffs from a sail maker and scoring discounted fiberglass rods from a place that sold tents, Don made kites one at a time. Insuring quality, Don built a reputation for excellence and grew his living room production enterprise into a legitimate business called Top of the Line. Later, Don followed up on the Hawaiian with his Spinoffs, North Shore, and Radical kites. By the late '80s, the majority of kites flown in competition were Top of the Line products, and they dominated and defined the stunt kite market of that era.

An integral part of Don's process was test flying his handiwork. A flier at heart, Don dedicated himself to flying. Looking back to "how team flying basically started," Don recalls, "I was designing kites during the week and I would go out to south of the Hilton in San Diego and I would test them." Sharing the beach with "maybe a half dozen other guys" with dual lines, Don started bringing extra kites and said, "'Would you fly these today and let me know what you think about it. I am trying to design a kite.'" The group would fly, then drink beer, and debrief. Don used their feedback to improve his kites, but one day he said, "Hey why don't we all stay here flying" together. Initially, lines tangled, but someone shouted, "You follow me" and they came up with the caterpillar. With their first follow the leader technique, "we were tickled pink" and cheered. Playing was fun and things "got crazier after that" as the group "latched onto the Blue Angels' kind of flying."

As Don's flying abilities improved and his company grew, he looked to his team as fellow kite enthusiasts and as a fun vehicle to advertise his company's products. "I was still of the mind that it took people seeing my product, what it could do, before they would shell out that much money for it." Making a name flying Hawaiians, Don and his Top of the Line teammates, Ron Reich, Eric Streed, and Pam Kirk, blazed trails in the new variation of the sport. For a few years, they flew without musical accompaniment before setting ballet routines to music. "That was a whole new thing" that the team got into about the time Ron Reich joined them. Ron "was a judge for ice skating," a natural with choreography, and he had a knack for building suspense and playing up quiet parts. "It is like a small play. You try to end up with a big finale." Practicing four to five times a week, three to four hours a session, the Top of the Line team won the AKA's first official team competition at the convention in San Diego in 1985 and the group helped advance the sport to new levels of performance.

At one point, Top of the Line, sold 1.5 million in kites, employed forty-five people, and Don achieved everything from scratch. "I never once made a bank loan. Everything was taken care of in-house." With an all-in attitude, Don and his wife Pat traded apartment life for a motorhome and rented a workshop. In the early days, the company had three or four employees, but as it grew Don hired more people. Unfortunately, Top of the Line's boom years went bust, when Don learned that his accountant and office manager made mistakes that led to an exceptionally costly audit. Tithing to shore up their fine, the Gulf War hit, and the business quieted while imports overseas began selling "cheaper than I could buy materials for." Up against the ropes, Don stopped advertising to divert funds and drastically shrunk staff down to a lone employee. "We had nothing except a name and ambition."

At the time, their rival and chief competitor, Frank Alonso, was looking to get into another business. He had just sold his company when he reached out to the Tabors with an offer that "helped Pat and I stay afloat, gratis." Without strings, Frank simply said, "'I want you to just think kites.'" Over time the partnership blossomed and "now we are selling better than a couple million kites a year." Focusing on entry-level recreational kites, Don designs mass-market kites at home and together they work with partners in Asia to oversee manufacturing. Don designed about two dozen kites, marketed under a half dozen brand names, each retailing for about $9.95 and sold at big box outlets like Costco and Target.

Don's involvement in kiting has changed over the years. "I myself stopped competing as my hearing got worse and worse, and I couldn't hear the music and the arthritis in my knees" flared and made backpedaling in the sand impossible. Loving the sport and community, Don stepped into a less active role. Though no longer competing, kiting always wins Don's attention. In 2003, the AKA honored Don with the Steve Edeiken Award to honor his significant lifelong contributions to kiting. Sadly, Don passed away in 2017 but fliers the world over think of him as they enjoy their sport.

Catherine "Cat" Gabrel

Long before hanging her hat in Oklahoma, and retiring into a second career selling DIY kites online, native Texan Catherine "Cat" Gabrel recalls only "fleeting experiences" with kites in her early years. Little hands from Cat's childhood circle made classic Eddy kites from newspaper comics and she recalls ferreting "as many balls of string as we could and put them out as far as we could." Their highfliers soared and took "more than an hour to bring back in," but the toil and time spent on the rewind created pleasant memories that later gave Cat something to build on in her kiting career.

As a dietitian and busy mom, Cat did not think much about kites until she was in her early 30s when her older brother Gary got the kiting bug and turned her and good friends Marti and Richard Dermer on to the fun. He picked up two early stunt kite models, a Peter Powell and a Skynasaur, and started to play. "I was just wowed by the Peter Powell and loved flying those," but the Skynasaur, "I found those pretty frustrating."

Unimpressed, but not defeated by the Skynasaur, Cat slowly found herself around kites more often and started attending festivals occasionally with Marti and Richard. In those days, her young daughter "tolerated" outings for only a few hours, but those short stints were long enough for Cat to meet people who encouraged and influenced her kite wanderings. Learning the ropes, she recalls hearing Richard's kiting "spiel probably a thousand times" and each rendition tugged her deeper into the kiting world and tightened Cat's friendship with the Dermers.

About ten years after playing with her brother's Peter Powell stunt kite, Cat joined the AKA in the mid–1990s and casually dabbled in kiting until the 2002 convention in Ocean City, Maryland. There she met Stafford Wallace, who gave her lessons in flying fighter kites and urged her to compete. She placed third, and the whirlwind convention "was just over the top ... and right there I was hooked." Abuzz with victory and enjoyment, Cat dug in and got involved in kiting.

Fast-forward to 2014, and Cat, ever ready to share kiting with others, won the AKA's Volunteer of the Year Award. Well-deserved, the honor speaks to the many

Cat Gabrel flying a Roloplan kite in Fanø, Denmark, 2015. Richard Steiff of Germany designed and manufactured Roloplans from 1909 to 1968, and Werner Ahlgrim made this replica in 2001 (photograph by Jim Day, courtesy Cat Gabrel).

ways Cat supports organized kiting. Active with her hometown club, over the years Cat has helped organize many Mother's Day flying events for the Tulsa Wind Riders. She served an abbreviated term as an AKA regional director to help spread kiting a little further, but Cat hit her stride and found her niche coordinating workshops for the AKA's annual conventions. "That's a fun job to have," and Cat is particularly adept at creating programs and recruiting instructors. Each year, she focuses on a particular slice of kiting and looks to the area where the convention is held to recruit regional kitemakers to teach workshops. Cat keeps the schedule fresh and helps kiters from across the country share their creative knowhow.

Around 2012, Cat ventured to Denmark, with Jim Day and Robert Brasington, to attend the Fanø International Kitefliers Meeting and was completely charmed by the kites and camaraderie between fliers. "We go every year. I plan to continue for as long as I am able." At each visit, Cat lends her skills and teaches kids kite making in the local school. "I've learned much from discussions and working with friends from Germany, the Netherlands, and Australia." With great enthusiasm, she delights in these interactions, finding it "incredible to watch how foreign adults relate to children" and for her, it is "a lot of fun to expand my teaching" and demonstrate kite making "in other cultures." Enjoying kites stateside or abroad, Cat cherishes the friendships she has made through kiting, and heading to festivals has something of the feel of a family reunion.

Around 2007, Cat took early retirement and traded in her career as a dietitian for kite making, and got more involved creating banners. About that time, Richard Dermer was swimming in kite kit orders and offered her his sled kit business. Cat realized she needed to sell more than just one style of kite to make a living. In 2008, after some thought and planning, she expanded the product line and launched her business Kites in the Sky. Just like IKEA, Kites in the Sky carries ready-to-assemble goods that come packaged with all their parts, cut to size and geared to go. Perfect for beginner and intermediate-level kite making. Cat offers about twenty-five types of kites and is "always looking for new kite kits" to entice the broad online market. When developing a new product, she "stops and thinks how kites work with other people" and adjusts the kit until it is simplified and streamlined even enough for first-time fliers. Cat typically sells in volume, and ships bundled orders to groups in classrooms, birthday parties, or adult team-building seminars. Strong sales from January through August keep Cat busy, but the slower fall allows her free time to fly and experiment. Work and play tend to blur and Cat says, "I forget I'm doing this for a living." For Cat, "My favorite thing is just playing with kites. I could just do that all the time."

Karl and Sara Longbottom

While other kids played football and rode bikes, a young Karl Longbottom dabbled in kite making. Although his childhood kites "never flew," Karl tucked memories of his bumbling attempts into a need-to-figure-this-out-later pile that he revisited as an adult. Around 1990, Sara and Karl Longbottom were vacationing with their children and family dog when they happened upon a kite shop and on a whim decided to give kiteflying a go. Purchasing a little sled, the family found that kiteflying perfectly matched the tempo of their leisurely beach routine: walk a stretch, stop and pop up the kite, reel it in and tuck it in a pocket, then walk some more and repeat. During those flies the "dog was always pulling ahead," although in the end, it was the new kite that tugged the Longbottoms' lives in a new direction.

Returning to their hometown in western England, the kids gave Karl a kite-making book as a gift. "We made one. It flew. We've never looked back since" and

Sara Longbottom with *Knickers* and Karl Longbottom with *Pants*, steerable single line fighter kites, at the Washington State International Kite Festival, Long Beach, Washington, in 2013 (courtesy Sara and Karl Longbottom).

kiting became another member of the family. Around that time, Karl learned about a nearby kiting event and said, "'Let's see what it is all about.'" The family spent the day with their backs on the grass, eyes to the sky, watching a variety of kites dance above. The outing encouraged Karl to experiment. Pre-internet, scouring libraries and bookstores for kite making instructions and inspiration, the Longbottoms started building their own kites because, "you can't buy interesting kites." Beginning with simple designs, Karl met kitemakers who generously shared tips, and his craft improved while he worked his way up to making advanced kites.

Looking back, "the first five to six years, we were very isolated and on our own, not knowing where to go." Karl and Sara eventually learned about the Midlands Kite Fliers, avidly read their newsletter, and began making connections that introduced the Longbottoms to a wider network of kitefliers. Their first trip to Dieppe, in 1996, was their turning point. On the French shores, the mind-blowingly creative kites and infectious camaraderie forever hooked them into kiting and inspired Karl to push forward with his kite making.

Successful kite projects elicited compliments from friends, and gradually fan-fare progressed "from people liking what we did" to people asking to buy the kites.

A flock of 22 *Dove* kites flown at the 30th annual RICV in 2016 in Berck-sur-Mer, France. Each dove has a wingspan of about 5' (1.5 m) and flap their wings in flight (courtesy Sara and Karl Longbottom).

Open to commerce, the Longbottoms tinkered with their production process for a few years, and in 2003, Karl left his desk job and Sara, a part-time mathematics instructor, dove full-time into kite making.

Although not lookers, the Longbottoms' Hawk "bird scarers" were their bread and butter stock item for many years. Farmers snatched up these tethered scare-crows to "scare birds away" and help them protect their crops. In recent years, though, "a Chinese company got hold of the design and started to produce a much cheaper and inferior kite." Unfortunately, the knockoff bit deeply into a very important part of their operations. "Our main achievement is still being able to make a living from kites. We are constantly trying to find new shapes and ideas for kites." Recently, the Longbottoms added a line of indoor kites and began offering historic kites they reproduce using durable modern materials. Business may not always be lucrative, but through kiting "we get to see the world." For the Longbottoms, at the end of the day, kite making is "a lifestyle choice more than a business" and it is their key to living life differently.

An engineer by training, Karl meticulously ensures that all his kites are top-notch, high-quality fliers, but the businessman in him realizes that "to have any kind of commercial viability you have got to produce something different." This insight allows whimsicality to color his work. From flying underwear to ptero-

Sara and Karl Longbottom's *Phoenix Number 5* soaring in the blue sky, 2016. Karl constructs his kites from Ripstop nylon and carbon fiber frames (courtesy Sara and Karl Longbottom).

dactyls, Karl's kites make you smile, yet aerial photographers seek out his workhorses for their uncompromising precision and flying stability. This combination of craft and imagination attracts admiration from seasoned kitefliers and the world at large. In recent years, theater designers and the London Olympic planners have approached the Longbottoms to create fabric sculptures. Venturing into stage work, the Longbottoms bring kite making techniques and ingenuity into their flightless commissions and wow stage audiences. At the 2012 London Olympics, the Longbottoms' impressively large *Empire Windrush* boat sculpture sailed through the opening ceremony festivities, and their ethereal *Butterfly Wings* piece fluttered through the ceremonial closing of London's Paralympic Games. These high-profile theatrical pieces led to other public sculpture commissions, and since then "we have made giant jelly fish and a flocks of doves on poles for Take That concert tours," stunning pop-up stage pieces for Benjamin Britten's *Noye's Fludde*, and the kites flown during Coldplay's performance at the 2016 Super Bowl halftime show.

   When not delighting spectators with theatrical kite-inspired creations, the Longbottoms teach kite making workshops for children and adults. Sara and Karl, the main organizers of the successful Herefordshire Kite Festival, were "involved with the festival from its beginning in 2000," but passed along the responsibility to the Midlands Kite Fliers in 2015. Their local council funded the event for a few years until subsidies dried up, and afterward, the Longbottoms ran "it with a zero budget." The school Sara worked at provided the flying venue for "a few years until we moved it to Berrington Hall," a National Trust Property with handsome grounds designed by noted traditional landscape architect Capability Brown.

Extending the fun indoors, the Longbottoms organized an indoor kite event in Swindon that ran from 2012 to 2015. The event typically drew "between ten and thirty participants" who enjoyed a new way to fly kites. During the Swindon events, "we did not include kite making, but we had a variety of kites" that people could test fly. Many "got hooked" and went on to purchase indoor kites. As the Longbottoms tap into emerging kite niches, such as indoor kiteflying, they expand the fun people can have with kiting and widen their kiting circle. For Cheshire natives Karl and Sara, kiting has an unquestionable pull on their lives, and upon reflection, "It's all about the people. Through kites, we have made friends from around the world. With the increasing use of social media, it is easy to see where all your kite friends are and what they are doing. Our daughter says she always knows where we are when we are travelling with our kites because of the pictures she sees."

Jan and Wayne Hosking

Native Aussie Wayne Hosking grew up skipping stones into the ocean under the Southern Cross until he moved overseas in early adulthood. Although kites weren't commonplace in Australia when he was young, Wayne recalls making a few from salvaged household materials with friends. Working without formal plans, Wayne and his pals fiddled and, inevitably, built tanks that flew only briefly, but created fun memories. Wayne left kites in the skies of his childhood and did not think much of them until the early-1970s when his wife Jan reintroduced him to kiting. Native to Long Island, New York, Jan fondly recalls her childhood kiting experiences. Each spring, her family flew Hi-Flier kites under the guidance of her father, an engineer with the Grumman Aerospace Corporation. There were successful flights, impromptu aerodynamic lessons, and cherished family times that Jan looks back on fondly. As an adult, Jan was on the lookout for a couple's activity and kiting came to mind. Wayne was warm to the idea, and together the Hoskings began experimenting with kite making.

Before long, the kiting bug bit the Hoskings and their pleasant leisure hobby evolved into making kites for sale. The cottage industry builders did pretty well with their weekend forays to craft markets, and Wayne remembers them selling over 300 kites at a single fair. This sales volume did not lead to a rock star lifestyle, but the business venture kept the couple afloat when Wayne was downsized from his day job in 1975. Making a go at commerce, the Hoskings launched their kite store, Inside-Out Kite Factory, and did well. An artist, drawn to creating kinetic sculptures, Jan is a natural kitemaker, while Wayne adopted the role of engineer who steadied and improved each kite's flight. The couple's skills complemented each other and they found success and pleasure in kite making. For three years Wayne and Jan "supplied all of Australia with kites." Looking back, Wayne recalls, "We didn't make a living off it, but we made an existence."

The merchant role eventually expanded and the couple began teaching others about kites. Three to five days a week, Wayne and Jan packed their kite bag and headed to area schools to teach the art of kite fighting. Students took to the sport rapidly and word traveled. The Hoskings' date book filled up quickly as school-children took to the skies to compete with kites. This person-to-person instruction was a tremendous amount of fun and it helped promote the Hoskings' business ventures. Soon, Jan and Wayne's passion for kiting broke out of the schoolyard and they organized a kite festival. The festival drew 20,000 people and subsequent events expanded rapidly. The kite festival caught the eye of the press and colorful multi-page spreads dazzled readers of the local paper. Free press coverage beats pricey print advertising costs, and the grateful Hoskings enjoyed the media attention.

At home, their young daughter was diagnosed with autism and the Hoskings faced a tough decision to either stay in Australian or to seek out medical attention for their daughter abroad. Researching treatment options, the family learned of doctors in Michigan who specialized in progressive treatments, and in 1979, the Hoskings sold their business and moved. Michigan is not necessarily the breeziest place, but the Hosking family managed to keep kites aloft in the upper midwest. There, Jan's kite making flourished and she won a kite art competition held at Central Michigan University and judged by legendary fine artist and kite art innovator Tal Streeter. Jan's kinetic sculptures and this kite making victory landed her a solo art show at CMU, as well as press in local newspapers and national magazines, such as *Southern Living* and *Better Homes and Gardens*.

While Jan's kite successes faced outward, Wayne looked inward with his kite-flying. Flying year-round to relax, Wayne recalls thinking that his new neighbors likely thought he needed a straightjacket as they watched him fly a red kite through a snowstorm. Contrary to imagined whispers, Wayne enjoyed the Zen of flying amid the relentless flurries, and kiteflying helped ease the emotional toll of the move around the globe and caring for a child with special needs. After awhile, though, kiteflying was not enough and Wayne consulted with a doctor who advocated medication. Not a fan of happy pills, Wayne headed to his basement to write. Writing suited Wayne and soon, he completed *Kites Aussie Style*, the first of his fourteen kite books. Writing did more than counterbalance a stressful time in his life. It redirected Wayne's kiting efforts and helped connect him with fliers from distant corners of the world. Kiting pioneers like Paul Garber and Dom Jalbert welcomed Wayne as a peer, while countless newcomers were introduced to kiting after stumbling upon his kite books. With a virtual kiting renaissance on the horizon, Wayne's books contributed to the rise of organized kiting.

The Hoskings' overall involvement with organized kiting picked up along with

Wayne's book sales and Jan's success in kite competitions. In the '80s, they discovered the AKA, began attending festivals, and soon kiting took them overseas. In 1987, the Hoskings moved to Houston and later in the year, Jan entered her "Seven-Sister" kite in the Black Ships Festival in Newport, Rhode Island and won a trip to Japan with Dave Checkley. The trip inspired the Hoskings and they began traveling internationally to promote and participate in kiting adventures. Their foreign trips fueled their imaginations and they eventually found their way to the page and to the kite. Wayne's book *Asian Kites* started with firsthand visits to Malaysia, and Jan picked up eastern kite making techniques that influenced her art.

International experiences may have wowed the Hoskings, but Jan and Wayne never lost interest in helping spread the joys of kiting locally. Back at home, they brought kites to nearby classrooms. Although Wayne encountered some initial resistance from school administrators, he and Jan eventually taught kite making and kiteflying at over 200 schools, colleges, and community organizations. Additionally, for four years the Hoskings enjoyed spending part of their summers at NASA's Johnson Space Center showing teachers ways to incorporate kiting into their lesson plans. Wayne turned his teaching experiences into another book and wrote, *Flights of Imagination*, a textbook for science teachers that uses kites to demonstrate aerodynamics and science principles.

In 1998, the Hoskings moved to Florida where Jan works at Walt Disney's EPCOT Center and for the past three years, Wayne has sold reclaimed sunken Spanish treasures from the *Nuestra Señora de Atocha* ship that sank in 1622 and the 1715 Fleet at treasure hunter Mel Fisher's store in Orlando. Offering mostly "artifacts and coins," Wayne enjoys talking with customers about the intrigue and history behind the booty.

Jan and Wayne continue their long involvement with kiting, and recently "finished *The World's Greatest Kiting* international kite art exhibition and celebration where we were presenters, displayed part of our kite collection, and conducted three workshops." Looking forward to retiring in the next year or so, the Hoskings hope to kick off "a new chapter in creating, teaching, and writing about kites." The sky is the limit to see how far Jan and Wayne will take kiting.

Daniel Prentice

Longtime kite businessman, kite magazine publisher, and kite club leader Daniel Prentice was born in Louisiana but spent the first four years of his life in Brazil with his family on a missionary trip. Fresh with memories of the Amazon, the Prentices returned to the States and eventually set roots in southeast Missouri. After graduating high school, Daniel headed to Duke University where he studied for a year before taking time off to seek his"fame and fortune"in California. Daniel landed in San Francisco and worked as a house painter. Shortly afterward, in late 1973, his girlfriend found a part-time job at Little People Kites and Daniel started hanging around the shop. Showing an interest in kites, Daniel was soon offered a job making Mylar box kites.

Daniel brought experience and ample hand skills to his new position. In junior high, a go-getting Daniel took up a quest to invent, and patent, a circular kite. His elder siblings ridiculed him mercilessly, but he wanted "to do something great and wonderful." Although Daniel missed the mark in his youth, as an adult his many accomplishments and contributions to the kite community are noteworthy, including earning several kite-related patents.

New to Little People Kites, Daniel learned the ropes and whet his entrepreneurial appetite. With aspirations of starting his own kite company, Daniel tested the waters and took a stab at distribution. He approached his bosses with a proposition and, after a handshake, became their distributor. By 1974, Daniel started Shanti Kites. Shanti is the Sanskrit word for inner peace and, as a part-time yoga teacher, Daniel liked the idea of using the irenic word for his business' name to remind him of life's greater values. Reflecting on this time in his life, Daniel is proud of the spark of "wisdom that teenagers sometime have" and still feels warmly about his company's poetic name.

Bitten by a dream, Daniel quickly set out to pursue the stars. He bought a 1950 Metro van with a three-foot loft built on top and painted a rising sun outside and lettered "Shanti Kites" on the back. He, his girlfriend, three cats, and a couple dogs piled into the van, along with fifty 45-foot Mylar dragon kites, and set off across the country to sell their wares. In the 1970s, dragon kites instantly drew a crowd, but getting people to part with their money during those inflationary days proved especially tough. Overall, the trip was a sales flop. Daniel returned to San Francisco with more than half of his inventory unsold, but Daniel learned a lesson on how to realistically evaluate a business plan.

Back home, a shrewder Daniel had a eureka moment and realized that the kiting world needed rugged kite lines and spools, and he turned his focus from wholesaling to creating quality gear at a time when flimsy accessories blanketed the market. Daniel's carpentry skills and kite making roots mixed perfectly to nurture his aspirations into a sustainable business venture. For decades, Daniel focused on producing high quality spools and lines that have raised standards across the industry.

Daniel joined the American Kitefliers Association in 1975 and in 1978 was elected vice president of its founding board of directors. In 1983, he helped create the Kite Trade Association to give the industry a professional foundation. "All the people in the kite business at this time were a little bit crazy. You know you couldn't very well go into a bank and say 'I'm in the kite spool making business' and have any credibility. There was no industry. There was no set formula for success. We were all on the edge of being real business people" and the KTA provided a much-needed forum for them to talk shop and come together to learn how to make their way through the larger business landscape. In the mid-'80s Daniel became the KTA's second president and during his tenure, he made a bold step and abandoned the jointly held AKA/KTA conventions. For some, the separation stung, but in the end, it allowed the KTA to spread its wings and focus on business matters while letting the AKA to keep club issues at the forefront.

Forever interested in pushing the envelope and venturing into unexplored territory, in 1988 Daniel created *American Kite Magazine* to document the American kiting experience. Organized kiting was hitting critical mass and the sport kite movement punctuated the drive behind new membership swells. As a kite person, Daniel thought the time had come for a new kiting magazine. As a businessperson, Daniel saw how the magazine would reach a wider customer base and create more advertising opportunities.

Setting out to fulfill this dream, Daniel enrolled in a magazine writing class at San Francisco State University. Taught by former *Rolling Stone* editor John Burks, Daniel hoped the course would get him to his publishing goal. During a break on the first night of class, Daniel approached John and told him he wanted to start a magazine but needed advice and help. John asked him a series of simple questions: "Do you know anything about publication?" "No." "Are you a journalism major?" "No." "Have you taken many writing classes?" "This is my first." John smiled and asked, "Do you have a lot of money?" "No, I'm pretty broke." "When do you want this publication out?" "I want it to be on the stands by June."

It was February.

John laughed and walked away. Daniel tried unsuccessfully to make appointments with him over the next month or so until John finally agree to hear him out over dinner. The two hit it off and before the check arrived, John signed on as editor and *American Kite* was on the stands in May.

Beyond covering the events of kiting, Daniel influenced them through his publication. Though not the originator of the idea to start a professional sport kite circuit, after careful thought, Daniel saw that the idea had legs. For two years, while president of the KTA, Daniel "pushed the idea of a KTA Pro-Am Kite Circuit" where the AKA would oversee the fliers and the KTA would fund the venture. He met stiff resistance from both clubs, so he used *American Kite* as a platform to create the first national sport kite circuit. Two years later, he expanded the idea to create the World Cup Sport Kite Championships, which unified the international rules and promoted national circuits worldwide. He personally ran the event for seven years, organizing World Cup competitions in six countries.

As kiting manufacturing began going overseas, small American kitemakers closed up their shops and canceled their standing orders for advertising space in trade magazines. For awhile, Shanti subsidized *American Kite*'s revenuc losses, but "eventually I couldn't afford to print it." In 1999, *American Kite* released its final issue, though Daniel never forgot how to run a magazine. In 2015, he became editor-in-chief at *Kiting* and redefined the look of the magazine and upped its readership. As a valuable outreach arm of the AKA, the magazine puts kiting news in the hands of veteran and new fliers alike.

Now in its fifth decade, Shanti continues to push boundaries in the kite industry as Daniel looks for innovative products to move kiting in new directions. While living on a sailboat, Daniel began wondering why sails were made of polyester, yet his kites were cut from nylon. "Polyester only stretches half as much as nylon, which makes it good for kite line but makes it very hard to weave." Quick to research the market, Daniel located a Japanese company that made high quality polyester Ripstop. He met with their silk weavers and then found a chemical company that could coat the fabric to reduce its stretch but keep the material soft and flowy. Holding its shape, even under the windiest tension, Daniel developed Icarex, the now ubiquitous modern-day industry standard for kite cloth.

Daniel's lifelong involvement with organized kiting has shown him the sport and its personalities from just about every angle. Through business, club advocacy, publication, and invention, Daniel celebrates and influences kiting as few others have ever done.

Sources

All interviews are by the author unless noted otherwise.

Bahadur, Dinesh. Tape-recorded oral history interview. Pacific Grove, California, 1995.

Bahadur, Dinesh. Telephone conversation with Rakesh Bahadur. 2017.

Barresi, John. Interview by Patti Gibbons and Kay Buesing. Tape-recorded oral history interview. Long Beach, Washington, 2017.

Barresi, John. Telephone conversation. 2017.

Bieck, Wolfgang. Email correspondence. 2016–17.

Bieck, Wolfgang. Tape-recorded oral history interview. Long Beach, Washington, 1995.

Bigge, Bill. Interview by Kay Buesing. Tape-recorded oral history interview. Ocean Shores, Washington, 1998.

Bigge, Bill. Mail correspondence. 2017.

Bigge, Bill. Telephone conversation. 2017.

Brockett, Steve. Email correspondence. 2017.

Brockett, Steve. Interview by [Kay Buesing]. Tape-recorded oral history interview. [Washington], 1998.

Burkhardt, Jon. Email correspondence. 2016–17.

Burkhardt, Jon. Interview by Kay Buesing Tape-recorded oral history interview. Port Townsend, Washington, 1997.

Burkhardt, Jon. Telephone conversation. 2016.

Carroll, Mike. Email correspondence. 2016–17.

Carroll, Mike. Tape-recorded oral history interview. Downers Grove, Illinois, 1997.

Checkley, David and Dorothea. Email correspondence with Leslie Morse Goldfarb. 2017.

Checkley, David and Dorothea. Telephone conversation with Leslie Morse Goldfarb. 2017.

Checkley, Dorothea. Tape-recorded oral history interview. Seattle, Washington, 1996.

Conrad, Ken, and Suzanne Sadow. Email correspondence with Suzanne Sadow. 2017.

Conrad, Ken, and Suzanne Sadow. Interviews by Kay Buesing. Tape-recorded oral history interviews. Seattle, Washington and Long Beach, Washington, ca. 2005.

Conrad, Ken, and Suzanne Sadow. Telephone conversation. 2017.

Daly, Pat. Email correspondence. 2017.

Daly, Pat. Tape-recorded oral history interview. Chicago, Illinois, 1997.

DeBolt, David, and Lois. Email correspondence with Mindy Hogg. 2017.

DeBolt, David, and Lois. Telephone conversation with Mindy Hogg. 2017.

DeBolt, Lois. Interview by Nancy Lockwood. Tape-recorded oral history interview. Tulsa, Oklahoma, 1995.

Dermer, Marti, and Richard. Email correspondence with Marti Dermer. 2016–17.

Dermer, Marti, and Richard. Interview by Melissa Brewster. Tape-recorded oral history interview. Stillwater, Oklahoma, 1996.

Dermer, Marti, and Richard. Telephone conversation with Marti Dermer. 2016.

Dietrich, Eva, and Ralf. Email correspondence with Ralf Dietrich. 2016–17.

Dietrich, Eva, and Ralf. Interview by Kay Buesing. Tape-recorded oral history interview. Port Townsend, Washington, 2006.

Dolphin, Pete. Tape-recorded oral history interview. Long Beach, Washington, 1995.

Dolphin, Pete. Telephone conversation. 2016.

Engvall, Gary. Email correspondence. 2017.

Engvall, Gary. Interview by Kay Buesing. Tape-recorded oral history interview. Long Beach, Washington, 2009.

Fieber, Paul. Email correspondence. 2016–17.

Fieber, Paul. Interview by Kay Buesing. Tape-recorded oral history interview. Seaside, Oregon, 2010.

Fieber, Paul. Mail correspondence. 2017.

Fieber, Paul. Telephone conversation. 2016.

Freeman, John. Interview by Kay Buesing. Tape-recorded oral history interview. Seaside, Oregon, 2010.

Freeman, John, and Marzlie. Email correspondence with Marzlie Freeman. 2016–17.

Gabrel, Catherine "Cat." Email correspondence. 2016–17.

Gabrel, Catherine "Cat." Interview by Kay Buesing. Tape-recorded oral history interview. Long Beach, Washington, 2014.

Gabrel, Catherine "Cat." Telephone conversation. 2016.

Gibian, Ron. Interview by Kay Buesing. Tape-recorded oral history interview. Dayton, Ohio, 2003.

Gibian, Ron, and Sandra. Email correspondence with Ron Gibian. 2016–17.

Gibian, Ron, and Sandra. Telephone conversation with Ron Gibian. 2016–17.

Gomberg, David. Email correspondence. 2017.

Gomberg, David. Tape-recorded oral history interview. Long Beach, Washington, 1995.

Gomberg, David. Telephone conversation. 2017.

Goodwind, Kathy. Email correspondence. 2017.

Goodwind, Kathy. Tape-recorded oral history interview. Long Beach, Washington, 1995.

Greger, Margaret. Email correspondence with Jan Gregor. 2017.

Greger, Margaret. Tape-recorded oral history interview. Long Beach, Washington, 1995.

Grys, Ed. Email correspondence. 2016–17.

Grys, Ed. Interview by Kay Buesing. Tape-recorded oral history interview. Seaside, Oregon, 2013.

Ham, George. Tape-recorded oral history interview. San Francisco, California, 1995.

Ham, George. Telephone conversation with Scott Seiwald. 2017.

Harris, Anne. Email correspondence. 2017.

Harris, Anne. Tape-recorded oral history interview. Long Beach, Washington, 1996.

Henderson, Charlie. Email correspondence with Chuck Holmes. 2016–17.

Henderson, Charlie. Interview by Kay Buesing. Tape-recorded oral history interview. Wildwood, New Jersey, 1997.

Hickman, Mel. Email correspondence. 2017.

Hickman, Mel. Interview by Kay Buesing. Tape-recorded oral history interview. Ocean Shores, Washington, 2007.

Hickman, Mel. Telephone conversation. 2017.

Hosking, Jan and Wayne. Email correspondence with Wayne Hosking. 2017.

Hosking, Wayne. Interview by Kay Buesing. Tape-recorded oral history interview. Port Townsend, Washington, 1997.

Ingraham, Bob. Email correspondence with Robert P. Ingraham. 2017.

Ingraham, Robert "Bob" M. Interviewed by [Kay Buesing]. Tape-recorded oral history interview. Silver Springs, New Mexico, 1995.

Jaspers, Don. Email correspondence. 2016–17.

Jaspers, Don. Interview by Kay Buesing. Tape-recorded oral history interview. [Florida, 2000].

Jaspers, Don. Mail correspondence. 2017.

Jensen, Corey. Email correspondence with Laurel Driskill, Neil Jensen, and Rick Kinnaird. 2017.

Jensen, Corey. Tape-recorded oral history interview. Monterey, California, 1995.

Jones, Billy. Email correspondence. 2016–17.

Jones, Billy. Interview by Kay Buesing. Tape-recorded oral history interview. Ocean Shores, Washington, 2007.

Jones, Billy. Telephone conversation. 2016.

Lamb, Steve. Tape-recorded oral history interview. Long Beach, Washington, 1996.

Lamb, Steve. Telephone conversation. 2017.

Leffler, Brooks. Email correspondence. 2017.

Leffler, Brooks. Tape-recorded oral history interview. Long Beach, Washington, 1995.

Lindner, Charm, and Ron. Interview by Kay Buesing. Tape-recorded oral history interview. Dayton, Ohio, 2003.

Lindner, Charm, and Ron. Telephone conversation. 2017.

Lochman, Chris, and Heloise. Email correspondence with Heloise Lochman. 2017.

Lochman, Chris, and Heloise. Interview by Kay Buesing. Tape-recorded oral history interview. Long Beach, Washington, 1998.

lockhart, bill. Mail correspondence with Tommy Lockhart. 2017.

lockhart, bill. Tape-recorded oral history interview. Long Beach, Washington, 1995.

Lockwood, Nancy. Email correspondence. 2016–17.

Lockwood, Nancy. Tape-recorded oral history interview. Long Beach, Washington, 1995.

Longbottom, Karl, and Sara. Email correspondence with Karl Longbottom. 2017.

Longbottom, Karl, and Sara. Interview by Kay Buesing. Tape-recorded oral history interview. Long Beach, Washington, 2013.

Lynn, Peter. Email correspondence. 2017.

Lynn, Peter. Interview by Kay Buesing. Tape-recorded oral history interview. Long Beach, Washington, 1997.

McAlister, Tom. Interview by Kay Buesing. Tape-recorded oral history interview. Seaside, Oregon, 2004.

McAlister, Tom. Telephone conversation. 2017.

Meyer, Barbara. Interview by Kay Buesing. Tape-recorded oral history interview. Long Beach, Washington, 2009.

Meyer, Barbara. Telephone conversation. 2017.

Miller, Jim. Interview by Kay Buesing. Tape-recorded oral history interview. Ocean Shores, Washington, 1998.

Miller, Jim. Telephone conversation. 2016.

Miller, Marla. Email correspondence. 2016–17.

Miller, Marla. Interview by Kay Buesing. Tape-recorded oral history interview. Long Beach, Washington, ca. 2010.

Miller, Marla. Telephone conversation. 2016.

Mitchell, Walter. Interview by Kay Buesing. Tape-recorded oral history interview. Seaside, Oregon, 2010.

Mitchell, Walter. Mail correspondence. 2017.

Mitchell, Walter. Telephone conversation. 2017.

Modegi, Masaaki. Email correspondence. 2017.

Modegi, Masaaki. Interview by Kay Buesing. Tape-recorded oral history interview. Long Beach, Washington, 1997.

Pollock, John. Email correspondence. 2017.

Pollock, John. Interview by Kay Buesing. Tape-recorded oral history interview. Seaside, Oregon, 2010.

Pollock, John. Mail correspondence. 2017.

Prentice, Daniel. Email correspondence. 2017.

Prentice, Daniel. Interview by Kay Buesing. Tape-recorded oral history interview. Santa Monica, California, 1996.

Price, Bob. Interview by Kay Buesing. Tape-recorded oral history interview. Tulsa, Oklahoma, 1995.

Price, Bob. Email correspondence with Marae Price. 2017.

Price, Bob. Telephone conversation with Marae Price. 2017.

Quinn, Cliff. Email correspondence. 2017.

Quinn, Cliff. Interview by Kay Buesing. Tape-recorded oral history interview. Long Beach, Washington, 2013.

Rogallo, Francis. Email correspondence with Ginny Darcey, Cathie Rogallo Fox, Bob Rogallo, and Carol Sparks. 2017.

Rogallo, Francis. Interview by Wayne Hosking. Tape-recorded oral history interview. Kitty Hawk, North Carolina, 1995.

Rogallo, Francis. Telephone conversation with Carol Sparks. 2017.

Sainz, Jose. Email correspondence. 2017.

Sainz, Jose. Interview by Kay Buesing. Tape-recorded oral history interview. Ocean Shores, Washington, 2007.

Sainz, Jose. Telephone conversation. 2017.

Sisson, Tom. Email correspondence with Jean Sisson. 2016–17.

Sisson, Tom. Interviewed by [Kay Buesing]. Tape-recorded oral history interview. [Seattle, Washington], 1993.

Skinner, Scott. Interview by Kay Buseing. Tape-recorded oral history interview. Long Beach, Washington, 1997.

Skinner, Scott. Telephone conversation. 2017.

Sonntag, Bill, Bob, and Marylu. Mail correspondence with Marylu Sonntag. 2017.

Sonntag, Bill, Bob, and Marylu. Tape-recorded oral history interview. Evansville, Indiana, 2012.

Sotich, Charlie. Email correspondence with John Brazzale. 2017.

Sotich, Charlie. Interview by Nancy Lockwood. Tape-recorded oral history interview. Tulsa, Oklahoma, 1995.

Spencer, Scott. Email correspondence with Mike Dallmer. 2016.

Spencer, Scott. Tape-recorded oral history interview. Long Beach, Washington, 1996.

Stanfield, Bobby. Interview by Kay Buesing. Tape-recorded oral history interview. [Port Townsend, Washington], 1998.

Stanfield, Bobby. Mail correspondence. 2017.

Streeter, Tal. Email correspondence with Lissa Streeter. 2017.

Streeter, Tal. Interview by [Kay Buesing]. Tape-recorded oral history interview. Ca. 2000.

Streeter, Tal. Skype conversation with Lissa Streeter. 2017.

Tabor, Don. Interview by Kay Buesing. Tape-recorded oral history interview. [Long Beach, Washington], ca. 2010.

Tabor, Don. Telephone conversation with Andrea Sheib. 2017.

Toki, Mikio. Email correspondence. 2017.

Toki, Mikio. Interview by Kay Buesing. Tape-recorded oral history interview. Long Beach, Washington, 2012.

Trépanier, Robert. Email correspondence. 2017.

Trépanier, Robert. Interview by Kay Buesing. Tape-recorded oral history interview. Long Beach, Washington, 1999.

Tumminia, Deb Cooley. Interview by Kay Buesing. Tape-recorded oral history interview. [Washington], ca. 2010.

Tumminia, Deb Cooley. Telephone conversation. 2017.

Vohs, Maggie. Email correspondence. 2016–17.

Vohs, Maggie. Interview by Kay Buesing. Tape-recorded oral history interview. Ocean Shores, Washington, 2007.

Weathers, Warren "Stormy." Email correspondence with Ann Weathers Ebelmesser, Nancy Weathers Nicholson, and Warren R. Weathers. 2017.

Weathers, Warren "Stormy." Interview by [Kay Buesing]. Tape-recorded oral history interview. [Washington], 1995.

Weathers, Warren "Stormy." Telephone conversation with Warren R. Weathers. 2017.

Wilson, Craig. Email correspondence. 2017.

Wilson, Craig. Interview by Kay Buesing and Patti Gibbons. Tape-recorded oral history interview. Dayton, Ohio, 2003.

Index